Glenn:

We both know
more than we agree, but at the end
of the day you're still a great
person! Thanks for the support since
I've bee in Kremen my friend,

MODELING MENTORING ACROSS RACE/
ETHNICITY AND GENDER

MENTORING
RACE EDUCATION
relationship
research academic
FACULTY WOMEN
gender UNIVERSITY
GRADUATE EXPERIENCES
support
COLOR MALE HIGHER SOCIAL
DEVELOPMENT professional STUDY CAREER PROFESSOR
ADDRESS AMERICAN HELP PROVIDE common PEOPLE Reference
PRESENTED ACADEMY know
theory State racism
COLLEGE RESPECT
FEMALE narratives UNDERSTANDING
racial EXAMPLE themes
PERSONAL ISSUES CENTER need
SERVE FIELD PROCESS
LEARNED PROJECTS BASED
CRITICAL POLICY SCHOLARS LITERATURE TEACHING CUSTOMS
SHARED GLASS DIVERSITY life COMPLETED CROSS WAY
practice PEER INDIVIDUALS PERSPECTIVE
TIME SCHOOL CHANGE
believe SPECIFIC interests
analysis opportunities PUBLICATIONS
chapter interactions MODEL
AFRICAN LATINA addition
INFORMAL YEARS GROUP WRITING
ADMINISTRATION discuss Black
SUCCESSFUL LEADERSHIP Reflections mentees RELATES BENEFITS degree
politics established wanted
REVIEW level
ADVISOR CHALLENGES INSTITUTIONS ethnic FAMILY

MODELING MENTORING ACROSS RACE/ETHNICITY AND GENDER

Practices to Cultivate the Next Generation of Diverse Faculty

EDITED BY

Caroline Sotello Viernes Turner and
Juan Carlos González

Foreword by Christine A. Stanley

STERLING, VIRGINIA

Published by Stylus Publishing, LLC
22883 Quicksilver Drive
Sterling, Virginia 20166-2102

Library of Congress Cataloging-in-Publication Data
Cataloging-in-Publication data for this title is available from the
Library of Congress.

13-digit ISBN: 978-1-57922-487-5 (cloth)
13-digit ISBN: 978-1-57922-488-2 (paperback)
13-digit ISBN: 978-1-57922-569-8 (library networkable e-edition)
13-digit ISBN: 978-1-57922-570-4 (consumer e-edition)

Printed in the United States of America

All first editions printed on acid-free paper
that meets the American National Standards Institute
Z39-48 Standard.

Bulk Purchases

Quantity discounts are available for use in workshops and for
staff development.
Call 1-800-232-0223

First Edition, 2015

10   9   8   7   6   5   4   3   2   1

Caroline Sotello Viernes Turner

To all of my life mentors: my family, my friends, my students, my colleagues.

Para todos mis mentores de vida: mi familia, mis amigos, mis estudiantes, mis colegas.

Para sa lahat ng mga naging mentors ko sa buhay: ang aking pamilya, ang aking mga kaibigan, ang aking mga mag-aaral, ang aking mga kasamahan.

Juan Carlos González

To my role models growing up: my cousins Jorge Espinoza and Horacio González and my brother Antonio González. May my work in the academy serve as a reminder of what we can accomplish and how we can overcome all obstacles.

Dedicado a mis primos Jorge Espinoza y Horacio González y a mi hermano Antonio González. Espero que mi trabajo en la Universidad sirva como recuerdo de todo lo que podemos alcanzar y como podemos sobresalir. ¡Sí se puede! Siempre.

CONTENTS

FOREWORD   *ix*
Christine A. Stanley

PREFACE   *xi*
Caroline Sotello Viernes Turner

1. WHAT DOES THE LITERATURE TELL US ABOUT MENTORING
   ACROSS RACE/ETHNICITY AND GENDER?   *1*
   Caroline Sotello Viernes Turner and Juan Carlos González

2. BUILDING CROSS-GENDER MENTORSHIPS IN ACADEME
   A Chicano–Latina Filipina Relationship Built on Common
   Scholarly Commitments   *43*
   Juan Carlos González and Caroline Sotello Viernes Turner

3. SOCIALIZATION IN ACADEME
   Reflections on Mentoring by a Latina Filipina Mentor and an
   African American Male Protégé   *59*
   J. Luke Wood and Caroline Sotello Viernes Turner

4. BREAKING THROUGH RACIAL AND GENDER BARRIERS
   Reflections on Dissertation Mentorship and Peer Support   *77*
   *Edward P. St. John, O. Cleveland Hill, Ontario S. Wooden,
   and Penny A. Pasque*

5. LATINA FACULTY AND LATINO MALE STUDENT
   MENTORSHIP PROCESSES
   Aprendiendo y Compartiendo Juntos   *107*
   Jeanett Castellanos and Mark A. Kamimura-Jiménez

6. A CRITICAL RACE JOURNEY OF MENTORING   *125*
   Dimpal Jain and Daniel Solórzano

7. CROSS-GENDER MENTORING FROM A CARIBBEAN
   PERSPECTIVE   *143*
   Christine A. Stanley and Dave A. Louis

8. AUTOETHNOGRAPHY, INSIDER *TESTIMONIOS*,
    COMMON SENSE RACISM, AND THE POLITICS OF
    CROSS-GENDER MENTORING   *161*
    Elvia Ramirez and Alfredo Mirandé

9. ANALYSIS OF THE MENTOR–PROTÉGÉ NARRATIVES
    Reflecting the Literature   *179*
    Juan Carlos González and Caroline Sotello Viernes Turner

10. ANALYSIS OF THE MENTOR–PROTÉGÉ NARRATIVES
    Contributing to the Literature and Emerging Mentoring
    Model for Practice   *197*
    Caroline Sotello Viernes Turner and Juan Carlos González

ABOUT THE EDITORS AND CONTRIBUTORS   *215*

INDEX   *221*

FOREWORD

Mentoring is gaining quite a bit of attention in the research literature, especially so because we know from experience that the outcomes of successful mentoring relationships can have a lasting and profound impact on one's professional career. Caroline Turner and Juan Carlos González contacted me to ask if I would consider writing a chapter and the foreword for *Modeling Mentoring Across Race/Ethnicity and Gender: Practices to Cultivate the Next Generation of Diverse Faculty*. I suspect that one of the reasons I was asked is that I wrote an article with Yvonna S. Lincoln in 2005, "Cross-Race Faculty Mentoring" (*Change*, Vol. 37, No. 2), which continues to be cited and used in higher education circles, most recently at the 2013 Management Development Program (MDP) at Harvard University. I accepted their invitation because mentoring, when examined as a process and product, brings fulfillment and excitement, especially when you have an opportunity, as I have had throughout my career, to help people attain their professional goals. Furthermore, Caroline is an accomplished and outstanding scholar on faculty diversity in higher education, so any writing project she undertakes promises to be insightful and informative. How could I refuse such an offer?

Caroline, now president of the Association for the Study of Higher Education (ASHE), is no stranger to the research literature in higher education. Caroline identifies as Latina Filipina. Over the course of her academic career, she has amassed a plethora of accolades for her work in faculty diversity, including the highly cited *Faculty of Color in Academe: Bittersweet Success* (with Samuel L. Myers Jr.; Allyn & Bacon, 2000). I met Juan Carlos González when I worked at The Ohio State University. He was pursuing his master's degree there. Juan Carlos identifies as Chicano. He is a scholar in his own right, garnering attention in this area as well. After completing his degree, Juan Carlos went to Arizona State to pursue his doctorate under Caroline's mentorship. I share this as an example to illustrate how our peers in higher education regard Caroline. She mentors graduate students and junior faculty exceptionally well. You will see clear evidence of this in this book.

The mentor–protégé relationship is complex and highly individualized. It can occur through formal and informal mechanisms and structures. Yet, amid this complexity, it remains clear from individual experience and the literature that we need to explore more deeply the interactions that occur across gender, race, and ethnicity. It is my humble opinion that only through the exploration and understanding of these infinite interactions will we become better equipped to cultivate the next generation of scholars and change the academic landscape in higher education for the recruitment and retention of women faculty and faculty of color. We also know from the literature that the experiences of women faculty and faculty of color present unique challenges and opportunities related to teaching, research, service, mentoring, collegiality, promotion and tenure, and succession planning, as well as sexism and racism. What remains clear from these encounters is— *Mentoring does make a difference!* Furthermore, the intersectionality across gender, race, and ethnicity offers a dynamic and unique window from which to observe the micro and macro processes and nuances that occur within a mentoring relationship. This is what this book aims to uncover. Two of the most fundamental questions about mentoring are as follows: (a) How do we know that mentoring makes a difference? and (b) What does effective mentoring look like or feel like?

Modeling Mentoring Across Race/Ethnicity and Gender is a book that speaks to these questions and examines them through phenomenology—from the lens of those who enter, experience, and benefit directly from mentoring relationships. If you are a graduate student, a faculty member, a college or university administrator, or an aspiring academic, this book will speak to you!

There are books on mentoring and mentoring relationships, yet few take a look at the relationship across gender, race, and ethnicity, as well as from other lenses and experiences such as what you will encounter in *Modeling Mentoring Across Race/Ethnicity and Gender*. This book has the potential to influence mentoring practice, processes, and policies by bringing issues that many of us still find uncomfortable talking about in academia—the micro- and macroaggressions associated with the experiences of women faculty and faculty of color in higher education—into focus. We espouse that cultivating the next generation of academics of color is important and a reality for countless reasons; however, we often underestimate the impact an effective mentoring relationship can have on that generation. *Modeling Mentoring Across Race/Ethnicity and Gender* is insightful and informative and can help us experience mentoring relationships in deeper and impactful ways to bridge the gender, social, and cultural divide.

—Christine A. Stanley
Texas A&M University

PREFACE

This book project emerged from years of experiencing, studying, and observing cross-gender and cross-race mentor relationships. As is indicated more than once in the literature and in the narratives presented here, in the case of academics of color, few are represented among the university faculties, and mentorship has been shown to be critical in helping many to enter, to remain in, and to succeed in their academic careers. Scholars doing research on students and faculty of color often cite mentorship as a key component necessary for success in a largely traditional academy that still operates on the age-old apprenticeship model (Blackwell, 1989; Singh & Stoloff, 2003; Turner, González, & Wood, 2008; Turner & Thompson, 1993). Mentoring across gender and race/ethnicity inserts levels of complexity that may facilitate or complicate this important process. This book proposes not only to add knowledge to a gap in the literature on race, ethnic, and gender differences in mentoring but also to provide an in-depth look at successful mentorship across gender and race/ethnicity between senior and emerging scholars of color.

Chapter 1 presents a review of the literature, and the following chapters were written by scholars who share in-depth descriptions of their cross-gender and/or cross-race/ethnicity mentoring relationships. Each chapter was coauthored by mentors who are established senior scholars of color and their former protégés with whom they have continuing collegial relationships. As the reader will see, these relationships are important in providing insights into how they influence the academic pipeline for scholars of color. The mentoring relationships of the scholars featured in this book demonstrate that the protégés not only are successfully mentored as graduate students but also continue to be mentored as they pursue professional lives in academe. As the relationship deepens and ages, the mentor–protégé relationship evolves into a reciprocal collegial relationship.

Stanley and Lincoln's (2005) reflective essay, contextualized in the related research literature, on their cross-race mentorship experience was adapted to include considerations across gender to form a starting point for an examination of cross-gender and cross-race/ethnicity mentorships in this book.

Examples of questions provided as guides to chapter contributors are as follows:

For mentees:

What have been the benefits of being mentored by your mentor?
How and why did you select this mentor?
What have been the challenges of being mentored by your mentor?
How were these challenges resolved?

For mentors:

What have been the benefits of mentoring your protégé?
How and why did you select this protégé?
What have been the challenges of mentoring your protégé?
How did you navigate the challenges?

For both:

How does your gender and race/ethnicity facilitate or complicate your mentor–protégé relationship?
What "lessons" have you learned from your mentor or protégé about mentorship and academic life?

Through a review of the literature examining mentoring across race, ethnicity, and gender, including 86 publications spanning 32 years (1981–2013), chapter 1 presents the results of a thematic analysis of factors that facilitate and/or challenge mentoring in higher education, primarily focusing on the experiences of graduate students and junior faculty. Using QSR NVivo 10, the editors conducted an analysis of the literature and created visuals reflective of themes found. Chapters 2 through 8 provide seven narratives of successful cross-race/ethnicity and/or cross-gender mentorships. These narratives make evident the unique ways by which these mentor–protégé relationships developed, explicating the rewards and challenges from the perspectives of the chapter authors. Themes emerging from these chapters portray unique insights shared from the lived experience of the authors, providing a close-up view of their mentoring relationships. The analysis of the narratives provided in this book results in insights to inform students who would be protégés and faculty who would be mentors. The editors hope that these reflective narratives will also contribute to a broadened, nuanced understanding of such mentorship relationships, as well as provide ideas for processes, practices, and policies that promote the presence of underrepresented groups in the professoriate.

González and Turner's chapter "Building Cross-Gender Mentorships in Academe: A Chicano–Latina Filipina Relationship Built on Common Scholarly Commitments" explores the factors facilitating and challenging their successful mentorship relationship over 14 years within the context of their similarities and differences. In "Socialization in Academe: Reflections on Mentoring by a Latina Filipina Mentor and an African American Male Protégé," Wood and Turner explore their cross-gender and cross-race mentorship relationship in the context of integrating into the academy and within the context of their own mixed-race identities. "Breaking Through Racial and Gender Barriers: Reflections on Dissertation Mentorship and Peer Support" presents the experiences of several scholars—Hill, Wooden, and Pasque—who share their dissertation mentoring and peer support experiences with senior scholar Edward P. St. John. In their group reflection, they discuss how one learns to be a mentor, exploring the concept of thought partners, the value of giving equal voice, the development of a caring community, and intentional mentoring. Castellanos and Kamimura-Jiménez address their experiences through a psychosociocultural framework in "Latina Faculty and Latino Male Student Mentorship Processes: Aprendiendo y Compartiendo Juntos," with particular attention to Latino male retention and academic success. In "A Critical Race Journey of Mentoring," Jain and Solórzano use a critical race theory and a critical pedagogy lens to reflect on issues of marginalization in the academy and the importance of mentoring in retaining faculty of color. Stanley and Louis in "Cross-Gender Mentoring From a Caribbean Perspective" examine their cross-gender mentoring relationship in the context of their shared common experiences as individuals, being born and raised in the West Indies—Jamaica and Trinidad and Tobago, respectively—bringing the uniqueness of their cultural heritage to the discussion. In "Autoethnography, Insider *Testimonios*, Common Sense Racism, and the Politics of Cross-Gender Mentoring," Ramirez and Mirandé use critical race theory and women-of-color feminist frameworks to present personal *testimonios* of how a politicized academic milieu shaped their mentoring relationship.

The concluding chapters compare issues and themes emerging from the narrative chapters to the thematic model developed from the literature review presented in chapter 1, noting similarities and differences. Chapter 9, "Analysis of the Mentor–Protégé Narratives: Reflecting the Literature," presents examples from the mentor–protégé narratives that mirror those found in the literature. Emerging from the mentor–protégé coauthored chapters are also themes that differ from those identified in the literature, resulting in an elaborated model presented in chapter 10, "Analysis of the Mentor–Protégé Narratives: Contributing to the Literature and Emerging Mentoring Model for Practice." The narrative chapters' themes and issues that differ from the literature are contributions to the extant literature. The final emerging model, including themes from the literature and additional critical insights from the seven narrative chapters, of mentoring across race/ethnicity and gender is presented in chapter 10, along with implications for practice.

In a time when higher education is experiencing a continued lack of representation for all academics of color, especially for males of color, this book examines cross-gender and cross-race/ethnicity mentorship. Because of the lack of faculty of color and the availability of large numbers of White faculty, students of color and faculty of color will likely experience mentoring across race/ethnicity and gender. This book aims to further the reader's understanding of the unique complexities inherent in successful cross-gender and cross-race/ethnicity mentorship relationships. The examination of ways in which academics can enhance the quality of mentorship across these dimensions is critical if a diverse professoriate is to be achieved.

—Caroline Sotello Viernes Turner
California State University, Sacramento

References

Blackwell, J. E. (1989). Mentoring: An action strategy for increasing minority faculty. *Academe, 75*(5), 8–14.

Singh, D. K., & Stoloff, D. L. (2003). *Mentoring faculty of color.* Paper presented at the annual meeting of the American Association of Colleges for Teacher Education, New Orleans, LA. (ED 474179)

Stanley, C. A., & Lincoln, Y. S. (2005). Cross-race faculty mentoring. *Change: The Magazine of Higher Learning, 37*(2), 44–50.

Turner, C. S. V., González, J. C., & Wood, J. L. (2008). Faculty of color in academe: What 20 years of literature tells us. *Journal of Diversity in Higher Education, 1*(3), 139–168.

Turner, C. S., & Thompson, J. R. (1993). Socialization experiences of minority and majority women doctoral students: Implications for faculty recruitment and retention. *The Review of Higher Education, 16*(3), 355–370.

I

WHAT DOES THE LITERATURE TELL US ABOUT MENTORING ACROSS RACE/ETHNICITY AND GENDER?

Caroline Sotello Viernes Turner and Juan Carlos González

To better prepare for an increasingly diverse society, campuses across the country remain engaged in efforts to diversify the racial, ethnic, and gender makeup of their faculties. The 2010 U.S. Department of Education, National Center for Education Statistics, Integrated Postsecondary Education Data System (IPEDS) data show that, for example, faculty of color, males and females combined, remain seriously underrepresented, composing 19.1% of total full-time faculty (see Table 1.1). These data reflect full-time faculty in degree-granting institutions that award associate's or higher degrees and participate in Title IV federal financial aid programs. When the data are compared across gender and rank, White males show an increase in numbers while all other groups are far less represented in all categories. Furthermore, across the ranks of lecturers to full professors, faculty of color, both men and women, have the lowest representation.

Mentorship has been cited as one of the most important factors in successful graduate and faculty careers by scholars, discussed in this chapter, who are interested in how students and faculty advance and thrive in academia. There is no agreed-on definition of *mentorship* because the concept and practice vary within and beyond academic institutions and fields of study. Mentoring theory is underdeveloped and likely to remain so, as studies of mentoring are conducted from multidisciplinary perspectives (Bozeman &

1

TABLE 1.1

Full-Time Faculty by Race/Ethnicity, Sex, and Academic Rank, Fall 2009

	White	Black	Hispanic	Asian/ Pacific Islander	American Indian/ Alaska Native	Total	% of Total Faculty by Rank/ Gender
Males							
Full	107,315	3,755	3,209	10,684	365	125,328	20.8
Associate	68,747	4,180	3,096	8,338	321	84,682	14.0
Assistant	59,607	4,568	3,422	10,658	306	78,561	13.0
Instructors	35,137	2,880	3,078	2,568	477	44,140	7.3
Lecturers	11,702	822	650	1,084	64	14,322	2.4
Females							
Full	42,253	2,331	1,474	2,600	215	48,873	8.1
Associate	48,523	3,983	2,287	4,294	280	59,367	9.8
Assistant	58,285	6,411	3,367	8,054	413	76,530	12.7
Instructors	43,192	4,926	3,499	2,998	525	55,140	9.1
Lecturers	13,193	990	933	1,234	74	16,424	2.7
Total	487,954	34,846	25,015	52,512	3,040	603,367	
% of Total faculty by race/ ethnicity	80.9	5.8	4.1	8.7	0.5		100

Note. Data from U.S. Department of Education, National Center for Education Statistics, Integrated Postsecondary Education Data System (IPEDS), Winter 2005–06, Winter 2007–08, and Winter 2009–10, Human Resources component, Fall Staff section. (This table was prepared August 2010.)

Fenney, 2007). For purposes of this chapter, we will refer to a definition that comes from within the academy. Blackwell (1989) defined *mentorship* as "a process by which persons of superior rank, special achievements, and prestige instruct, counsel, guide, and facilitate the intellectual and/or career development of persons identified as protégés" (p. 9). (The terms *protégé* and *mentee* are used interchangeably in this book.) In essence, the mentoring relationship is one that is built on trust and bidirectional benefits between the mentor and the protégé, who both largely depend on successful relationships for their intellectual, social, and career advancements.

In the case of academics of color, mentorship has been shown to be critical in helping many to attain and to succeed in their academic careers.

For example, in a metasynthesis of 252 papers related to faculty diversity published over a 20-year period, the importance of positive mentoring experiences was a dominant theme (Turner, González, & Wood, 2008). However, even though mentoring emerged as a dominant theme in this work, few of the publications examined cross-race/ethnicity or cross-gender mentor relationships. Building on the methods used in this metasynthesis, this chapter provides a thorough examination of publications over a 31-year period that document both successes and challenges for mentorship across gender and race/ethnicity. Mentoring across gender and race/ethnicity inserts levels of complexity that may facilitate or complicate the mentorship process. Examining mentorship across race/ethnicity and gender is critically important because, as documented previously, the lack of faculty of color and women to serve as mentors and the availability of large numbers of White males to be mentors ensure that students and faculty of color will likely experience mentoring across race/ethnicity and gender. The literature presented in this chapter, as well as the chapters to follow, focusing on cross-race/ethnicity and cross-gender relationships, sheds light on the nuances of the mentoring process for would-be mentors and protégés.

In the past 32 years, authors have addressed mentoring experiences as a critical and complex facet of career development. From 1981 to 2013, there was a continued rise in publications addressing mentoring processes as they contribute to or detract from the development of a racial/ethnic- and gender-diverse faculty. This chapter presents the results of a literature review and syntheses of 86 publications, with the goal of informing scholars and practitioners of the current state of the field. We reviewed 68 journal articles, 3 book chapters, 7 dissertations, 6 technical reports, and 2 conference papers published from 1981 to 2013. In 1981, from the perspective of 62 mentors surveyed, Blackburn, Chapman, and Cameron found that mentors were of major importance in the academic career placement and development of their protégés. Blackburn et al. concluded that there is a need for in-depth examination of cross-gender mentor processes and how productive mentorship relationships are fostered at the institutional level. In 2012, Reddick and Sáenz used a scholarly personal narrative approach to reflect on their journeys as faculty of color in the professoriate. The importance of mentorship was extensively highlighted throughout their article. On the basis of our analysis of these articles and the 84 other journal articles, book chapters, dissertations, technical reports, and conference papers, several themes emerged. These themes are captured in Figures 1.1 and 1.2. These figures were created for use as visual and interpretive models reflecting findings from literature reviewed for this chapter.

Figure 1.1 delineates successful pathways and challenges in mentoring relationships across race/ethnicity and gender. Figure 1.2 (p. 27) delineates successful pathways and challenges in mentoring relationships in general, with implications for cross-race/ethnicity and cross-gender mentorships. The two figures serve as a guide for the discussion of our findings from the literature review.

Successful Pathways Across Race/Ethnicity

In our analysis of the literature, as shown in the top-left quadrant of Figure 1.1, themes related to the successful pathways based on race/ethnicity were identified. According to Brinson and Kottler (1993), successful cross-relationships result in benefits to both mentors and mentees because they provide mutual learning and increased cross-cultural understanding. Similarly, in a study by Beverly (2011), three African American scholars stated that cross-race mentorships were quite significant to their success. Examining the literature on successful pathways across race/ethnicity, we identified 11 themes, which will be explicated in this section.

The first theme was related to the ways in which racial/ethnic minority faculty identify *allies* at their institutions to assist them in navigating their

Figure 1.1 Successful pathways and challenges in mentoring relationships across race/ethnicity and gender.

	Successful Pathways	Challenges
Race/Ethnicity	• Ally Identification • Demystifying the Academy • Diverse Mentoring Programs • Not Academic Cloning • Peer Mentoring • Respect Leads to Openness • Mentoring as Healing • Psychosocial Support • Rich Legacy of Cross-Race/Ethnicity Mentoring • E-mentoring • Cross-Cultural Support	• Dominant Culture Assimilation • Isolation and Marginalization • Racism and Institutional Racism • Power Dynamics Affect Relationships • Stigma With Seeking Help • Negative Cross-Cultural Interactions • Language, Racial, Cultural Barriers • Mentees Prefer Same-Race Mentors
Gender	• Feminist Mentoring • Politics of Gender • Support Social Needs • Respect Leads to Openness • Developing a Culture Supporting Diverse Mentoring and Demystifying the Academy • Characteristics That Support Relationships • E-mentoring	• Sexism • Tokenism and Marginalization • External Perceptions (Sexual Liaisons and Favoritism) • Lack of Professional Interactions • Politics and Power Relations • Gender Stereotypes • Gender Differences (Mentoring Expectations and Effects on Careers)

departments, schools, and institutions (Beverly, 2011; Johnson-Bailey & Cervero, 2008). Identification of allies is done with the assistance of other faculty of color, within or outside of their respective department. Allies do not always have to be faculty of color, as stated by Stanley and Lincoln (2005); sometimes they can be White faculty and/or administrators. Stanley and Lincoln noted that when faculty of color identify White allies, building these relationships requires extra sensitivity and understanding due to potentially different cultural understandings but also requires mutual respect, admiration, and an understanding of the meaning of "White privilege." Lechuga (2011) found that graduate students of color characterized faculty as potential allies when trying to develop professional relationships that can facilitate their mentorship into academe.

Second, the theme of *demystifying the academy* was related to the ways in which aspiring faculty of color are socialized on the values, unwritten rules, and culture of academe. Hill, Castillo, Ngu, and Pepion (1999) talked about this demystification within, for example, the context of understanding the process and culture of academic writing. In general, demystifying the academy relates to learning the nuances of how the academy works from an insider perspective. This knowledge is critical in facilitating successful academic careers. Reddick and Sáenz (2012) identified the value of demystification as vital to learning ways to increase scholarly productivity and institutional research collaborations. Stanley and Lincoln (2005) and Stanley (1994) also discussed how senior White faculty could serve as the voices of junior faculty of color when equity issues need to be addressed, thus protecting junior faculty from exposing themselves to scrutiny prior to tenure and promotion. Blackwood and Brown-Welty (2011) addressed the reliance of junior faculty on senior faculty in order to gain greater visibility and understand the political culture of their work environment.

Third, *diverse mentoring programs* were also found to contribute to successful pathways for faculty of color (see Hall & Sandler, 1983; Hill et al., 1999; Tillman, 2001). Hill et al. (1999) described one doctoral student mentoring program that included training for the mentors in the program to increase their awareness and sensitivity of differences in worldviews of their mentees, particularly when the mentor and mentee were of different culture and race/ethnicity. While providing training for mentors, scholars also underscore the importance of training mentees to voice their concerns and ideas. Both contribute to creating successful pathways for doctoral students of color to enter academe as faculty (Hill et al., 1999).

The fourth way to help create a successful pathway for faculty of color to succeed in academe is discussed in the literature as a need to resist *academic cloning*, which includes the process by which the mentor has the desire to mentor the mentee in a way that will result in the mentee thinking and acting in the same fashion as the mentor. In their seminal article, Stanley and Lincoln (2005) stated that for mentor relationships to work across race/ethnicity, the mentors need to be aware of academic cloning and understand that faculty of color may not want to think and act like them. When mentors are aware of their tendencies toward creating others just like them (Light, 1994) and are committed to rejecting the propensity to remake mentees into their own image, then cross-race/ethnicity relationships are more likely to be successful and result in helping institutions retain their faculty of color (Stanley & Lincoln, 2005). Research by Thomas (1993) found that when mentors viewed racial differences as positive and as enhancing the relationship with their mentees, cross-race mentorship was more successful because there was not a desire to change the mentees but a desire to learn from them.

Fifth, Reddick and Sáenz (2012) provided evidence for *peer mentoring* as a key to success for faculty of color. Through peer mentoring, faculty of color can increase their scholarly productivity and increase their understanding of academic culture. Peer mentors, if close in age and hired around the same time, can share mutual challenges in navigating academe and also exchange strategies for overcoming such challenges (Reddick & Sáenz, 2012). Hiring a critical mass of faculty of color can also help institutions retain them because they essentially help support each other (see Smith, Turner, Osei-Kofi, & Richards, 2004).

Sixth, several scholars talked about how *mutual respect can lead to openness* for cross-race/ethnicity relationships. If faculty are genuine and sincere in their interactions with each other, enhanced communication can ensue (see Hill et al., 1999; Stanley & Lincoln, 2005). In Hill et al. (1999), the authors discussed a scenario where cross-race faculty and students spend years developing mentorships prior to students of color approaching White faculty to voice their concerns. Stanley and Lincoln (2005) also described their cross-race relationship as developing and achieving success over time, as they both achieved a comfort level for genuine interactions to take place. As shown in research by Thomas (1993, 2001), cross-race mentorships are most likely to be successful when both mentor and mentee have respect for each other and acknowledge race as a potential barrier in their relationship but are open to discussing racial issues that may arise. As stated by the aforementioned authors, openness across race/ethnicity is easier and leads to more meaningful dialogue when there is mutual respect, understanding, and admiration.

Seventh, Espinoza-Herold and Gonzalez (2007) identified mentoring for faculty and students of color as having a *healing power*. This healing power of mentoring is described as ways in which mentors affirm and validate the experiences of their mentees of color. Mentors can also mentor in a way that affirms the professional and diverse identities of their mentees of color. In a narrative shared in Johnson-Bailey and Cervero (2008), one of the coauthors described how as a graduate student seeking mentors, she confided in a White male professor about her aspirations to become faculty someday. She explained how he laughed at her, stating, "Juanita, you're aiming mighty high" (p. 316). This experience led her to shut down and become hesitant about sharing her aspirations with other faculty, until she met her coauthor, another White male faculty member. Juanita shared her aspirations, and Ron did not laugh; instead, he became her mentor, and mentoring became positive rather than negative for Juanita.

Eighth, *psychosocial support* was also identified as important in the mentorship of faculty of color. Singh and Stoloff (2003) stated that psychosocial mentoring requires emotional support and encouragement. Specific for cross-race/ethnicity mentorships, this support requires awareness by White faculty of the basic beliefs and worldviews of their mentees of color. Understanding cultural differences is important not only for mentors in providing psychosocial support (Crutcher, 2007; Singh & Stoloff, 2003) but also for mentees to strengthen their relationship with their White mentors (Singh & Stoloff, 2003). In addition, in a study of African American faculty at predominantly White institutions, Tillman (2001) found that mentors can provide important psychosocial functions to their mentees in order to increase the success of these mentorships, such as providing the mentees with a sense of competence and identity. As role models, mentors can demonstrate the importance of positive acceptance, pointing out and highlighting their protégés' strengths while challenging them to shore up weaknesses in a context of support. By doing so, mentors may provide a safe space that encourages mentees to speak openly about their anxieties, concerns, and struggles in coping with work and life demands (Tillman, 2001).

Ninth, the literature review also documented the *rich legacy of cross-race/ethnicity mentoring* (Reddick, 2009). Reddick (2009) described his own successful mentoring experiences with African American and White faculty. Willie, Reddick, and Brown (2005) addressed the successes of cross-racial mentorship in higher education. Lynch's (2002) research supports the contention that Black faculty receive excellent mentorship from White faculty.

The tenth area of note in the literature is *e-mentoring*, which was studied by Bernstein, Jacobson, and Russo (2010) and found to be beneficial to racial/ethnic minority faculty, in part, because through online communication mentors may be less likely to have and/or express behaviors based on stereotypic assumptions. Bernstein et al. (2010) stated that communicating via e-mail nullifies visual or auditory cues so that there is less potential for negative emotional tones to be communicated as in the case of in-person cross-race/ethnicity interactions. However, these authors cautioned against generalizations as a result of their findings, as mentors who participate in e-mentoring may be more dedicated and knowledgeable than mentors who do not participate. Nonetheless their findings underscore the importance of commitment and genuine interaction as critical to successful mentoring of women in the sciences.

Last, because of the continued underrepresentation of faculty members of color in counseling and other programs, the most likely *cross-cultural mentoring relationship* will be between a White mentor and a mentee of color (Casto, Caldwell, & Salazar, 2005; Dinsmore & England, 1996). Mentors who recognize how issues such as cross-cultural communication styles and power differences based on race/ethnicity may influence the mentoring relationship can positively address such challenges in striving to create a mutually supportive and satisfying mentoring relationship (Brinson & Kottler, 1993). In successful cross-cultural mentoring, mentees of color have described receiving from their mentors a sense of genuine concern for their personal welfare and for their professional development. Demonstrating cultural sensitivity and willingness to learn about a mentee's ethnic heritage and appreciation of an individual mentee's differences within his or her culture is vital for the growth and transformation of both mentor and mentee (Brinson & Kottler, 1993; Thomas, 2001).

Successful Pathways Across Gender

Themes emerging from an analysis of identified literature related to successful pathways based on gender are listed in the bottom-left quadrant of Figure 1.1. These seven themes will be described here. Blackburn, Chapman, and Cameron (1981), as noted previously, found women mentors named twice as many successful female and male protégés as male mentors, prompting them to ask for further research about cross-gender mentorship relationships. This section will describe what the literature says about successful pathways across gender as reflected in the literature.

Schramm (2000), using a feminist analysis of faculty mentor–protégé relationships, acknowledged the detrimental effects of power differentials based on sexist assumptions in mentoring relationships between a male mentor and a female protégé. Schramm called for a *feminist mentoring* approach to support the academic development of women faculty. She described feminist mentoring as emphasizing "interpersonal relationships, empowerment, personal development, self-esteem, political awareness, personal autonomy, and the *politics of gender*" (p. 1, italics added). According to Schramm,

In typical mentoring programs, inherent inequalities lead to imbalanced mentor-protégé relationships. Many mentors do not have adequate training in cross-gender mentoring. Feminist mentors should help to identify sex bias as problematic. Mentors of both sexes should participate in understanding, working within, and transforming sexist culture. (p. 1)

Casto et al. (2005) implied that if a feminist mentoring approach is not used, an example of the potential negative effects for female academics is that "male mentors have the edge when it comes to helping their protégés be known and recognized by the right people . . . [allowing] them to more effectively sponsor and promote their protégés" (p. 336).

Schramm (2000) and Parker and Kram (1993) suggested that each protégé have more than one mentor to obtain different perspectives and to meet various needs, such as professional and *social needs*. Parker and Kram (1993) also recommended that organizations develop ways to recognize and reward senior women faculty, given their small numbers and likely large demands made on their time, who mentor others in the organization, particularly junior women faculty.

When these approaches are taken with cross-gender mentoring relationships, protégés can be nurtured within an openness *emanating from mutual respect*. For example, as noted previously but also relevant here, a woman graduate student indicated that she confided her secret wish to become a professor to a second White male professor, who did not laugh at her:

Then, I shared it with my professor, Ron. He did not laugh; he said that he thought it was a great idea. This pivotal event, which I don't think Ron even remembers, opened a door in my mind and let me know that I could safely confide in him. And maybe, I reasoned, he could be my ally. He could possibly help me fulfill my dream. (Johnson-Bailey & Cervero, 2008, p. 316)

Stanley (1994) noted that White male mentors can provide a positive professional mentoring experience for female students of color if they are honest, interested in their development, confident in their abilities, invested in their success, and demand excellence.

The next themes were *developing a culture that supports diverse mentoring* and *demystifying the academy*. Blackwood and Brown-Welty (2011) concluded, "Mentors, including those who are supervisors, can work to develop a culture where cross-gender and cross-cultural mentoring is embraced" (p. 130). This discussion also noted that protégés within the California Community College System, who participated in this study, "indicated they experienced both male and female mentors of different races" (p. 130), but there was a consensus that neither the race nor gender was significant. The main distinction that emerged from this study was that women mentors could provide more emotional support as it related to balancing family and professional roles. One Mexican American woman respondent noted, "With a female, I can let my guard down and deal with family issues, but I never felt I could show that weakness to a man" (p. 122). In Hill et al. (1999), the Western Interstate Commission of Higher Education's (WICHE) Doctoral Scholars Program is described as providing both external funding and strategies designed to encourage faculty–student mentoring. WICHE was credited with the creation of a successful cross-race and cross-gender mentoring program, one that supports diverse mentoring and the demystification of the academy. More will be said about this program in later sections of this book.

Crutcher (2007) and Mansson and Myers (2012) described *characteristics that support cross-gender relationships*. Crutcher concluded, "Mentors need not have the same cultural or social background as their mentees. But they must pay close attention to the implications of the differences" (p. 44). She also stated, "Because of the complexity of cross-cultural mentoring, mentors need certain attributes or abilities, including selflessness, active listening skills, honesty, a nonjudgmental attitude, persistence, patience, and an appreciation for diversity" (p. 45).

Last, *e-mentoring* is cited by Bernstein et al. (2010) as beneficial to female faculty for some of the same reasons that are given for its benefit to faculty of color, because through online communication mentors may be less likely to have and/or exhibit sexist beliefs and behaviors. Bernstein et al. also stated that e-mentors in their study assisted women to overcome difficulties they may have in identifying themselves as potential scientists and in understanding their options when considering a career related to science, technology, engineering, and mathematics (STEM).

Challenges Across Race/Ethnicity

While literature on the benefits of cross-race/ethnicity mentorship was found, there was also a body of literature describing challenges experienced when faculty engage in cross-race/ethnicity mentorships. In academe, with the larger representation of White male faculty compared with women faculty and faculty of color (see Table 1.1), it is not possible that all faculty of color receive mentorship from other faculty of their own racial/ethnic group. Thus, if mentors are part of the formula for academic success, and faculty of color are to succeed in academe, it is important that successful mentorships across race/ethnicity be understood. Examining the dissatisfaction of faculty new to the professoriate, Kanuka and Marini (2005) suggested,

Mentoring initiatives can meet the individual needs of new faculty for growth, recognition, support, and a sense of belongingness . . . while converging with the institutional needs for stability, expansion, renewal, and an opportunity for senior faculty to influence and guide new and early faculty. . . . Given the well-documented benefits of successful mentoring relationships, there is a need to better understand the issues involved in and the barriers to implementing mentoring programs. (p. 14)

Given Kanuka and Marini's observations and that faculty of color will likely be new faculty, the careers of faculty of color may be affected by factors that do not affect the careers of White faculty who populate much of the tenured ranks of the professoriate. In this section, eight themes found in the literature that negatively affect the careers of faculty of color will be presented.

The first theme deals with faculty of color experiencing pressure to assimilate into the current culture of academe (*dominant culture assimilation*) from White faculty serving as their mentors. Cox (1993) described this type of assimilation as mentors having expectations that members of racial/ethnic groups will integrate into the social and economic life of the dominant racial group and embrace its behaviors and values. In the main, the newcomer is expected to embrace the values of higher education institutions that reflect the cultural norms of the majority. This includes the acceptance by faculty of color that what they may be interested in, if not widely valued in the current academic climate, remains on the margins. Brinson and Kottler (1993) described that one of the challenges in cross-race/ethnicity mentorships is that both the mentor and the mentee must learn about one another's cultural values and be responsive to and respectful of their differences. For mentees, one key challenge in mentorship is finding the right balance between receiving the type of professional socialization to be successful in their field and not having to relinquish their cultural heritage in favor of adapting White cultural norms (Brinson & Kottler, 1993).

Second, faculty of color are more likely than White faculty to feel *isolated and marginalized*, with or without mentors (see Aryan & Guzman, 2010; Mark et al., 2001; Stanley & Lincoln, 2005; Williamson & Fenske, 1992). Stanley and Lincoln (2005) wrote that when faculty of color are the first to be hired in departments, they feel isolated, alienated, and marginalized and are less likely to be mentored. Furthermore, Aryan and Guzman (2010) stated that one of the primary reasons faculty of color are isolated, get fewer professional opportunities than Whites, and are less likely to advance professionally is that, in part, they lack mentors of color.

Third, societal *racism and institutional racism* are factors that marginalize and exclude faculty of color in academe. Griffin and Reddick (2011) described the idea of hypersurveillance felt by Black male faculty as stemming from racially charged higher education environments. They wrote that Black male faculty restricted their interactions with their mentors out of concern that they may be misinterpreted and because they felt like they were being watched closely, in large part because of how Black males are perceived as dangerous in the larger society. This hypersurveillance not only affected their relationships with their mentors but also affected their students, as they tried to limit their interactions with students for the same reasons. Hall and Sandler (1983) pointed to the same underlying racist environment as a major reason for why faculty of color are frequently marginalized and undermentored in higher education. Last, Thomas (2001) found that because of the prevalence of racism, mentors of minorities need to approach mentoring of faculty of color with an understanding that they may have challenges, such as those described here, that they must strive to overcome in their mentorship.

Fourth, *power dynamics are more likely to affect faculty of color than Whites* because senior White faculty are more likely to be the mentors, and faculty of color are more likely to be graduate students or junior faculty mentees. Unbalanced power dynamics may have the senior faculty mentors assuming that they always know what is best for the protégé (Brinson & Kottler, 1993; Casto et al., 2005). These power dynamics are more likely to emerge when issues of race/ethnicity and diversity are at the forefront, such as when they affect the curriculum (Hill et al., 1999) or when issues arise in cross-race/ethnicity mentorships (Casto et al., 2005; Hill et al., 1999).

Fifth, many faculty of color may not seek mentorship because of the *stigma associated with seeking help.* Gothard (2009) wrote that seeking mentorship support is perceived to involve a loss of personal autonomy and a weakening of one's self-efficacy. Such a stigma may be especially traumatizing to mentees from minority groups (Ponce, Williams, & Allen, 2005). Furthermore, Brinson and Kottler (1993) explained that many faculty of color, like White faculty, succeeded as students because they had a single-minded determination and persistence and did it with little mentoring and therefore may perceive mentoring as unnecessary and as a sign that they are less than capable. In their study of Latino male students, using gender male role conflict as a theoretical guide, Sáenz, Bukoski, Lu, and Rodriguez (2013) shed light on this phenomenon as expressed by their respondents, finding "that pride and fear can prevent men from seeking academic help and support when needed" (p. 82).

Sixth, Brinson and Kottler (1993) and Thomas (2001) reported that *negative cross-cultural interactions* between White faculty and faculty of color can compromise the formation, development, and maturation of such mentorship relationships. When attempting to communicate intimately and respectfully, members coming from diverse cultural backgrounds make mistakes out of ignorance. Sometimes these mistakes can be minor and still lead to overreactions and perceived slights (Brinson & Kottler, 1993). In a study of cross-race faculty mentorships, Tillman (2001) found that while some African American faculty in predominantly White institutions had been successfully mentored by White faculty, there were just as many who had negative experiences with their White mentors. Tillman (2001) concluded that junior faculty "sought same race mentors with similar personal and cultural backgrounds and who could provide them support in coping with feelings of professional and social isolation" (p. 323). Study results also noted that the traditional mentoring dyad model needs to be expanded, as same-race mentors could serve as either a primary or a secondary mentor in order to meet the career and psychosocial needs of faculty. Psychosocial functions were described as enhancing "the protégé's sense of competence, identity, and work-role effectiveness . . . acceptance and confirmation . . . and counseling . . . in coping with job stress and work demands of the new faculty role" (p. 298).

Seventh, in the literature describing faculty being mentored by people outside of their race/ethnicity, many stated experiencing *language, racial/ethnic, and cultural barriers* (Sands, Parson, & Duane, 1992). Crutcher (2007) when writing about White faculty stated that to be good mentors to faculty of color, they must overcome their fears, biases, and stereotypes about people of other races/ethnicities. In addition, some faculty of color have been socialized to view Whites cautiously, which may lead to distrust of White mentors by faculty of color (Brinson & Kottler, 1993). Crutcher (2007) also stated that cross-race mentorships can be difficult and therefore mentors and mentees need to understand that successful cross-race mentorships can present a slippery slope "because if the mentor distances him or herself too much, the relationship can suffer. Clearly, mentors should get to know their mentees. Yet we must preserve appropriate power balances and ethical boundaries" (p. 47). As stated by Davidson and Foster-Johnson (2001), part of the reason for many of the cross-cultural issues and problems in higher education is that few graduate students learn about these issues through their formal course work.

Eighth, the last theme emerging from the literature related to challenges across race/ethnicity mentorship documented how *mentees prefer mentors of the same race* (see Lechuga, 2011; Sands et al., 1992; Wunsch, 1994). Lechuga's (2011) research addressed preferences that graduate students of color have for mentors of the same race/ethnicity. Similarly, Wunsch (1994) found that faculty of color may prefer same race/ethnicity backgrounds in their mentors. One reason stated for why students of color prefer mentorship from faculty of color is they have the capacity and ability to relate to them culturally (Patton, 2009). Thomas (1993) also found that when African Americans who have cross-race mentors were compared to those who had same-race mentors early in their career, those with cross-race mentors were generally more dissatisfied with their advancement. While this literature supports that mentees prefer same race/ethnicity in their mentors, many mentees also find success in cross-race/ethnicity relationships.

Challenges Across Gender

Several of the studies reviewed in this section identify challenges that women experience in academe. As shown in Table 1.1, women at all ranks and races/ethnicities are the least represented. Thus, the chances for women, in graduate school or as a junior professor, to be mentored by another woman are slim, because women are especially missing at the associate and full professor ranks. In our review of the literature, seven primary challenges are documented for mentor relationships across gender. These are identified and summarized next.

Sexism was the first theme found throughout the literature related to challenges across gender. The *Merriam-Webster's* (2013) online dictionary defined *sexism* as "prejudice or discrimination based on sex" and "behavior, conditions, or attitudes that foster stereotypes of social roles based on sex." Articles reviewed for this book document the challenges faced by women mentored by men (mentoring across gender). These authors described a sexist environment that constrains mentorship relationships across gender in higher education.

In 1983, Hall and Sandler described a mentoring system that supports the professional development of men but one that denies women the same assistance. They concluded that as senior faculty and administrators are predominantly White and male in higher education, women and minorities are "excluded from the long-established informal systems through which senior persons socialize their successors. . . . These systems have tended to function as 'old boys' networks' in which male mentors guide and foster male mentees. Women often don't receive the same support for professional achievement as men do" (p. 2). Hall and Sandler further reported, "Many senior men may hesitate to mentor women because they fear rumors of sexual involvement" (p. 13). This is the case especially "where mentoring of women is not supported by institutional policies that make the mentoring of all junior persons a part of senior professors' responsibilities" (p. 3).

In 1993, Parker and Kram concluded, "Though many [women] have found senior men to be effective and helpful mentors, cross-gender mentor relationships have several complexities that often limit their usefulness" (p. 42). In 1994, Wunsch suggested, "One would also do well to assess the institutional mores and culture in doing cross-racial or cross-gender pairing, and be aware of the potential for sexual harassment or exploitation" (p. 30).

In 2000, Schramm demonstrated that mentoring relations are problematic for women faculty, who are marginalized in patriarchal institutions because of power dynamics and cross-gender interactions. Furthermore, Schramm (2000) contended that male mentors who mentor women should have training to explicate issues and concerns related to cross-gender mentoring. Casto et al. (2005) stated that male mentors with female mentees must support them in overcoming pervasive or unaddressed sexist attitudes toward women in the department and the differential power relations that are part of the workplace environment, particularly placing women at a disadvantage.

In their study, Aryan and Guzman (2010) concluded that the experiences women of color have with sexism due to their gender intersect with their experiences of racism due to their race. In 2001, Tillman provided an example of issues emerging from a cross-gender, cross-race relationship, stating,

> There was only one female protégé in this study in a cross-gender mentoring relationship. Rosemary, a protégé in University A, was being mentored informally by a White male. Although Rosemary expressed no concerns about her cross-gender mentoring relationship, her mentor was concerned about how his mentoring relationship with an African American female would be perceived by other faculty members in their department. This mentor was not only concerned about the reactions from his colleagues, but he also seemed to anticipate that gender and race differences would prevent him and his protégé from interacting positively. (p. 315)

Through narrative inquiry, Griffin and Reddick (2011) revealed the troubling tendency for Black women to assume a greater load of mentoring responsibilities, engaging in a form of mentoring that is more personally taxing and time-consuming. They further concluded that women may have an additional "'gender tax,' . . . demonstrated by an expected level of personal support to students . . . expectations that women will serve as 'academic caretakers' (Aguirre, 2000; Gregory, 2001; McKay, 1997), meeting students' educational and social needs" (p. 1050). Griffin and Reddick (2011) contended that this situation could hinder the career advancement of Black female faculty members. Their research indicated that "Black women may be expected to engage with students in close familial ways, regardless of their desire to do so and despite the personal costs . . . [thereby] maintaining the disparities we see in the professoriate" (pp. 1051, 1052). They also discussed the following finding:

> Black male professors operate under the cloak of surveillance not unlike their experiences in society generally . . . [recommending that] departments and campuses should engage in frank conversations about historical and societal influences that affect Black men and women in academic settings and strategize about how these communities can challenge stereotypical perceptions . . . [setting] clear protocols for advising and mentoring for all members of the academic community. (p. 1053)

Unfortunately, these studies, conducted from 1983 to 2013, reveal that many of the issues described by Hall and Sandler in 1983 remain in academe today, and their recommendations for addressing these challenges are also quite similar. The major difference is that more recent work addresses the intersectionalities of multiple discrimination, examining race/ethnicity and gender in higher education mentoring relationships.

The second theme was *tokenism and marginalization*. The work of Kanter (1977) provides a theoretical lens for interpreting the tokenism and marginalization experienced by women faculty when engaged in a mentoring relationship with male faculty. Kanter concluded,

> Women in the minority inhabit a context characterized by: being more visible and on display, feeling more pressure to conform, needing to make fewer mistakes, finding it harder to gain credibility, being more isolated and peripheral, having fewer opportunities to be sponsored, facing misperceptions about their identity and role in the organization, being stereotyped, and facing more stress. Those in the majority faced the opposite social context, such as being seen as one of the group, and being preferred for sponsorship by higher level colleagues. (pp. 248–249)

Kanter's results imply that "the more ways in which one differs from the norm, the more social interactions will be negatively affected, and women of color, because of their multiple marginality, are generally far from the norm among the ranks of the professoriate" (Turner, González, & Wong, 2011, p. 200). For women and men, understanding the social context in which one another lives within their institutional workplace environment is invaluable to creating successful mentorship relationships. When defining *success*, Tillman (2001) suggested going to the mentor and protégé for their unique definitions. She contended that success could have different meanings for protégés and mentors, stating,

A successful mentoring relationship [can be defined as] whether the protégé was granted (or would be granted) promotion and tenure. In other cases, a successful relationship meant that [they] had a "good" relationship—that is, they liked each other and had a collegial relationship. (p. 305)

Nonetheless, Tillman (2001) stated, "Cross-gender mentoring relationships can be affected by the organizational culture—the values, norms, and attitudes that shape the organization" (p. 299). This is similar to Noe's (1988) work, which identified six potential barriers in cross-gender relationships: (a) lack of access to information networks, (b) tokenism, (c) stereotypes and attributions, (d) socialization practices, (e) norms regarding cross-gender relationships, and (f) reliance on ineffective power bases.

Related to the experience of tokenism, Hall and Sandler (1983) described the situation for women as "women's over visibility. . . . Where women are few, they tend to stand out because of their difference." This may lead senior scholars to avoid the risk of choosing a woman as a protégé. Whereas a male protégé may fail without anyone noticing, "a woman's mistakes are often loudly broadcast"; consequently, to protect their own reputations, men may "maintain higher standards for female protégés than for male protégés, or exclude women altogether" (p. 4). This situation is also reflected in some cases of women mentoring women, as will be discussed later in this chapter.

Schramm (2000) found that untenured women faculty experience marginalization and, if they are perceived as feminists, the marginalization may increase. Furthermore, Ellis (2001) found that women of color within the academy report both gender and race marginalization. One example is provided in the words of a graduate student in the WICHE Doctoral Scholars Program reported in an article by Hill et al. (1999). Castillo shared this student reflection:

The mentor-mentee relationship between a female doctoral student of color and a White male faculty member is complex. For this reason, we have also struggled in our relationship, and there have been times that I was clearly aware of our differences. As an example, our program and department experienced a recent conflict over multicultural issues . . . with regard to the program's gender and ethnic balance. Some women and women of color graduate students in the program found that they were unable to openly express their views. This systemic struggle played out in our relationship, which became symbolic of the larger conflict over marginality and power differentials. However, because we had previously developed mutual respect for our differences, I was able to talk openly with Dr. Hill about many of my concerns. (p. 839)

In the same article, a White male mentor, Dr. Hill, reflected on his mentoring relationships:

> From the very beginning of our relationship, she [Castillo] was eager to help me see her point of view and learn about her unique needs as a female ethnic minority doctoral student in counseling psychology in a predominantly White university. Although I realize that there are limitations to our mentor-mentee relationship (e.g., our research interests differ), I have helped Linda [Castillo] get started on her dissertation research, supervised her as part of a teaching practicum, and involved her in some of my own research that has overlapped with her interests. (p. 835)

Hill et al. (1999) described in detail some of the critical dynamics influenced by tokenism and marginalization in a cross-gender mentoring relationship. This level of detail informs others of potential issues and possible solutions to such challenges in cross-gender relationships.

Third, literature reported on *external perceptions* of sexual liaisons and favoritism as detrimental to cross-gender mentorships. Hall and Sandler (1983) stated,

> The sexual issue in a mentoring relationship can be especially problematic in the postsecondary setting. Both women students and male faculty may sometimes misinterpret each other's interest. . . . Should problems arise, faculty women are often in a more difficult situation than women students because their career may be threatened. Women students and faculty need ways to make their own professional concerns clear, and institutions need policies to clarify appropriate relationships. (p. 8)

Clawson and Kram (1984) suggested the types of relationships emerging from productive and unproductive levels of intimacy (see Table 1.2). They concluded that productive levels of intimacy lead to accomplishment of scholarly goals and development of respect between the mentor and the protégé. Distance between the mentor and the protégé leads to a lack of productivity and reinforced prejudices.

For example, one of Crutcher's (2007) respondents who is a mentor advises faculty to avoid intimacy with their mentees. She said, "Maintaining appropriate boundaries is challenging, because if the mentor distances him or herself too much, the relationship can suffer. Clearly, mentors should get close to their mentees. Yet we must preserve appropriate power balances and ethical boundaries" (p. 47). Another mentor in Crutcher's (2007) study suggested, "As a man, I need some different guidelines for how to mentor women than how to mentor men. . . . In mentoring women . . . not to

TABLE 1.2
Some Outcomes of Three Levels of Intimacy in Two Kinds of Relationships

	Unproductive Intimacy	*Productive Levels of Intimacy*	*Unproductive Distance*
Internal relationships	Sexual liaisons likely Less than desired growth	Desired levels of productivity and development	Less than desired productivity development
External relationships	Perceived favoritism and distrust	Development of respect for boss, subordinate, and other sex	Reinforced prejudices

Note. From "Managing Cross-Gender Mentoring," by J. G. Clawson and K. E. Kram, 1984, *Business Horizons, 27*(3), p. 25.

intrude in ways that can be misinterpreted or that open the doors to inappropriate kinds of relationships" (p. 47).

Despite this early work, the challenges to cross-gender mentoring based on external perceptions of the relationship still provide hindrances, according to studies conducted post-1984. For example, O'Neill and Blake-Beard (2002) stated,

> There are few female mentor/male mentee relationships because people are worried about perceptions and therefore prefer to interact with members of the same sex because they hold similar attitudes, values, and experiences. . . . The potential for real or perceived sexual involvement partly explains why females and males don't like to enter into mentoring relationships. . . . Even the possibility of unfounded rumors may deter female/male relationships. (p. 54)

Casto et al. (2005) reported, "Cross-gender mentorship may lead some mentors to worry that others may perceive them as having ulterior unethical motives in the relationship, and thus they may be reluctant to engage in mentoring relationships" (p. 336). For example, Griffin and Reddick (2011) indicated Black male faculty members were particularly cautious with female students. They kept female students at a distance, limiting the necessity of having to explain even the suggestion of sexual impropriety. "Black men by choice or fear of accusation are not engaging in close mentoring relationships with women generally, and Black women specifically" (Griffin & Reddick, 2011, p. 1052). Taken as a whole, and coupled with the demographic data presented at the beginning of this chapter, these studies suggest fewer mentorship opportunities for women who aspire to the professoriate.

A fourth theme was *the lack of professional interactions*. In the areas of engineering and medicine, researchers grapple with ways in which mentoring across gender might address the lack of women as faculty in these areas. For example, examining the context for women faculty in engineering, Chesler, Single, and Mikic (2003) reported, "Women faculty members often report lower levels of social support and fewer intra- and inter-departmental professional interactions than their male counterparts. . . . There are few women in positions of academic leadership who can act as role models for women faculty" (p. 257). Chesler et al. (2003) reported on adventure education, composed of linked intellectual and physical challenges in an outdoor setting, as a peer mentoring innovation designed to establish communication and trust among women engineering faculty members from different academic institutions. Adventure education "was chosen as the vehicle to transform the group into a highly functioning team" (p. 257).

Mark et al. (2001) examined mentoring programs needed to establish faculty gender and racial/ethnic equity in medicine. The Office on Women's Health (OWH) within the U.S. Department of Health and Human Services established the programs reviewed. They were National Centers of Leadership in Academic Medicine, one at each of four medical schools: MCP Hahnemann School of Medicine; the University of California, San Diego, School of Medicine; East Carolina University School of Medicine; and Meharry Medical College School of Medicine. These programs were formed with "institutional commitment and [included] institutional rewards and recognition for mentors [in order to] . . . foster the advancement of a diverse faculty, a more supportive academic environment, and the education of providers who are sensitive to the needs of all their patients, staff, and colleagues" (p. 39).

Fifth, the literature provides examples of how *politics and power relations* create challenges for women in academe. O'Neill and Blake-Beard (2002) indicated, "Since men are seen as more powerful than women, there may be a perception that they have more access to resources and opportunities, therefore more likely to be chosen as mentors" (p. 58). Furthermore, Casto et al. (2005) identified "challenges for male mentors of female mentees to overcome, such as pervasive or unaddressed sexist attitudes toward women in the department, gender politics, and power relations" (p. 335). Gibson (2006) found that women faculty described "the political climate of the organization as an essential attribute of their experience. Women faculty identified organizational culture and gender issues that affected the mentoring they received. This study suggests the need for human resource and organization development initiatives to facilitate the provision of academic mentoring for women faculty" (p. 63).

In Hill et al. (1999), one of the protégés described the power differentials she felt within her mentoring relationship:

> We have very few personal characteristics in common; he is a 40-year-old White male in a position of authority in the program, and I was not aware of any experience he had working directly with ethnic minority students. . . . Dr. Hill was open to learning about mentoring an ethnic minority student. . . . Initially, I had difficulty trusting Dr. Hill's stated interest in multiculturalism and his commitment to diversity. . . . I was very aware of cultural and power differentials between us that were contrary to experiences with my previous faculty mentor, who, I believe, had a personal connection to my ethnic identity. (p. 838)

Such power differentials are characterized by privilege for the majority and lack thereof for the minority, as dramatically exemplified by Johnson-Bailey and Cervero in their 2008 article. Johnson-Bailey, a Black female professor, and Cervero, a White male professor, contrast their academic lives by exploring the influence of race and gender. Cervero was Johnson-Bailey's mentor when she was a student and at an early stage in her career. They are now colleagues and collaborators. They are both full professors. Their study revealed a situation where

> White men and Black women are regarded and treated differently by colleagues and students. . . . Overall, the Black woman is often relegated to a second-class existence characterized by hostility, isolation, and lack of respect, while the White man lives an ideal academic life as a respected scholar who disseminates knowledge, understands complexity, and embodies objectivity. (p. 311)

They ended their article saying, "Ron cannot think of a time when race and gender have interfered. Juanita cannot think of a time when race and gender have not mattered. . . . Ours is a story of contrasts and of lives lived in parallel worlds" (p. 329). In the end, they stated that they are both working toward the elimination of such contrasts in experiences based on race and gender.

Kalbfleisch and Davies (1993) concluded that those individuals who need help the most (e.g., visible minorities, nontraditional faculty, and women) are the least likely to find it. Wunsch (1994) advanced this argument further by asserting that when individuals agree to enter into a mentoring relationship related to academic and career goals, the relationship moves from the personal to the institutional realm; this can result in inequity of opportunities, which the institution must address. To be exact, when some individuals have access to certain career advantages (e.g., mentoring relationships) and others do not, inequity of career opportunities (e.g., advancement, promotion) occurs. Kanuka and Marini (2005) asserted, "It is the responsibility of the institution to ensure that all individuals have equity of access to the same career opportunities. Structured mentoring relationships, such as the mosaic [group] mentoring model, are key to ensuring equity of access to mentoring" (p. 33). These studies demonstrate that men and women have very different life experiences within the same context, influencing not only their career trajectories but also their mentoring relationships.

As pointed out by Crosby (2007), "Those in positions of power (men) may not be as interested in keeping women out of good jobs as they are in bringing other men into their in-group" (p. 50). They concluded, "Discrimination in favor of men has the same effect as discrimination against women" (p. 50). Supportive of the commitment made by Johnson-Bailey and Cervero (2008), Bernstein et al. (2010) stated, "The goal of mentoring is not simply to teach the system, but also to change the system so that it becomes more flexible and responsive to the needs and pathways of its members—mentors and protégés" (p. 58).

Sixth, O'Neill and Blake-Beard (2002) examined *gender stereotypes*, concluding that males seeking mentors may perceive women to be less powerful, influential, and qualified so may not seek to have them as mentors. Crutcher (2007) suggested, "Mentors coming from the dominant culture must overcome their fears, biases, and stereotypes about other races and ethnicities, and they need to find a way to empathize with and understand their mentee's personal life situation" (p. 45). In addition, Crutcher (2007) stated,

> It is imperative, however, given the lack of diversity in higher education, that we support students from minority and underrepresented groups. Because few mentors, especially in the higher ranks of academe, come from non-majority backgrounds, we especially need to focus on strategies to make cross-cultural mentoring work. The lessons taught by the experienced mentors in my study are good starting points. When we become culturally competent and practice relationship behaviors that foster trust and growth, then we can become the mentors our students need. (pp. 47, 48)

Bernstein et al. (2010) stated, based on their research on women in the sciences,

> Mentors need to understand the subtleties, range, and impact of the various forms of sexism and racism that women and minorities continue to

encounter even in the 21st century. The more blatant and egregious forms of discrimination that were visible and documentable have been replaced by more subtle forms of marginalization and discouragement of women in the sciences. . . . Gender stereotypes differ among subcategories of women (e.g., stereotypes of white, black, and Hispanic women differ; they also differ for women physicists and women artists). In particular, stereotypes of women change when they become mothers such that they are both more liked but also seen as less competent. (p. 54)

In Hill et al. (1999), Dr. Hill, a White male mentor, provided a clear example of unlearning stereotypes that took place for him within a cross-gender and cross-race mentoring relationship:

A problematic, albeit tacit, assumption that I held prior to mentoring Linda and Le was that ethnic minority doctoral students would most likely benefit from an ethnic minority mentor. I suppose, in some respects, this rigid mindset on my part was perpetuated by my personal decision to culturally encapsulate myself by choosing mentees who were White. . . . I learned . . . that ethnic minority doctoral students share many of my personal values about academia even though our worldviews differ (e.g., both Linda and Le had a strong desire that our new faculty hire should be a highly skilled researcher). In sum, I have learned a great deal about professional mentorship . . . and this has included an increased flexibility in my attitudes and opinions about the kinds of students with whom I believe I can be an effective mentor. (p. 836)

The last theme addressed *gender differences*, particularly in terms of mentoring expectations and how they affect the careers of male and female faculty. With implications for success in science, mathematics, and engineering, Chesler and Chesler (2002) provided an overview of predominant socialized gender differences between women and men (see Table 1.3).

Chesler and Chesler (2002) stated that the "dominant mentoring style in science and engineering based on a traditional model of male socialization [within an environment of competition and individual achievement] is not the only impediment to successful mentoring of women scholars. It is also true that in these male dominated fields there are few senior female faculty available to act as mentors and models" (p. 51). Along this same vein, Mark et al. (2001) referred to similar issues to establish gender and racial/ethnic equity in the field of medicine.

Reflective of the work described previously, Ferreira (2003) described the male culture of STEM fields, stating, "The culture of science has been shaped by the masculine ideal of 17th century England and has yet to fully adapt to contemporary realities" (p. 122). Ferreira listed myriad factors that serve

TABLE 1.3
Outcomes of Female and Male Socialization on Characteristics and Goals

	Female	*Male*
Motivation	Encouragement	Challenge
Group interaction	Integrated	Separated
Task engagement	Collaborative	Competitive
Vision of success	Group affiliation	Individual achievement

Note. From "Gender-Informed Mentoring Strategies for Women Engineering Scholars: On Establishing a Caring Community," by N. C. Chesler and M. A. Chesler, 2002, *Journal of Engineering Education,* *91*(1), p. 50.

to undermine the advancement of women in STEM, including "the lack of support for women with family commitments; sexual harassment; and subtle stereotyped beliefs, attitudes, and cultural biases that operate beyond conscious awareness and that are often discipline- and department-specific" (p. 122). Bernstein et al. (2010) concluded, echoing the findings of Chesler and Chesler (2002), "Women aspiring to STEM careers find themselves in highly competitive male-dominated environments, with few female role models, mentors, or guidance for how to negotiate their ideals for their careers and personal lives" (p. 53). They reported on study findings that identify four areas of concern identified as particularly discouraging to doctoral student women in STEM fields, stating, "In addition to trouble managing the relationship with their dissertation advisor, students reported lack of timely . . . progress with dissertation research, difficulty balancing the demands of academic work with a personal life, and coping with an unfriendly professional climate" (p. 58).

Blackwood and Brown-Welty (2011) also found that mentoring had a positive influence on the careers of 11 women administrators who were leaders in the California Community College System. They found that women faced identity issues and discrimination, which were factors unique to women and not to their male counterparts. Although all of their women of color respondents felt that there were still gender equity issues in higher education, 66% of the respondents felt that these issues have improved over the years. In their view, this indicated that the culture of public community colleges had "made more progress and opened up for women more rapidly than other sectors of society. However, it also shows there is more work to be done to encourage an inclusive culture that embraces female leadership" (p. 125). They contended the need for exposure to a more broad definition of *mentoring* so that individuals can move from the definition primarily concerned with a formal, structured relationship toward a definition inclusive of the range of relationships that indicate mentoring is taking place. They concluded that mentoring relationships need to be defined broadly so as to capture their many facets.

As women have become a small but visible part of the departmental landscape, studies indicate that expectations of them as a mentor and a protégé are very different. Crutcher (2007) provided one example of the perception of gender differences when mentoring. One of the study's participants, Ross, a mentor, said that he is "'more comfortable with a less directive approach. I don't think it's my job to come up with the answers. I think it's my job to help others come up with the answers they need.' Although Ross is a man, he operates in what he deems a more feminine style of interaction—one that is less direct and more holistic" (p. 47). Gibson (2006) reported, "Male mentors were not seen as people with whom female faculty could address certain issues, such as concerns related to having children" (p. 72) and their "expected roles in the family and society," as noted by Bernstein et al. (2010, p. 58). Griffin and Reddick (2011) found that women in their study engage in close, personal relationships and face high gender-based expectations regarding student contact and that men describe more formal and compartmentalized relationships, partly because of their perceptions, as noted previously, of "surveillance" and potential accusations of inappropriate relationships with female students. In this case, women bear most of the mentoring responsibilities, to the potential detriment of their careers. However, Griffin and Reddick (2011) also stated, "Not all women will be able or willing to serve as 'academic caretakers'" (p. 1053). Findings complementary and extending these perceptions are reflected in a study by O'Neill and Blake-Beard (2002), which reported that women in roles of leadership are more likely to behave in a masculine manner, taking on the traits of those in the majority so that they may be successful.

Bernstein et al. (2010) presented three specific interventions for transforming institutional culture in the sciences but that have implications for all fields. First is getting involved with the Association for Women in Science (AWIS), an organization that provides an institutional structure for peer networking and mentoring across scientific fields and access to mentoring resources. A new mentoring handbook can be ordered from the AWIS website. The second is learning about the variety of opportunities for electronic mentoring, for mentors and for protégés. They listed the Society of Women Engineers, which has a professional development program that includes webinars and podcasts that are free to members. They also mentioned MentorNet, a nonprofit e-mentoring network that pairs motivated protégés (male and female) in STEM fields with mentors in higher education, government, and industry. They also noted the *Career*WISE project, a resource supported by the National Science Foundation for protégés that seeks to develop and evaluate a web-based personal resilience development program. The online *Career*WISE project is designed to equip STEM graduate women with skills that will help them find well-suited mentors and more generally deal with a variety of problems that can be encountered in STEM educational and occupational contexts, including problems in the mentor or advisor relationship. The third intervention is the ADVANCE program, which is supported by the National Science Foundation and targets university projects designed to increase the participation and success of women in STEM fields.

Again, these studies are reflective of Hall and Sandler's (1983) early work when they stated, for all disciplines and fields, that "the mentoring system as it currently operates in academe generally tends to bolster the professional development of men, but to deny women the same help in advancement. . . . Encouragement from others can be especially influential" (p. 2). In fact, when one is struggling as a student or a faculty member, hostility may not be the final straw causing one to walk away; indifference may be the primary culprit. An encouraging word or an empathetic response can reenergize one's resolve to stay.

Research on Mentorship That Can Affect Cross-Race and Cross-Gender Relationships

In addition to the literature described previously that specifically addresses the pros and cons of cross-race/ethnicity and cross-gender mentorships, we found extensive literature on mentoring that affects faculty of color and women. Figure 1.2 shows the ways in which mentorship can offer supportive pathways and challenges to faculty of color and women. In the middle of the figure are themes found to support or challenge faculty of color and women in mentoring relationships.

The area at the top of Figure 1.2 lists themes (e.g., shared power) of support for both faculty of color and women, and the area at the bottom lists themes (e.g., traditional [informal] mentoring) associated with challenges for both faculty of color and women. In this section, the literature on successful pathways (for race/ethnicity, for gender, and for both) will be presented first, followed by a discussion of the literature on the challenges.

Figure 1.2   Mentorship that can affect cross-race/ethnicity and cross-gender relationships, successful pathways, and challenges.

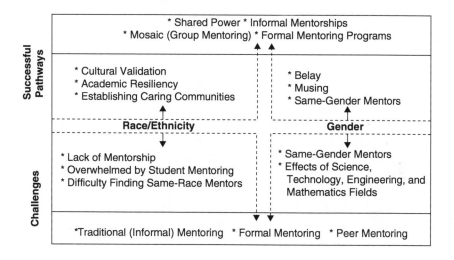

Successful Pathways That Affect Cross-Relationships

The mentoring literature on successful pathways addresses issues of race/ethnicity and gender but does not address pathways specific to cross-race/ethnicity and cross-gender relationships. This section will first present the literature on mentoring with implications for race/ethnicity, then present literature with gender implications, and conclude with literature that addresses both race and gender.

Regarding race/ethnicity. As shown in Figure 1.2, the literature addressed three themes: (a) cultural validation, (b) academic resiliency, and (c) establishing caring communities. *Cultural validation* was mentioned by faculty of color, who stated that regardless of the race or gender of their mentors, they need to be appreciated, their cultural views and values understood, and their responsibilities to their family and heritage affirmed (Okawa, 2002). Reddick and Sáenz (2012) described this cultural affirmation as a mentorship that includes nurturing the intellectual and personal self. In "Diving for Pearls: Mentoring as Cultural and Activist Practice Among Academics of Color," Okawa (2002) used "diving for pearls" as a metaphor in support of cultural validation within same-race mentorships, which can also be applied to mentorship where both mentor and mentee have significant commonalities. Okawa stated, "If you're both skin divers and you know how to find the pearls, then you can get into a deeper level" (p. 509), meaning that like those with similar knowledge about diving can be more effective as a team, those with similar cultures (or other similarities) can be more effective as a team. *Academic resiliency* in mentoring is the idea that when a senior scholar provides junior scholars with mentorship and networking opportunities, they develop resiliency to resist adverse cultural and ideological forces that have negative effects on their academic careers (Espinoza-Herold & Gonzalez, 2007). It has been said that when mentors teach mentees how to use coping strategies, mentees can develop the resiliency to overcome challenges (Espinoza-Herold & Gonzalez, 2007). And when mentees succeed because of their resiliency, research has shown that organizations benefit by having more productive faculty (Gothard, 2009; Kanuka & Marini, 2005; Schrodt, Cawyer, & Sanders, 2003). *Establishing caring communities* entails having mentors who truly care and act on the behalf of mentees to establish a connection with them, affirm who they are, and provide friendship and/or collegiality (Gibson, 2006).

Regarding gender. The literature reviewed here addressed three examples of successful same-gender mentoring programs and relationships: (a) belay, (b) musing, and (c) same-gender mentors. First, *belay* is the mountaineering term that refers to being physically supported in a harness that is attached to the harness of another person known as the *belayer* (Chesler et al., 2003). Belayers are used in mountain climbing such that the person being supported derives (a) informational benefits through learning opportunities, (b) psychosocial support through increased self-awareness and self-confidence, and (c) individual achievement through encouragement of the belayer (Chesler et al., 2003). Second, *musing* is a process of creating peer communities that facilitate connections in naturally developing relationships, which are more beneficial than mandated mentoring relationships (Angelique, Kyle, & Taylor, 2002). In musing relationships, power is shared between the mentor and the mentee, multiculturalism of individuals is respected, and mentees support one another toward collective action (Angelique et al., 2002). Last, research supports *same-gender mentors*. For example, Reddick and Sáenz (2012) addressed the importance of males mentoring males in documenting their own experiences from being graduate students to serving as faculty at their alma mater. In addition, Ceja and Rivas (2010) addressed the importance of women mentoring women in the case of Latinas, and Johnsrud (1994) explicated the important role women mentors play in the academic lives of women, such as mentorship on academic politics and academic writing.

Regarding race/ethnicity and gender. The literature addressed four factors that contribute to success in cross-race/ethnicity and cross-gender mentorships: (a) shared power, (b) informal mentorships, (c) mosaic (group) mentoring, and (d) formal mentoring programs. First, *shared power* was described by Angelique et al. (2002) as an element in musing presented earlier, but Johnsrud (1994) also described shared power as a way for female mentors to empower their female mentees. Mentorship based on power sharing has senior scholars working in collaboration with junior scholars (Johnsrud, 1994). Second, *informal mentorships* were said to sometimes work better for faculty of color and women than formal mentorships (see Peterson-Hickey, 1998). Peterson-Hickey (1998) wrote that informal mentoring proves to be more successful than formal programs for American Indian faculty, who highly value mentorship but also value authentic mentorship that evolves over time. Third, Kanuka and Marini (2005) wrote that *mosaic mentoring* programs "have no agendas to preserve hierarchies and power imbalances" and "view all faculty members as continuing learners, [attempting to] reduce feelings of dissatisfaction among new and early faculty members" (p. 12). Group mentoring relationships composed of faculty members with diverse and complementary skills and knowledge can result in greater benefits than traditional mentoring dyads and can avoid many of the potential problems. Mullen (2000) called this type of group mentoring *mosaic mentoring*. In mosaic mentoring, there are multiple mentors, which means less chance of cloning, when faculty mentors impose on a mentee what they view as normative and good, which more likely can occur in the traditional one-on-one mentorships (Sandler, 1993). Last, *formal mentoring programs* were also noted as important in the mentoring of students of color, faculty of color, and women (Boyle & Boice, 1998; Gothard, 2009; Kanuka & Marini, 2005; Strayhorn & Saddler, 2009). Formal mentoring programs were said to provide formal, structured, and goal-oriented opportunities that are important to the academic success of students of color, faculty of color, and women (Strayhorn & Saddler, 2009). If formal mentoring programs exist, where the institution or department takes on the responsibility to provide mentoring, the possibility of everyone attaining a mentor may increase.

Challenges That Affect Cross-Relationships

For race/ethnicity. Lack of mentorship was the first of three themes on challenges that affect cross-race and cross-gender relationships. First, Ceja and Rivas's (2010) review of the literature and interviews with Chicana students found the need for same-race and same-gender faculty–student mentorships for academic success. In addition, Lovell, Alexander, and Kirkpatrick (2002) also indicated that the presence of same-race, same-gender faculty role models is important for the satisfaction and success of students of color. More recently, according to Aryan and Guzman (2010), women students of color express feelings of frustration and isolation when describing a lack of mentorship and advising in their graduate programs. They suggested more research to determine how to recruit and retain professional staff of color so that "women of color can have mentors and advisors that support and understand them" (p. 76).

Contesting the perception of Asian and Pacific Island Americans as model minorities who are not in need of mentoring, Sands et al. (1992) reported on a survey of 71 Asian tenured or tenure-track faculty and 301 White faculty regarding their perceptions of mentoring. Of this sample, White faculty are broadly represented across fields, whereas Asian faculty are clustered in specific fields such as engineering, math, and the physical sciences. Asian faculty appeared to receive adequate amounts of mentoring (when compared to their White counterparts) in graduate school and as postdocs, but survey results suggest that Whites reported receiving more mentoring opportunities than Asians as faculty. Of the Asian faculty who didn't have and didn't seek mentoring, some perceived mentoring as "hitching myself to somebody else's coattails" (p. 127) and felt that they needed to figure it out for themselves, buying into the model minority myth, according to the authors. Others merely reported they were never presented with the opportunity to be mentored. Sands et al. (1992) concluded that although Asians have made progress they "have not achieved equity with Whites" (p. 129).

Stein (1994), in his survey of 22 American Indian faculty, found that many had mentors while pursuing graduate studies but rarely were these mentors American Indian. Once they secure faculty positions, finding mentors at this level proves to be difficult. Only 50% of American Indian faculty surveyed had mentors. Those who had mentors described how they helped them overcome obstacles. Those who did not have mentors expressed frustration as they made career decisions (p. 104). On the basis of her interviews with 28 American Indian faculty, Peterson-Hickey (1998) reported on the critical need for mentoring specifically for American Indian faculty. She stated that only two of the American Indian faculty in her study talked about the existence of formal mentoring programs that helped them on their way to the professoriate. If they had a mentor, they had to seek him or her out.

According to Stein (1994), these faculty are also expected to serve as mentors, advisors, and role models to all American Indian students, even for all other minorities on campus and off campus. If American Indian faculty are to serve communities inside and outside the institution, an overwhelming responsibility, Stein suggested that this service must be counted toward the tenure decision. In a similar vein, Griffin (2012) discussed the management of mentoring of students by Black professors. However, Griffin's study concluded that if mentoring included collaborative project activities, then both mentor and protégé may benefit. On the other hand, mentoring with a focus on student development generally might detract from scholarly research.

Her findings suggest that the type of mentoring interaction determines whether it might be detrimental to a faculty member's research productivity.

Calhoun (2003) remarked that Native students (and faculty) need to acquire sufficient social and cultural capital to do more than survive but to also thrive academically. Her research showed that "we need mentors who are willing to take the time to explain the way college is done. . . . The mentoring we require is not the same as that required by Euroamerican students who come with multiple resources available to them for mentoring" (p. 136). One of her study participants provided an example:

> If you're a Native woman who gets into graduate school, . . . there's at least one professor who wants you, the individual, to succeed. But that potential mentor is swamped and has very little time for mentoring. . . . Without one-on-one mentoring, which many of us have not had, we miss learning the little details that make the difference between just getting an education and knowing what to do with one. This is huge—HUGE. (p. 136)

Calhoun (2003) noted that, in her personal response to an unsupportive academic environment, she sought a position at a minority-serving institution, one where "respect is more important than any other idea" (p. 145). She challenged individuals and institutions to "respect and honor diversity" (p. 146).

For gender. The first of two challenges was *same-gender mentors*. Although studies report on the benefits of women mentoring women, research also demonstrates challenges stemming from the dynamics of tokenism (visibility and high risk), discussed previously. For example, Parker and Kram (1993), who began their study based on initial discussions of their own mentor–protégé relationship, reported, "Because there are so few senior women in business . . . their mentee . . . may be seen as a reflection of themselves, so they may have higher expectations of their mentees. . . . They cannot afford to have a woman protégé fail" (p. 45). In addition, these scholars provide a list of problems that may underlie "disconnections between women" (p. 42). They reported, "Women [in business] often discover that mentoring relationships with other women are unsatisfying. Senior women report feeling either discounted or overburdened as mentors" (p. 43). They also report that junior women need too much hand-holding and nurturing. Furthermore, women mentees complain that their women mentors want them to be dependent and to pursue career over family. Mentees also feel that senior women are too busy trying to break the glass ceiling to be effective mentors and are too competitive and unreceptive to them. Strategies that they proposed to address such challenges include increase self-awareness of projections and transferences; make undermining dynamics potentially barring a stronger alliance discussable; challenge untested assumptions about needs, availability, and expectations; build multiple relationships so as not to depend solely on one mentor; and create a supportive culture (pp. 49–50).

The second theme revolved around the *challenges that STEM fields provide for women.* Chesler and Chesler (2002) reported that undergraduate women, compared to men, have negative experiences in the classroom and with their peers, leading them to leave the sciences for other fields, termed "switch rates" (p. 50). In line with this finding, Bernstein (2011) and Bernstein and Russo (2008) suggested that some women decide to change course because of the disillusionment and discomfort they experience once in the program. This is coupled with the lack of senior female faculty available to act as mentors and models.

In addition, Nolan, Buckner, Marzabadi, and Kuck (2008) conducted a survey of 455 (135 women) graduates comparing women's and men's retrospective perceptions of the mentoring they received during their training and career development in chemistry. Of the 135 female chemists, only 11% had undergraduate female advisors, 7% had graduate female advisors, and no women had a female advisor for both undergraduate and graduate experiences. Their results "suggest that women perceived that they received less mentoring than men at the undergraduate, graduate, and post-doctoral levels of training, likely related to gender differences in eventual career success" (p. 235). For example, women noted that men were more likely to get help from advisors in obtaining postdoctoral positions, and men were more likely to say that their postdoctoral advisors were interested in their research. Interventions at the individual and the institutional level are recommended. Awareness of these varying perspectives is critical for both female protégés and male mentors if change is to take place. Formal mentoring programs are also recommended in an attempt to transform a negative climate as perceived by women in this study.

For race/ethnicity and gender. Three themes were identified that addressed mentoring challenges for faculty of color and women that do not necessarily relate to cross-race and cross-gender relationships: (a) traditional (informal) mentoring, (b) formal mentoring, and (c) peer mentoring. Whether we are examining traditional one-on-one informal mentoring practices or formal programs based within the protégé's campus or outside the campus, throughout this section challenges across race/ethnicity and gender include references to the isolation, lack of advising, and marginalization that students and new faculty encounter in their places of study and work. The potential and challenge of peer mentoring are also noted. Of particular importance is the benefit and cost of being mentors to minority faculty. Unless this service is valued for promotion and tenure, several of the articles reviewed here refer to mentoring as a potential constraint to the careers of minority faculty.

In our first theme that addresses traditional mentoring, contrasting findings in the literature regarding the need for same-race and same-gender faculty–student mentorships for academic success are revealed. For example, Herr (1994) contended, "There is no convincing evidence that same-gender, same-race, or same-ethnicity mentorship is any more likely to be successful than a relationship formed without such commonality" (p. 85).

On the other hand, Ceja and Rivas (2010) indicated that the presence of same-race, same-gender faculty role models is important for the satisfaction and success of students of color. In the narratives of 17 Chicana students, Ceja and Rivas (2010) documented the important role that strong connections with Latina faculty plays in the motivation of aspiring Chicana scholars. Although faculty of color and Latinas referred to in this study willingly volunteered their time to mentor these students, Ceja and Rivas (2010) concluded with an important charge: "Knowing that student-faculty interactions can form along racial and gender lines, and given the dearth of faculty of color in academia, future research should also examine . . . how can we improve the educational experience for students of color without doing so at the expense of faculty of color?" (p. 93). A multiplicity of mentoring approaches might be implemented.

Other scholars have provided a list of drawbacks found in traditional mentoring approaches: In their review of the literature, Boyle and Boice (1998) concluded that newcomers who are women and minorities are less likely to have spontaneous support and that "the single biggest advantage of natural mentoring in the professoriate goes exclusively to white males already in the old-boy network" (p. 159). They supported a systematic mentoring approach. Such programs may involve those who might otherwise be left out, and mentors can learn the nuances of mentoring from each other.

Angelique et al. (2002) challenged the traditional mentoring model as limited because people need more than one mentor to fulfill their needs and as equaling assimilation into an existing system with little or no incentive to change an institutional culture. Sandler (1993) agreed, maintaining that a person does not have to be older, or middle-aged, to be an effective mentor and that having multiple social networks can expand a mentee's ability to develop allies and alliances. Mullen and Lick (1999) advocated for mentoring models as reciprocal partnerships, valuing the contributions of both mentors and mentees.

On the basis of their work, Angelique et al. (2002) suggested that traditional mentoring approaches must evolve from mentoring into musing, "a process of creating peer communities that facilitates connections between naturally developing relationships, shared power, and collective action. Through mentoring as musing new faculty have the potential to evolve as change agents in the institution, instead of assimilating into the existing system" (p. 195).

Our second theme addressed *formal mentoring*. Formal mentoring institutes such as the National Summer Institute held at the University of Denver described by Aryan and Guzman (2010) may be one effective way to mentor doctoral students of color. The institute, founded in 2004, brings together doctoral students in various disciplines to participate in a four-day workshop that addresses issues peculiar to doctoral programs, such as completing a dissertation, building a résumé and curriculum vitae, becoming a faculty member, developing job talks, learning salary negotiation strategies, and publishing. According to their interviews, women students of color at the institute described how they also benefited from interactions with established scholars of color and students of color from across the nation. However, when referring to the specific graduate programs, they expressed feelings of frustration and isolation because of a lack of mentorship and advising. Consequences of this situation for them potentially extend into a lack of experience making presentations and authoring publications that are now critical to compete even for entry-level faculty positions. Aryan and Guzman suggested more research to determine how to recruit and retain professional staff of color so that "women of color can have mentors and advisors that support and understand them" (p. 76).

Johnsrud (1994) described a mentoring program funded by campus leaders to support women faculty at the University of Hawaii. On the basis of the assessment of their needs, the program was designed to meet their specific identified needs. For example, social interactions and connections, such as brown-bag lunches, with other women on campus and writing groups for junior women faculty were initiated to help them progress toward their tenure and promotion.

On the other hand, according to Kanuka and Marini (2005), there are possible drawbacks to formal mentoring programs. Mentors and mentees need to meet on a regular basis to complete various activities, which means a significant time commitment by both parties. This may be difficult to ensure in a formal mentoring program where no one is accountable. In mentoring, many feel that spontaneity is best, where those of similar interests are drawn together. In addition, there can be a stigma attached to mentees who participate in the mentoring program because they are labeled as people who need help. Providing incentives for a mentor and a mentee to participate in a formal mentoring program is also of concern. Issues for formal mentoring programs at the institutional level include that "there is too much variety among departments for an external mentoring program to be effective" (p. 19). A call to assess the effectiveness of any formal mentoring program is acknowledged.

The final theme addressed the importance of *peer mentoring*. Ong, Wright, Espinosa, and Orfield (2011) reported that peer support networks were a key factor in the long-term success of minority women students in STEM fields. However, peer study groups were difficult to enter, especially if there were no other minority women in the group. In these cases, women of color will likely go outside their department to seek support. On the other hand, Angelique et al. (2002) noted that if such support networks were inclusive, "peer mentors are relative equals in terms of their institution's hierarchy. . . . Peer mentors may be able to offer greater feedback concerning how work, personal, and family commitments have an impact on one another" (p. 199). Ong et al. (2011) also called for expanded research and programmatic support, concluding, "Research . . . on underserved students has focused on women and minorities . . . as *distinct* groups without . . . addressing the intersection between gender and race/ethnicity" (p. 200).

Crawford and Smith (2005) concluded, "Mentoring has shown promise as an appropriate intervention for advancing . . . careers. . . . Those with mentors . . . reported a greater satisfaction with their career development . . . greater productivity as leaders in professional associations, received more competitive grants, and have published more articles in their field" (p. 64). Regardless of all these challenges, the combined work of the scholars identified here inspires one to continue to explore ways in which mentoring can work for diverse communities within various roles and contexts in higher education. To do otherwise, as Crawford and Smith so aptly asserted, means that for those not mentored "their individual academic institutions have not capitalized on their talents" (p. 64).

Discussion

This chapter attempted to capture the breadth, depth, and complexity of various cross-race/ethnicity and cross-gender mentoring relationships as described in the literature. Although Blackwell's (1989) definition of *mentoring*, as a process by which a person of superior rank, achievement, and prestige counsels and guides the intellectual development of his or her mentee, still remains relevant for many mentoring relationships, the literature reviewed here expands that definition to include several other models of effective and successful mentoring relationships. The literature documents elements of programs and approaches, both formal and informal, used to achieve success in cross-race/ethnicity and cross-gender relationships. Positive, facilitative aspects were reported, as well as challenges and problems encountered. In addition, the literature documents the varied needs of protégés and the ways in which they can also potentially contribute to the intellectual development of their mentors.

Unfortunately, on the basis of the review of the extant literature on cross-race/ethnicity and cross-gender mentorship, racism and sexism continue to be identified as offering challenges to faculty of color and women, as well as to their allies who attempt to counter differential opportunities based on race, ethnicity, and gender. Discussion on how to remedy these concerns continues to be recommended throughout the higher education literature, but little, if any, real progress has been made, resulting in the continuing trend of underrepresentation of faculty of color and women, especially at the tenured and full professor levels. More must be done to address this issue across all forms of diversity remaining in the margins of academe. It is hoped that the insights and ideas presented in this book will provide further understanding of what can be done to make a difference.

Narratives coauthored by mentors and protégés will now be presented. Through detailed biographical sketches, these narratives provide the reader with nuanced descriptions of cross-race/ethnicity and/or cross-gender mentorship relationships. From the authors' unique perspectives, each narrative not only provides contemporary reflections of what is currently documented in the literature but also adds other insights and depth of understanding into what occurs in the development of a mentorship relationship that can be lifelong.

References

Aguirre, A. (2000). *Women and minority faculty in the academic workplace: Recruitment, retention, and academic culture* (ASHE-ERIC Higher Education Report, 27[6]). San Francisco, CA: Jossey-Bass.

Angelique, H., Kyle, K., & Taylor, E. (2002). Mentors and muses: New strategies for academic success. *Innovative Higher Education, 26*(3), 195–209.

Aryan, B., & Guzman, F. (2010). Women of color and the PhD: Experiences in formal graduate support programs. *Journal of Business, 1*(4), 69–77.

Bernstein, B. L. (2011). Managing barriers and building supports in science and engineering doctoral programs: Conceptual underpinnings for a new online training program for women. *Journal of Women and Minorities in Science and Engineering, 17*(1), 29–50.

Bernstein, B. L., Jacobson, R., & Russo, N. F. (2010). Mentoring women in context: Focus on science, technology, engineering, and mathematics fields. In C. A. Rayburn, F. L. Denmark, M. E. Reuder, & A. M. Austria (Eds.), *The Praeger handbook for women mentors: Transcending barriers of stereotype, race, and ethnicity* (pp. 43–64). Westport, CT: Praeger.

Bernstein, B. L., & Russo, N. F. (2008). Explaining too few women in STEM careers: A psychosocial perspective. In M. Paludi (Ed.), *Obstacles and the identity juggle* (Vol. 2, pp. 1–33). Westport, CT: Praeger.

Beverly, C. (2011). *African American faculty and administrator success in the academy: Career mentoring and job satisfaction at predominantly White institutions.* Bethlehem, PA: Lehigh University.

Blackburn, R. T., Chapman, D. W., & Cameron, S. M. (1981). "Cloning" in academe: Mentorship and academic careers. *Research in Higher Education, 15*(4), 315–327.

Blackwell, J. E. (1989). Mentoring: An action strategy for increasing minority faculty. *Academe, 75*(5), 8–14.

Blackwood, J., & Brown-Welty, S. (2011). Mentoring and interim positions: Pathways to leadership for women of color. *Diversity in Higher Education, 10,* 109–133.

Boyle, P., & Boice, B. (1998). Systematic mentoring for new faculty teachers and graduate teaching assistants. *Innovative Higher Education, 22*(3), 157–179.

Bozeman, B., & Fenney, M. K. (2007). Toward a useful theory of mentoring: A conceptual analysis and critique. *Administration and Society, 39*(6), 719–739.

Brinson, J., & Kottler, J. (1993). Cross-cultural mentoring in counselor education: A strategy for retaining minority faculty. *Counselor Education and Supervision, 32*(4), 241–253.

Calhoun, J. A. (2003). "It's just a social obligation. You could say 'No!'": Cultural and religious barriers of American Indian faculty in the academy. *The American Indian Quarterly, 27*(1), 132–154.

Casto, C., Caldwell, C., & Salazar, C. F. (2005). Creating mentoring relationships between female faculty and students in counselor education: Guidelines for potential mentees and mentors. *Journal of Counseling and Development, 83*(3), 331–336.

Ceja, M., & Rivas, M. (2010). Faculty-student interactions and Chicana Ph.D. aspirations. *Journal of the Professoriate, 3*(2), 78–98.

Chesler, N. C., & Chesler, M. A. (2002). Gender-informed mentoring strategies for women engineering scholars: On establishing a caring community. *Journal of Engineering Education, 91*(1), 49–55.

Chesler, N. C., Single, P. B., & Mikic, B. (2003). On belay: Peer-mentoring and adventure education for women faculty in engineering. *Journal of Engineering Education, 92*(3), 257–262.

Clawson, J. G., & Kram, K. E. (1984). Managing cross-gender mentoring. *Business Horizons, 27*(3), 22–32.

Cox, T. (1993). *Cultural diversity in organizations: Theory, research and practice.* San Francisco, CA: Berrett-Koehler.

Crawford, K., & Smith, D. (2005). The we and the us mentoring African American women. *Journal of Black Studies, 36*(1), 52–67.

Crosby, F. (2007). Sex discrimination at work. In J. E. Chrisler, C. Golden, & P. D. Rozee (Eds.), *Lectures in the psychology of women* (pp. 42–57). Long Grove, IL: Waveland Press.

Crutcher, B. N. (2007). Mentoring across cultures. *Academe, 93*(4), 44–48.

Davidson, M. N., & Foster-Johnson, L. (2001). Mentoring in the preparation of graduate researchers of color. *Review of Educational Research, 71*(4), 549–574.

de la Luz Reyes, M., & Halcón, J. J. (1988). Racism in academia: The old wolf revisited. *Harvard Educational Review, 58*(3), 299–315.

Dinsmore, J. A., & England, J. T. (1996). A study of multicultural counseling training at CACREP-accredited counselor education programs. *Counselor Education and Supervision, 36*(1), 58–76.

Ellis, E. M. (2001). The impact of race and gender on graduate school socialization, satisfaction with doctoral study, and commitment to degree completion. *The Western Journal of Black Studies, 25*, 30–45.

Espinoza-Herold, M., & Gonzalez, V. (2007). The voices of senior scholars on mentoring graduate students and junior scholars. *Hispanic Journal of Behavioral Sciences, 29*(3), 313–335.

Ferreira, M. M. (2003). Gender differences in graduate students' perspectives on the culture of science. *Journal of Women and Minorities in Science and Engineering, 9*(2), 119–135.

Gibson, S. K. (2006). Mentoring of women faculty: The role of organizational politics and culture. *Innovative Higher Education, 31*(1), 63–79.

Gothard, K. A. (2009). *Faculty mentoring in higher education: How can the institution benefit?* (Unpublished doctoral dissertation). Capella University.

Gregory, S. T. (2001). Black faculty women in the academy: History, status, and future. *The Journal of Negro Education, 70*(3), 124–138.

Griffin, K. A. (2012). Black professors managing mentorship: Implications of applying social exchange frameworks to analyses of student interactions and their influence on scholarly productivity. *Teachers College Record, 114*(5), 1–37.

Griffin, K. A., & Reddick, R. J. (2011). Surveillance and sacrifice: Gender differences in the mentoring patterns of Black professors at predominantly White research universities. *American Educational Research Journal, 48*(5), 1032–1057.

Hall, R. M., & Sandler, B. R. (1983). *Academic mentoring for women students and faculty: A new look at an old way to get ahead.* Project on the Status and Education of Women, Association of American Colleges, Washington, DC.

Herr, K. U. (1994). Mentoring faculty at the departmental level. *New Directions for Teaching and Learning, 57*, 81–90.

Hill, R. D., Castillo, L. G., Ngu, L. Q., & Pepion, K. (1999). Mentoring ethnic minority students for careers in academia: The WICHE Doctoral Scholars Program. *The Counseling Psychologist, 27*(6), 827–845.

Johnson-Bailey, J., & Cervero, R. M. (2008). Different worlds and divergent paths: Academic careers defined by race and gender. *Harvard Educational Review, 78*(2), 311–332.

Johnsrud, L. K. (1994). Enabling the success of junior faculty women through mentoring. *New Directions for Teaching and Learning, 1994*(57), 53–63.

Kalbfleisch, P. J., & Davies, A. B. (1993). An interpersonal model for participation in mentoring relationships. *Western Journal of Communication, 57*(4), 399–415.

Kanter, R. M. (1977). *Men and women of the corporation.* New York, NY: Basic Books.

Kanuka, H., & Marini, A. (2005). Empowering untenured faculty through mosaic mentoring. *Canadian Journal of University Continuing Education, 30*(2), 11–38.

Lechuga, V. M. (2011). Faculty-graduate student mentoring relationships: Mentors' perceived roles and responsibilities. *Higher Education, 62*(6), 757–771.

Light, P. (1994). Diversity in the faculty "not like us": Moving barriers to minority recruitment. *Journal of Policy Analysis and Management, 13*(1), 163–186.

Lovell, N. B., Alexander, M. L., & Kirkpatrick, L. A. (2002). *Minority faculty at community colleges: Fastback 490.* Bloomington, IN: Phi Delta Kappa Educational Foundation.

Lynch, R. V. (2002, November). *Mentoring across race: Critical case studies of African American students in a predominantly White institution of higher education.* Paper presented at the annual meeting of the Association for the Study of Higher Education, Sacramento, CA.

Mansson, D. H., & Myers, S. A. (2012). Using mentoring enactment theory to explore the doctoral student-advisor mentoring relationship. *Communication Education, 61*(4), 309–334.

Mark, S., Link, H., Morahan, P. S., Pololi, L., Reznik, V., & Tropez-Sims, S. (2001). Innovative mentoring programs to promote gender equity in academic medicine. *Academic Medicine, 76*(1), 39–42.

McKay, N. Y. (1997). A troubled peace: Black women in the halls of the White academy. In L. Benjamin (Ed.), *Black women in the academy: Promises and perils* (pp. 11–22). Miami: University Press of Florida.

Mullen, C. A. (2000). Constructing co-mentoring partnerships: Walkways we must travel. *Theory Into Practice, 39*(1), 4–11.

Mullen, C. A., & Lick, D. W. (Eds.). (1999). *New directions in mentoring: Creating a culture of synergy.* London, UK: Falmer Press.

Noe, R. A. (1988). An investigation of the determinants of successful assigned mentoring relationships. *Personnel Psychology, 41*(3), 457–479.

Nolan, S. A., Buckner, J. P., Marzabadi, C. H., & Kuck, V. J. (2008). Training and mentoring of chemists: A study of gender disparity. *Sex Roles, 58*(3–4), 235–250.

Okawa, G. Y. (2002). Diving for pearls: Mentoring as cultural and activist practice among academics of color. *College Composition and Communication, 53*(3), 507–532.

O'Neill, R. M., & Blake-Beard, S. D. (2002). Gender barriers to the female mentor-male protégé relationship. *Journal of Business Ethics, 37*(1), 51–63.

Ong, M., Wright, C., Espinosa, L. L., & Orfield, G. (2011). Inside the double bind: A synthesis of empirical research on undergraduate and graduate women of color in science, technology, engineering, and mathematics. *Harvard Educational Review, 81*(2), 172–209.

Parker, V. A., & Kram, K. E. (1993). Women mentoring women: Creating conditions for connection. *Business Horizons, 36*(2), 42–51.

Patton, L. D. (2009). My sister's keeper: A qualitative examination of mentoring experiences among African American women in graduate and professional schools. *The Journal of Higher Education, 80*(5), 510–537.

Peterson-Hickey, M. M. (1998). *American Indian faculty experiences: Culture as a challenge and source of strength* (Unpublished doctoral dissertation). University of Minnesota, Minneapolis.

Ponce, A. N., Williams, M. K., & Allen, G. J. (2005). Toward promoting generative cultures of intentional mentoring within academic settings. *Journal of Clinical Psychology, 61*(9), 1159–1163.

Reddick, R. J. (2009). Fostering cross-racial mentoring: White faculty and African American students at Harvard college. In S. Sánchez-Casal & A. Macdonald (Eds.), *Identity in education* (pp. 65–102). New York, NY: Palgrave Macmillan.

Reddick, R. J., & Sáenz, V. B. (2012). Coming home: Hermanos académicos reflect on past and present realities as professors at their alma mater. *Harvard Educational Review, 82*(3), 353–380.

Sáenz, V. B., Bukoski, B. E., Lu, C., & Rodriguez, S. (2013). Latino males in Texas community colleges: A phenomenological study of masculinity constructs and their effect on college experiences. *Journal of African American Males in Education, 4*(2), 82–102.

Sandler, B. R. (1993, March 10). Women as mentors: Myth and commandments. *The Chronicle of Higher Education*, p. B3.

Sands, R. G., Parson, L. A., & Duane, J. (1992). Faculty-faculty mentoring and discrimination: Perceptions among Asian, Asian American, and Pacific Island faculty. *Equity and Excellence in Education, 25*(2–4), 124–129.

Schramm, S. (2000). *Thinking thrice: A feminist response to "mentoring" that marginalizes* (ED 446463). doi:http://www.eric.ed.gov/PDFS/ED446463.pdf

Schrodt, P., Cawyer, C. S., & Sanders, R. (2003). An examination of academic mentoring behaviors and new faculty members' satisfaction with socialization and tenure and promotion processes. *Communication Education, 52*(1), 17–29.

Sexism. (2013). *Merriam-Webster's online dictionary*. Retrieved from http://www.merriam-webster.com/dictionary/sexism

Singh, D. K., & Stoloff, D. L. (2003, January). *Mentoring faculty of color*. Paper presented at the annual meeting of the American Association of Colleges for Teacher Education, New Orleans, LA. (ED 474179)

Smith, D. G., Turner, C. S. V., Osei-Kofi, N., & Richards, S. (2004). Interrupting the usual: Successful strategies for hiring diverse faculty. *The Journal of Higher Education, 75*(2), 133–160.

Stanley, C. A. (1994). Mentoring minority graduate students: A West Indian narrative. *New Directions for Teaching and Learning, 1994*(57), 121–125.

Stanley, C. A., & Lincoln, Y. S. (2005). Cross-race faculty mentoring. *Change: The Magazine of Higher Learning, 37*(2), 44–50.

Stein, W. J. (1994). The survival of American Indian faculty. *Thought and Action, 10*(1), 101–113.

Strayhorn, T. L., & Saddler, T. N. (2009). Gender differences in the influence of faculty-student mentoring relationships on satisfaction with college among African Americans. *Journal of African American Studies, 13*(4), 476–493.

Thomas, D. A. (1993). Racial dynamics in cross-race developmental relationships. *Administrative Science Quarterly, 38*(2), 169–194.

Thomas, D. A. (2001). The truth about mentoring minorities. *Harvard Business Review, 74*(5), 99–105.

Tillman, L. C. (2001). Mentoring African American faculty in predominantly White institutions. *Research in Higher Education, 42*(3), 295–325.

Turner, C. S. V., González, J. C., & Wong (Lau), K. (2011). Faculty women of color: The critical nexus of race and gender. *Journal of Diversity in Higher Education, 4*(4), 199–211. doi:10.1037/a0024630

Turner, C. S. V., González, J. C., & Wood, J. L. (2008). Faculty of color in academe: What 20 years of literature tells us. *Journal of Diversity in Higher Education, 1*(3), 139–168.

Williamson, M. J., & Fenske, R. H. (1992, April). *Mentoring factors in doctoral programs of Mexican American and American Indian students.* Paper presented at the 73rd annual meeting of the American Educational Research Association, San Francisco, CA.

Willie, C. V., Reddick, R. J., & Brown, R. (2005). *The Black college mystique.* Lanham, MD: Rowman & Littlefield.

Wunsch, M. A. (1994). Developing mentoring programs: Major themes and issues. *New Directions for Teaching and Learning, 57*, 27–34.

2

BUILDING CROSS-GENDER MENTORSHIPS IN ACADEME

A Chicano–Latina Filipina Relationship Built on Common Scholarly Commitments

Juan Carlos González and Caroline Sotello Viernes Turner

This chapter focuses on a cross-gender mentorship between two scholars of color, both of whom are dedicated to access, equity, and social justice in academe. Caroline S. Turner has over 20 years of experience as a senior faculty of color in higher education, and Juan Carlos González is a junior faculty of color in administration and research. Both share a 14-year mentoring relationship that has produced numerous presentations, publications, laughs, and conflict resolution exchanges where both had to agree to disagree. Beginning as a doctoral advisor and advisee/research assistant and evolving into faculty colleagues working together, they built this relationship, most important, based on mutual respect, trust, and friendship. A strong mentoring relationship is forged in good times and in challenging times. This chapter will present autobiographical sketches depicting some of the experiences contributing to the creation of a long-lasting and mutually beneficial professional relationship, as well as an enduring friendship.

Autobiographical Sketch Approach

In a 2007 article, Turner used a biographical sketch approach to examine the pathways to the university presidency for three women of color. This approach is described as capturing the themes in the interview and other data collected. However, it does not attempt to portray the entire lives of these women. Instead, critical life factors leading to their present positions are the focus of this analysis. Biography was used as a form of inquiry, which Creswell (1998) described as the "study of an individual and her or his experiences as told to the researcher or found in documents and archival material" (p. 47). For this chapter, we will use a form of autobiography as we examine our recollections of the development of our mentorship relationship. *Autobiography*, as defined by Creswell (2007), is "written and recorded by the individuals who are the subject of the study" (p. 55). Howarth (1974) described this approach as the presentation of a *self-portrait*:

> Each of those italicized words suggests a double entity, expressed as a series of reciprocal transactions. The self thinks and acts; it knows that it exists alone and with others. A portrait is space and time, illusion and reality, painter and model—each element places a demand, yields a concession. A self-portrait is even more uniquely transactional. No longer distinctly separate, the artist-model must alternately pose and paint. (p. 364)

In this chapter, we are presenting not full autobiographies but ones focused on the emergence and continued growth of our mentorship relationship. As an outcome of our approach, we hope to provide the reader with the highlights we remember as cornerstones of our relationship from the time we met to the present. We tell our story as we remember it.

Although the autobiographical sketches presented here are not life histories, both of us adhere to the comments describing this genre of writing by Tierney (1999):

> One of the purposes of life history research is not to come to terms with an individual cohesive identity, but rather to see the greater complexity that exists across societies, across individuals . . . to see connections across differences, across identities. . . . Stories are told not in fixed time, but rather are synchronous, updated, and ever-evolving. . . . Authors are involved in the creation of texts to develop the conditions of agency—their own, the individuals with whom they are involved in the creation of the text, and with the reader. (pp. 310–311)

Our goal is to demonstrate the complexity of our relationship from each one of our lived perspectives, to examine the connections across our similarities and differences, to note the evolved and the ever-evolving nature of our relationship, and to create text as an outlet for our own agency in this collaborative writing process.

Even though this chapter emphasizes cross-gender relationships, there are many other layers of diversity within this broad umbrella. For instance, differences extend to include such factors as rural and urban experiences, generational contexts, employment experiences, language abilities, cultural contexts, gendered socialization, and special skills and talents. We also believe that race and ethnicity are socially significant characteristics and that there will be occasions when a person's experiences will be affected by his or her race or ethnicity, contributing to a diversity of ideas and values. Given all the significant ways we differ from each other, we share a critical commonality in advancing a scholarly and personal commitment to access, equity, and social justice in higher education.

Caroline Sotello Viernes Turner

"Walking together with company" is a phrase that comes to mind when thinking of my journey to this moment. The journey toward accomplishment and achievement in any endeavor is not done in isolation but with the support of others willing to travel with you, providing encouragement along each step of the journey; and helping one to overcome self-doubt, to achieve more than they thought was possible for them, and to overcome challenges and celebrate milestones.

—Caroline Turner

I am very fortunate to have many in my life whom I have crossed paths with and with whom I can walk together. One of these individuals is my colleague and friend, Juan Carlos González. I am a Latina Filipina from a large, very close-knit family. I grew up on farm labor camps in Northern California. I am the oldest child in my family and the first to obtain a college degree. Leaving home for the University of California, Davis, was a giant leap from one world to another. I was a senior in high school when I was pulled from class one day and asked to meet with the dean of girls. I was sure I had done something wrong but could not think of what that might be. Why else would she be calling me into her office?

I sat down, and she asked me if I had considered applying to college. I asked her, "What is college?" I had a very similar experience to that described by Juan Carlos. Both of us were not aware of college as an option for us or even the meaning of the word. This dean of girls was one of my first mentors, although I did not know this at the time. She selected the college I would attend and helped me fill out the application to the University of California, Davis. She even took the time to arrange for me to travel with another family so that I could take the college entrance aptitude tests. My father worked all day, from sunup to sundown, and my mother did not drive. I never knew who paid the testing fee.

She was changing the trajectory of my life without my fully realizing what this would mean. However, I was a risk taker and willing to take an opportunity to venture into the unknown, away from my family and the life I knew in Hollister, California. But now I also realize how brave my family was, especially my mother, who did not want me to leave home but who let me go, knowing I would likely not return home. To this day, I remember how jarring the transition was from my life on the farm to my life as a freshman at UC, Davis, but that is another story.

Unlike Juan Carlos, I did not participate in high school sports, mainly because I was not allowed to stay after school for any extracurricular activities. I know now that I am athletic, as I briefly ventured into competition in fencing and dancing later in my life. But in high school, I had to go straight home after class. I had to take the bus home every day, because missing the bus home (which I did only once because I was concentrating on a biology project) created a major problem, as there was no one to give me a ride from the school in town to our labor camp. I believe that my lack of experience with team sports, in part, made it hard for me to understand Juan Carlos's love of sports and how it was so much a part of his identity, especially when he felt that basketball games and other athletic pursuits were more important than meeting to work on his dissertation or on other research projects. For example, one day Juan Carlos was to meet with me as soon as I returned from a business trip so we could work on his dissertation. After waiting an hour for him, I called and asked if he was on his way. He answered that he was in the middle of the finals at a racquetball tournament, which he went on to win. He had not thought he would be in the finals. We did not meet then. On the other hand, I understood his independent nature. For example, when he decided to marry, he informed others and me by telephone weeks after the wedding ceremony attended by the bride and groom. I was surprised at the announcement but happy for him and his new bride. This is the way he approaches life.

As I write this chapter, I am also conversing with Juan Carlos, and we are realizing that the times of conflict and misunderstandings that we experienced as faculty advisor and student also emanated from the fact that we are both competitive and fiercely independent in our own ways. Otherwise, neither one of us would have been where we were then and where we are now. I am glad that we worked through these challenges in order to get to where we are now in our comentorship relationship.

He, like me, has a very driven personality. Recently, both professors now, we were working on a paper along with one of my doctoral students. We decided that we needed at least 5 days together to finish this paper (which was published and was one of the top-cited articles for the journal the year it came out). We wrote day and night with few breaks. I decided to take a walk to relax my mind, and I remember Juan Carlos calling out after me, saying, "Think about our analysis while you are walking," to which I remarked, "Don't tell me what to think when I am trying to relax." He had planted a seed, though, and while I was on my walk, I could not stop thinking about our analysis.

Another area of misunderstanding, due primarily to our different circumstances, was that Juan Carlos had the flexibility to take on more course work and participate in extracurricular activities that, in my view, took him away from completing his dissertation. I encouraged him to focus more. As a doctoral student and a new faculty member, I was a single parent and felt the pressure of having to move through my program and the tenure process quickly. Juan Carlos, on the other hand, was single with no children. He enjoyed his time as a doctoral student and could stay in his doctoral program as long as he learned what he felt he needed to learn. He could take extra courses and include international travel and other activities within the role of a doctoral student. However, this does not mean he was without different challenges. In our present conversations, he indicated that his negative attitude presented several barriers he had to overcome in his graduate student life. He was reading writings by Malcolm X, Che Guevarra, Nelson Mandela, Fidel Castro, Paulo Freire, the Black Panthers, and the Brown Berets and told me he had developed a lot of anger over the oppression of people of color by Whites in the United States. He had to move from a negative attitude to a positive one to successfully complete this part of his schooling and funnel this anger into academic pursuits.

As for me, while pursuing my doctorate, a professor encouraged me to embark on a career in the professoriate. Upon graduation, I became a professor at the University of Minnesota, Twin Cities. I was there for 12 years and then a professor at Arizona State University for 10 years. Now, I am in my fourth year as a professor at California State University, Sacramento. I met Juan Carlos during my first month at Arizona State University. After an orientation to the doctoral program, a few students were going to have dinner and see a movie. I found myself joining them and was seated next to Juan Carlos. We talked about our mutual interests in access, equity, and social justice issues in higher education. Juan Carlos had also just completed his master's degree with a colleague of mine at The Ohio State University. We had a good conversation and made plans to speak again at a later date. I enjoy meeting with students inside and outside of the classroom to engage in discussions with them about their research and their goals in life. I feel that I learn as much from my student interactions as they learn from me.

My mentorship approach is based on the belief that each mentor–protégé relationship is an emerging learning context and that these relationships are reciprocal with both parties contributing their perspectives to create their unique relationship. For me, the mentoring process has a reciprocal component in that students certainly challenge me to grow intellectually and help me maintain meaning and purpose in my work. It is very rewarding to see students grow and develop. In helping others realize their talents and dreams, they also help me realize mine. For example, Juan Carlos taught me a great deal about the use of technology in the research we were doing together. Because of his influence, although I still prefer reading from hard copy, I am much better at using digital resources, creating PowerPoint presentations, and understanding the application of computer software to create visuals depicting models based on our research findings. Beyond the use of technology, he also taught me to see things from his perspective, thereby broadening mine.

It is very important to get to know someone before embarking on work-related conversations, so I always enjoyed catching up on what is happening within our respective families. Juan Carlos enjoyed speaking about his family and the path that he took to come to college. We both had stories to share about our families, and I totally understood the importance of his visits to his family during times of celebration and challenges. We had similar dedication to our respective families.

I also believe that during transitions from leaving home to attending college, and from becoming a student and then a professional, one must not lose sight of knowledge gained during early life experiences. Our intellectual development from childhood to the present is of great value and must be wholly drawn on as people move through their doctoral student experience and onward. It is important to acknowledge who we are and how this affects our approaches to research. In other words, who you are shapes the types of questions you ask, the kinds of issues that interest you, and the ways in which you go about seeking solutions.

Besides gender and race/ethnicity differences, I believe that age, rural and urban differences, and the strict, regimented upbringing I experienced affected our interactions over the course of the 14 years I have known Juan Carlos. For example, in one of our writings together, we came to realize that Juan Carlos's inspirational mentors are scholars of his same ethnic background and that he eventually came to meet and know them personally, whereas my inspirational mentors were scholars who did not share my ethnic background and I would not come to meet and know them. Inspirational mentors are not necessarily those one has met but those whose scholarly accomplishments serve as a source of inspiration for the career path we have chosen. Partly because of generational differences, when I was an undergraduate in the 1960s and a doctoral student in the 1980s, I was largely unaware of scholars who shared a similar racial/ethnic and gender background to mine, Latina Filipina. When I was an undergraduate, the Farm Labor Movement, led not by scholars but by Mexican and Filipino laborers, had an impact on me as I began to awaken to the social and economic injustices that my family and others endured as they toiled in the fields. I am part of a large immigrant farm labor family. My parents believed in the importance of family, hard work, honesty, and education as an important way to achieve in this country. They were very proud of me and all I tried to accomplish, providing me with love and a strong foundation for everything I achieved in life.

During my undergraduate years, I began to see that injustices that created societal inequities based on race/ethnicity must be fought. This realization caused me to stay in college and dedicate myself to help others like me to succeed on campus as well. When I was in graduate school, reading the work of Erving Goffman and Rosabeth Moss Kanter, whom I have never met but who have made lasting impressions on me, I gained a further understanding of the power of individual and organizational influences that shaped my (and others') educational experiences. Goffman's research on total institutions and Kanter's examination of a corporation's structural determinants of workplace status for women led me to perceive that I was being heavily socialized and shaped by institutional factors inherent in my doctoral education. For example, my learning was shaped by who was and who was not teaching in my program, by who was and who was not a student in my program, by what we were and what we were not assigned to read, and so on. This led me to my interest in the study of higher education institutions and their impact on students and faculty. Juan Carlos did eventually meet his inspirational mentors. This, we concluded, was largely due to our generational differences, as fewer scholars of color were in academe when I received my doctorate as were around when he received his doctorate.

Juan Carlos and I both have learned to have respect and patience with each other's point of view and, bottom line, we value the colleagueship and friendship that we have developed over the years. Because I view each graduate student's education experience as uniquely his or her own, I work together with students to guide their progress. Helping each student realize his or her special intellectual talents, achieve his or her dreams, and be ready to successfully compete for the professional role(s) he or she has chosen is very important to me. Juan Carlos also keeps me focused on what is important in the work I have chosen to do. One day I was feeling disappointed because I was not selected for an award, and he said to me,

> Personally, I don't see this as a setback at all. While it's a nice award, it's extra. It's like ordering ice cream and not getting the cherry on the top. The

people that you mentored, the reward is the mentoring. Me, for example, you've profoundly changed my life forever, award or no award.

During recent years, I believe Juan Carlos has been my mentor. He continues to be someone whose company I enjoy along the journey we are both continuing to take.

Juan Carlos González

> *The mediocre teacher tells.*
> *The good teacher explains.*
> *The great teacher demonstrates.*
>
> —Unknown

This quote reminds me of Caroline and the mentoring model she has taught me to use on the students I mentor. Not only did she guide me into a career in academe, but she also integrated me in all her research so that I could watch firsthand as she collected data in the field. But before I talk about Caroline and myself, it's important to talk about my background and how I was guided to the professorial track.

I, Juan Carlos, am a Chicano, first-generation college student from a working-class background in Southern California. My socialization comes from living in all-Black, all-Chicano, and predominantly White neighborhoods in Southern California. I learned Ebonics growing up in South Central. When we left to move more inland, Chicanos from La Puente would make fun of me when I would say, "I'm funna go to the store." "We don't understand you aye," said my Chicano friends. A third move from La Puente to Fontana also became problematic because of the language that I spoke, and my English-only-speaking Chicano friends from Fontana were convinced I was in a gang in La Puente because I would say things like, "Wha's up aye!"

I was definitely on a trajectory to becoming a gang member, but I had two things going for me that shifted me from the school-to-prison pipeline to the barrio-to-college pipeline: family and an internally strong sense of survival and success. Family influence centers on Joaquina González, my mother, a Mexican Spanish-only-speaking immigrant who moved from Jalisco, Mexico, to East Los Angeles in the 1960s to become the live-in babysitter for her brother already living there. She never saw not knowing English as a barrier, spending entire days at my school volunteering to do anything the school asked of her: running copies, watching a class, and serving students during lunch. Her free services endeared her and her children to the school leaders and teachers, and her children were also expected to be better behaved.

The second important factor was something internal that told me I can be successful. But an internal drive was insufficient without some type of external force promoting academic success. I found this on the high school running track at a time when most Chicanos who went to my school began to check out. My older brother, Antonio, was also a runner. I idolized him and wanted to be just like him. In South Central Los Angeles, I did a lot of running to get home in order to keep from being assaulted. In La Puente, when I misbehaved my mom would send Antonio to chase after me and catch me so I could get my beating, and sometimes it would take several miles before he captured me. I was skinny, tall, and determined early on that I didn't like to lose and would rather run and fall from exhaustion than lose. I also thought during my high school years that perhaps I was gifted with running legs and lungs from my ancestors, whom I had never met, but I was sure they were Aztecs and Mayans, because it could not be a coincidence that all the fast long-distance runners on the various Southern California teams I participated in were Mexicans.

I still remember; it was during cross-country practice that I first heard the word *college*. Before, I did not know what this was, but now, the seniors were talking about going to college, and I became interested in finding out more. I still remember the day I heard the word *college*. It was during my freshman year in high school, it was our first practice, and I showed up early to practice that day as a 105-pound skinny kid. I didn't have friends, but everybody knew me because I was Antonio's kid brother, and therefore there were expectations because he was one of the top runners on the team. I overheard the seniors talking about "college." "What is college?" I asked. "It's a place you can go if you run fast enough," responded Edwardo, the team captain. And, so, practice was never the same. From this point forward college was something I would aspire to and could get there if I ran fast enough.

Family and sports got me out of the barrio, where as a youth I was so tired of the adults telling us every day not to become gang members. And I could see why they persisted. I'm sure that they knew we had something to do with spray painting the Bassett 13 (the well-known local gang) insignia all over the walls and were throwing gang signs to each other the same way other kids threw baseballs. Family and sports got me through graduate school and life in general, and I always appreciated their foundation role in my life and the institutions that taught me my values for how I needed to behave and what I needed to do—trust others with care, cherish competition, and have a vision for how your work can profoundly change the world.

With this said, I continue to be surprised that I am a professor at a university. I believe that being a professor at a Hispanic-serving institution gives me the liberty to write this chapter with Caroline and say that I am a professor but could have been a gang member, and that I engage in an intellectual fight for social justice when I could have been engaging in physical fights for street justice.

Although family and sports helped put me on the college trajectory, the college-student-to-college-professor trajectory required a third factor: mentoring. As a professor in Fresno, California, one of the areas of the country with the highest levels of poverty and unemployment, I find it heartbreaking to know the number of Chicano males in this region without mentors, lacking serious interest in education and pegged by schools, early on, as dropouts and future prison inmates. And I try to think about why I'm different, and how I'm similar, and much of it had to do with mentoring.

Despite always being ultracompetitive, hardworking, and hungry for success, all important American values, I still always struggled as a college student because I did not know how to translate this to writing books, developing theories, and having a deep love for the culture of knowledge creation and consumption. This is how Caroline's mentorship was so critical: I observed her as an academic and tried to emulate and learn from her. But a good mentor can only do so much for the academic success of a working-class Chicano like me, because there are forces that exist in universities that work against Chicano males, such as institutional racism and hostile campus climates, particularly from colleagues. To me, such is the nature of American higher education, which historically has hardwired its values and practices to maintain traditions of White dominance and the marginal existence of people of color.

What does my history as a youth have to do with my values and perspectives about higher education? Because by the time I met Caroline Turner, my coauthor, mentor, and friend, I had not had meaningful, enduring, or successful mentoring relationships as a college student. I believed what a majority of working-class Chicano doctoral students who prematurely exit their programs believe: If you want to be successful, you had better work hard and do it yourself. I met Caroline during my first year as a doctoral student, which means I had been a college student for nine years (seven as an undergraduate, two as a master's student). I believe that I had mostly myself to thank for my academic success, and I was not too trusting of people who might want to help me. She was a nice person and seemed to have more "familial-like" relationships with her students, but I still was not convinced that I needed mentorship to be successful. I was highly individualistic, highly skeptical of higher education, and somewhat turned off by authority figures. But I have always had a deep hunger for success, and I was inspired by Caroline's own success as a professor, especially how she had made a career by writing about social justice and equity for students and faculty of color.

As you have heard from Caroline, the details of her life reveal the similarities her life has with mine, despite how different we might be based on gender, race/ethnicity, age, knowledge, values, and personality. We are highly similar based on our love and respect for social justice, equity for communities of color in higher education, family and cultural values, and people and friends. And although our differences created conflict, it was ultimately our similarities that created the opportunity for us to form a friendship initiated by her mentorship over the past 14 years. Not dwelling on conflict, I think it is important to note, especially because it helped us to become such good friends after I completed my doctorate and entered the professoriate. At times I felt we were on different planets, and I would go in circles trying to understand her and her expectations of my work. I do remember that as I was completing my doctorate, Caroline was talking about me staying to do a postdoc with her, and in my mind, I felt I needed to move to another institution and make a name for myself, to stop being Caroline's student and become my own person. But I also wanted to move on because, given my history of independence, I wanted to do things the way I wanted. I am glad I left for the University of Missouri, Kansas City, upon graduation. I believed this strengthened our friendship because I now had the flexibility to be my own person and develop my own name.

Adding to our struggles, which I believe was a foundation to our friendship, when we were professor-student, I thought her to be unreasonable at times, and I didn't feel I had the voice to express this to her because as a Latino I was taught to respect our elders. But, also because she had power over me as my dissertation chair, and I knew this as a student wanting to graduate, trying to disrupt our relationship could affect the ultimate goal of graduating. Developing the ability to successfully and strategically navigate and understand power relations and still not compromise your vision and values is, I believe, one of the most important lessons there is to learn to be successful in higher education. For example, when I was in my last year of writing the dissertation, I decided to go to South Korea to teach English for a month, purposely not informing Caroline in order to avoid a conversation about why I should not go and instead focus on writing the dissertation. I figured I would tell her when I returned. These were the types of experiences that created conflict, with Caroline solely focused on my progress to degree and my focus solely on finishing my way. Caroline is a lifelong learner, always growing, but she also is a person who is focused on how things need to be done. This confused me as a doctoral student, but, ultimately, she taught me that although some things must follow protocol, there are always bigger goals and a bigger vision to strive toward. In the end, she was very supportive of what I did while always maintaining a focus on my finishing my dissertation and my doctoral program.

Upon completion of my doctorate, Caroline and I discussed my need to break away from the scholarship we forged together in order for me to develop my own professional scholarly identity, even if we continued to have some overlapping research agendas. For example, I do work on urban education across K–postsecondary education and am involved in a major initiative addressing issues for men of color, two areas that differ from Caroline's current research agenda.

By most measures, Chicanos, and minority males in general, are struggling in academe. They are extremely underrepresented in their college-going and degree-completion rates within all institutional types and at all levels. In their work, Sáenz and Ponjuan (2009) concluded that even as the number of Latinas and Latinos attending college and attaining degrees has increased steadily in recent decades, the proportional representation of Latinos continues to decline relative to their female peers. These scholars noted that Latino males are "an untapped resource in our intellectual marketplace" and underscored that the nation's best interests would be better served if U.S. colleges and universities improved pathways to success for both Latinas and Latinos at the student, faculty, and administrative levels of higher education (pp. 79, 84). When Caroline and I discussed this situation, we remarked on the need to understand how cross-gender mentoring, as in our case, works to increase Latino male graduates. We concluded that cross-gender mentoring can serve as a critical relationship for increasing men of color in academe, as women faculty may play important roles in advancing their trajectory as students and professionals.

This said, a notable experience that highlighted our differences based on gender provides one insight into a challenge for a cross-gender mentoring relationship such as ours. One day, as Caroline and I were beginning a committee meeting with a high-level male college administrator, Caroline said something to me about what I should do after the meeting. The administrator said, "You're his dissertation advisor, not his mother." Caroline interpreted this comment as a devaluation of her gendered identity, whereas I understood and somewhat agreed that the male administrator's perception had to do with how men should and should not be treated. In other words, males need to develop independently, not nurtured (or [s]mothered). Now, as we coauthor this chapter, we understand each other's reaction. In fact, this difference of perspective is noted in Table 2.1, from Chesler and Chesler (2002), who stated,

> An encapsulation of socialized gender differences between women and men in our culture is given in [Table 2.1]. We readily acknowledge that this rubric does not apply to everyone; a bell-curve distribution likely exists

allowing significant individual variation and crossover between socialization patterns. (p. 49)

In our case, most of what Chesler and Chesler present in Table 2.1 applies. Specifically, Caroline is expected to motivate her students by encouraging them, preferring to collaborate with them in her research endeavors. I, on the other hand, have also learned to do these things from Caroline but still find it hard to motivate students through encouragement rather than by challenging them. I also see successful students as those who produce individual achievement, even though I am starting to learn from and integrate more collaborative models of interaction, engagement, and success.

Caroline included me in several of her data collection trips out of state. I was envied by other research assistants who did not get to accompany their professor out into the field. These trips not only provided me with firsthand knowledge of interview, audiotaping, and videotaping techniques but also provided times of inspiration and laughter. For example, on one of our first trips, we interviewed Dr. Karen Swisher, then president of Haskell Indian Nations University (HINU). Moments of laughter ensued when I thought that our camera was not working and Caroline noticed that I still had the lens cap in place. Also, as a new researcher, I was in charge of videotaping her interview with President Swisher. Later, when viewing the tape, we noticed a constant tapping noise in the background, which was a distraction. We both realized that the noise was from my tapping my fingers on a hard surface, not realizing that this would be picked up on the tape. At first it was an annoyance, but then we laughed about it, treating these glitches as part of a learning experience. As a high school

TABLE 2.1

Outcomes of Female and Male Socialization on Characteristics and Goals

	Female	*Male*
Motivation	Encouragement	Challenge
Group interaction	Integrated	Separated
Task engagement	Collaborative	Competitive
Vision of success	Group affiliation	Individual achievement

Note. From "Gender-Informed Mentoring Strategies for Women Engineering Scholars: On Establishing a Caring Community," by N. C. Chesler and M. A. Chesler, 2002, *Journal of Engineering Education*, *91*(1), p. 50.

cross-country runner, I visited HINU, which also was a source of inspiration to me because I knew about Billy Mills, the famous Native American long-distance runner, Olympic gold medalist, and alumnus of HINU when it was called Haskell Institute. The first thing I wanted to do when I arrived at HINU was to visit the stadium on the campus where Mills had taken up running and set several high school track and field records. I ran around the track once, and that was enough for me to feel my connection to history and to someone I idolized.

Conclusion

Today, Caroline and I have a stronger friendship than ever, even though our communication is complicated by our busy schedules, our distinct research interests, and our commitment to be student focused and to provide peer mentoring. We remain committed to coproducing scholarship, which is easier because we now both live and work in our home state of California, within a three-hour drive. We also both remain rooted in our values, understand each other's challenges more than ever, and have created one of my most important professional, social, and familial (because I see her as family) relationships—all because of the power of her mentorship and her commitment to work with me even though I have a natural inclination to clash with authority. And it is this mentorship and independence, and my reflections on them, that inspire me as a professor to try to build on them as I try to inspire my Chicana and Chicano students to reach for excellence in their dreams to become higher education leaders and professors.

As we conclude the telling of our stories, we understand not only how we have challenged each other but also how we have broadened each other's perspectives. We have learned from each other how mentoring relationships can lead to creation of scholarship that is expressive, contributory to academe, and personally and professionally gratifying. But we have also learned that the growth and changes stemming from a strong mentorship relationship can have their challenges. It is easier now to talk to each other and write about these experiences because we're reflecting on them and not living them. We hope that our reflections provide useful insight into the development of the diverse mentorships that are so critical in academe. For us, our relationship has ultimately led to the production of important scholarship and a continued affirmation of the values we share, fueling our continued dedication to academe. We continue to grow and share experiences, challenges, and opportunities, both about our professional lives and in our friendship.

References

Chesler, N. C., & Chesler, M. A. (2002). Gender-informed mentoring strategies for women engineering scholars: On establishing a caring community. *Journal of Engineering Education-Washington, 91*(1), 49–56.

Creswell, J. W. (1998). *Qualitative inquiry and research design: Choosing among five traditions.* Thousand Oaks, CA: Sage.

Creswell, J. W. (2007). *Qualitative inquiry and research design: Choosing among five traditions* (2nd ed.). Thousand Oaks, CA: Sage.

Howarth, W. H. (1974). Some principles of autobiography. *New Literary History, 5*(2), 363–381.

Sáenz, V. B., & Ponjuan, L. (2009). The vanishing Latino male in higher education. *Journal of Hispanic Higher Education.* Retrieved from http://jhh.sagepub.com/content/8/1/54

Tierney, W. G. (1999). Guest editor's introduction: Writing life's history. *Qualitative Inquiry, 5*(3), 307–312. Retrieved from http://qix.sagepub.com/content/5/3/307

Turner, C. S. (2007). Pathways to the presidency: Biographical sketches of women of color firsts. *Harvard Educational Review, 77*(1), 1–38.

3

SOCIALIZATION IN ACADEME

Reflections on Mentoring by a Latina Filipina Mentor and an African American Male Protégé

J. Luke Wood and Caroline Sotello Viernes Turner

First and foremost, I would like to acknowledge my mentor and friend, Dr. Caroline Sotello Viernes Turner. . . . Your patience, constructive criticism, rigor, high expectations, and authentic care have made me the scholar and person who I am today. Your devotion to me and others has had and will continue to have a long-lasting impact on access, equity, and diversity in higher education. (Wood, 2010, p. vi)

My name is J. Luke Wood; I am an African American male faculty member, community college researcher, and advocate for educational equity and ethics in postsecondary education. The opening quote is taken directly from my dissertation, where I lauded Dr. Turner's[1] mentoring qualities (e.g., rigor, high expectations, care), which I believe contributed, at critical times, to my development as an academician. Dr. Turner is my former doctoral advisor, continued mentor, colleague, and lifelong friend. Her investment in my success as a doctoral student and now as a faculty member has been invaluable.

My name is Caroline S. Turner; I am a Latina Filipina and have been a faculty member for almost 30 years, with a lifelong interest in access and equity in higher education. I am fortunate to have interacted with many students over the years, including J. Luke Wood. Luke was a doctoral student at Arizona State University (ASU), whom I met in Minnesota and worked with in California before he joined me at ASU. Luke and I have known one another for six years. We have collaborated and continue to collaborate on publications, conference presentations, teaching, and supporting each other as we continue our careers as faculty of color. Although I appreciate Luke's kind comments, I have to say that, in his own right, he is very talented and focused on his growth as an academic. I was fortunate to have him as a student and continue to work with him. He has contributed much to my career as well. In this chapter, we tell our story.

This chapter provides an opportunity for us to reflect on and provide a glimpse of our experience and also discuss the cross-gender and cross-race challenges we faced and overcame, particularly while establishing initial trust in one another. Before we begin our reflections on our mentoring relationship, we will present an overview of the status of Black males in higher education and of two mentoring frameworks used to shed light on the nature of our relationship.

Black Males in Doctoral Education: A National Context

Faculty support of their doctoral students should not be taken for granted. I (Luke) have seen how my experience differed from that of many of my doctoral student peers. Although many of them would anguish over a lack of communication with their dissertation chairs, I had a direct line of communication with my mentor (Dr. Turner) at all times. I also received support in understanding and navigating the politics of doctoral education and continual encouragement for my research endeavors. On the basis of discussions with other doctoral students, I realize this kind of commitment is rare. However, further underscoring the importance of mentorship, my story is embedded within a greater sociocultural context with a critical underrepresentation of Black males in academe.

Black males are severely underrepresented in all levels of postsecondary education. This lack of representation becomes more acute when examining the movement of Black males into the professoriate. Drawing from literature in public affairs, Flowers (2003) discussed the importance of representative bureaucracy, using proportional representation ratios (PRRs) as a framework for understanding underrepresentation. This framework asserts that "the more diverse the constituent group is, the greater the diversity of the leaders of persons making policy decisions on behalf of the constituent group" should be (p. 38). I (Luke) support the use of PRRs in higher education (Wood, 2008). I am not recommending the use of a quota but suggesting that these ratios serve as a marker of what a more equitable and just representative distribution should be.

We calculate PRRs by dividing the representative group by the constituency. A ratio less than 1.0 indicates a lack of proportional representation, whereas a ratio greater than 1.0 indicates overrepresentation. For example, Black males represent 7.1% of the U.S. population (U.S. Census Bureau, 2010); thus, they should theoretically account for the equivalent proportion of collegians. However, data from Cominole, Riccobono, Siegel, Caves, and Rosen (2008) indicated that these men accounted for only 4.6% of public four-year collegians (*PRR* = .74). This underrepresentation continues into graduate study. Although Black men accounted for 4.56% of undergraduate students, they represented only 3.4% of master's of arts and science students (*PRR* = .75). In 2008, 2.3% of Black males were pursuing research doctorates; given that the majority of students in these programs transitioned from master's programs, this percentage indicated even greater underrepresentation (*PRR* = .68). Furthermore, in comparison to the general U.S. population, research doctorates were greatly underrepresented in American higher education (*PRR* = .37).

This lack of proportionality can have a negative impact on students. For instance, research suggests that Black faculty are more likely than their White peers to interact with students, employ collaborative teaching techniques, concentrate efforts on higher order thinking (Umbach, 2006), spend time advising students, engage in reflexive praxis (Johnson, Kuykendall, & Laird, 2005), and serve as "student-centered" mentors (Guiffrida, 2005). In addition to these benefits, literature on faculty of color indicates that they create affirming campus environments (Kee, 1999; Knoell, 1994; Lovell, Alexander, & Kirkpatrick, 2002), enable academic success for diverse constituencies (Opp & Smith, 1994), and foster higher aspirations for academic achievement. Thus, the quality of life for Black students may suffer when they don't have access to a diverse faculty, particularly professors of color. Literature on faculty of color is replete with discussions on the value of mentoring for doctoral students and faculty as a method for enhancing their success (e.g., Arnold, 2006; Dixon-Reeves, 2003; Peterson-Hickey, 1998; Stanley, 2006; Turner & Myers, 2000; Williams & Williams, 2006). My mentoring experience as a doctoral student and as a junior faculty member is one such case.

Theoretical Underpinnings

Mentoring relationships are unique, crafted by the individuals involved but also requiring patience, constructive criticism, high expectations, authentic care, and trust. We link our experiences related to these elements to Holland's (1993) faculty–student mentoring taxonomy and Bragg's (1976) model of socialization. Holland's (1993) framework aids in understanding the nature of our mentoring relationship by articulating a nomenclature of mentor–protégé relationships commonly encountered in the academy. Bragg's (1976) model further delineates the essence of how mentoring serves to facilitate socialization for a successful career as a faculty member.

Our mentor–protégé relationship can be understood through Holland's (1993) taxonomy of relationships. Holland identified four types of faculty–student mentoring relationships between African American doctoral students and their advisors. Table 3.1 presents an overview of the primary components of each mentoring relationship.

The mentor relationships include formal academic relationships, academic guidance relationships, quasi-apprenticeship relationships, and academic mentoring relationships. Each successive type of mentorship is on a continuum from a routinized and technical advisement relationship with minimal personal commitment and inflexible communication to one that illustrates personal investment and a high level of mentor commitment.

As noted in the table, the final relationship type is referred to as the *academic mentoring relationship*. In this relationship, the mentor provides extensive one-on-one guidance, counsel, and direction to the protégé. The focus of this relationship is to prepare the protégé for an academic career. The relationship itself is intensive, whereby the mentor is personally invested in the career success of the mentee. As such, the mentor provides the protégé with enhanced insight on the politics and culture of the profession. This latter form of mentorship typified my doctoral mentor–protégé relationships with Dr. Turner.

Bragg's (1976) model of socialization also offers a nomenclature for understanding our mentor–protégé dyad. This model has been widely used by scholars as a starting point for understanding the distinct aspects of socialization among graduate students. This model is typified by five stages. The first stage, referred to as *observation*, involves the prospective protégé's identification of an individual who can serve as a role model. In stage two, *imitation*, the protégé carries out the behaviors, actions, and mores of the role model. This imitation is overt, even including minute aspects of vocal intonation and visual cues. In stage three, *feedback*, the role model provides the protégé with feedback on his or her actions; if "the behavior is reinforced [by the role model], the individual begins to see himself in the role he has tried on" (p. 7). However, behaviors and actions can also be negatively assessed by the role model, resulting in the protégé's *modification* (stage four) or elimination of operations. In the final stage of the model, *internalization*, the protégé transitions from imitating behaviors, actions, and mores of the role model. Instead, the protégé begins to adopt them as his or her own. This

TABLE 3.1
Primary Mentoring Relationships and Key Attributes

Description	Formal Academic Relationship	Academic Guidance Relationship	Quasi-Apprenticeship Relationship	Academic Mentoring Relationship
Type	There is minimal faculty–student interaction.	Emotional support and enhanced interaction are provided; student's perceptions are more valued.	Research opportunities are extended that are available only to the protégé.	Mentor provides extensive one-on-one guidance.
Purpose	Technical and routinized advice is provided regarding program requirements.	General guidance is provided on career matters, with a primary focus on technical advisement.	Relationship is centered on academic opportunities.	Relationship is designed to prepare the protégé for an academic career.
Contact	Contact with mentor is inflexible; there are strictly designated office hours.	Faculty-student contact is more flexible; they can meet outside office and arrange times.	Research is conducted if focused solely on mentor's areas of interest.	Relationship itself is intensive, and the mentor is personally invested in the protégé's career success.

becomes incorporated into the protégé's personal and professional identity. Internalization is an essential stage; without it, the process is one of professionalization, not socialization.

These frameworks intersect, as mentorship is a critical facilitator of socialization. To better explain our mentor–protégé relationship, it is important to address the socialization that resulted from it. Guided by the aforementioned frameworks, we now discuss the intricacies of our unique mentor–protégé relationship. This discussion focuses on six areas: (a) origins of our relationship, (b) initial experiences in the mentor–protégé dyad, (c) opportunities for growth, (d) points of demographic distinction, (e) areas of commonality, and (f) benefits accrued for protégé and mentor.

Our Mentoring Dynamics

Origins of a Mentor–Protégé Dyad

In 2000, I (Luke) began my studies at California State University, Sacramento (CSUS), where only 3.7% of Black students graduated within four years (CSU Analytic Studies, 2006). I was heavily involved in the student government, serving as vice president for three consecutive terms, working arduously to encourage the university administration to focus on investing in a campus-wide student retention center. Recommendations extended to the campus administration for enhancing student outcomes were dismissed as lacking in research to warrant the viability of student support programs. After five and a half years I graduated, dismayed and critical of the campus administration, so I decided to pursue a career in higher education as a faculty member to learn more about, and to do research that could inform, practice. Shortly after graduating, I enrolled in a master's program. It was during this time that I read numerous articles written by Dr. Turner that articulated the benefits of a diverse faculty and the unique challenges that students of color face in the academy. Her words provided a source of encouragement during the formative stages of my scholarly development.

I entered the doctoral program at Arizona State University in 2007, and by 2008, Dr. Turner and I (in collaboration with J. C. González and K. Ryujin) presented on the concept of inspirational mentorship. We suggested that sometimes mentors and protégés do not have the benefit of direct contact; however, this does not prevent mentors from serving as an inspiration to students by virtue of their existence as successful scholars, authors, lecturers, teachers, leaders, and administrators. In this presentation, I commented on how Dr. Turner served as my inspirational mentor prior to actually meeting and working with her. Her scholarship bolstered my confidence in advocating for the increase of faculty of color in higher education. Her written ideas around diversity, equity, and social justice provided me with encouragement, affirmation, and renewed passion regarding my concern for inequities in education. Moreover, Dr. Turner's research helped me solidify my plans to pursue doctoral study.

Prior to 2007, I (Caroline) had met Luke at a "Keeping Our Faculties of Color" symposium in Minnesota. In 1998, I cofounded this symposium, featuring research focused on the recruitment and development of faculty of color in higher education. In the process of coauthoring this chapter, I found out that Luke flew to Minneapolis for a day in hopes of having a meeting with me. Having spent all of his discretionary funds on his flight, he could not stay more than the day and had no money for food. Luke explained that his goal in attending the conference was to meet and impress me as best as he could. Our initial interactions were limited, given the demands on my schedule throughout the day. There was even no guarantee that I would have a chance to meet with him. At the end of the day, I had a chance to spend several hours talking with him about his research and plans for the future. I was interested in helping him attain his educational goals. Luke said that he felt I displayed authentic care, making him feel welcome and important. His goals were achieved, and he flew home assured that he had made an intellectual connection. This demonstrates the lengths Luke would go to in order to pursue his educational aspirations. His focus, perseverance, and determination remain the same today.

Initial Mentor–Protégé Experience

As part of Luke's preparation for doctoral study, he applied to the California State University (CSU) Sally Casanova Predoctoral Fellowship. Given that CSU is a teaching university system, the Sally Casanova program is designed to provide students interested in doctoral study with the skills necessary to be successful. As a fellow, Luke was awarded monies for conference travel, provided with funding to purchase research software, and designated a mentor to support his research activities. One important element of this program is a summer fellowship program, where students are fully funded to work on research with any scholar or scholars throughout the country. Upon meeting me at the University of Minnesota, Luke changed his plans to work at another university.

Luke learned that I would be on sabbatical at the Institute for Higher Education Research at Stanford University. After several interactions (e.g., in-person meetings, phone calls, e-mail), he asked me to serve as his fellowship mentor at Stanford. This worked out well for both of us, as Luke was a new doctoral student who required hands-on experience with research projects.

I was involved with completing numerous projects related to my research on administrators of color and needed assistance with collecting and analyzing interview data. I also involved Luke in the development of a complex analytic method for reviewing extant literature, a meta-synthesis relevant to the experiences of faculty of color. In every way, although new to these methodological approaches, Luke was dependable and willing to do the work needed to complete all tasks involved. The literature meta-synthesis paper was eventually published, with Luke as the third author (Turner, González, & Wood, 2008). During this time frame, Luke and his wife, Idara, both received acceptance to doctoral study at ASU. I was his assigned program chair and eventually his dissertation chair. This made for a smooth transition from the predoctoral fellowship into doctoral study at ASU.

Opportunities for Personal Growth

Luke had high expectations of himself; and this, coupled with my expectations, required immeasurable dedication on both our parts. This is a primary component of formal academic mentorship (Holland, 1993). For example, as part of his graduate assistantship, Luke served as the co-coordinator of the Arizona Education Policy Fellowship Program (Arizona EPFP). I founded and coordinated this program, which brought together state leaders from multiple sectors (e.g., education, nonprofit, business, government) to discuss state and national policy challenges facing education. Luke provided invaluable support in building the curriculum for this nine-month program, including constructing an online resource website and coordinating program retreats, speakers, and miniconferences. He also assisted in the selection of fellows and in building in an extensive mixed-method assessment of all activities and events. Although this was primarily an administrative experience, the readings assigned on ethics and leadership as part of the Arizona EPFP were used in a future book publication (Nevarez & Wood, 2010).

As part of this academic mentorship, I (Luke) was prepared for a career in academe by having opportunities to copresent at conferences and copublish with Dr. Turner. Like most scholars, Dr. Turner was involved in numerous projects. As such, I always had numerous items to work on at any given time and was constantly writing literature reviews, data mining from federal data sets, and assisting with publication and presentation preparation.

The intensity of the work was exhausting for both Dr. Turner and me. I wondered how she was able to maintain her energy level and focus. I found balancing my personal life and my formal studies with the apprenticeship experiences to be difficult, and I sometimes begrudged these circumstances, feeling severely overextended. However, as metal is forged in a crucible to rid itself of impurities, I realized that without this intensity, I would not have the self-efficacy and proficiencies needed to succeed as a faculty member of color in academe. In fact, other doctoral students often told me that they were envious of the close relationship I had with my doctoral program advisor and dissertation chair.

Points of Demographic Distinction

Dr. Turner is a woman of Mexican and Filipino descent, and Luke is an African American man.[2] Given the dearth of Latina and Filipina scholars in academe and the low numbers of African American males in higher education, our mentor dyad is exceptionally unique.

In a doctoral program environment, our mentoring relationship encountered several challenges due to the inherent stress associated with doctoral work, mostly based on gender rather than race. We never really viewed our racial/ethnic difference as anything substantial. As a minority, I (Luke) was pleased to have the opportunity to work with another person of color, particularly one concerned with issues of equity and diversity. Although I had several wonderful and life-changing mentoring relationships with White men and women prior to working with Dr. Turner, the benefit of having another person of color as a mentor was essential for supporting my research interests. For example, Dr. Turner was an advocate for my research focused on minority students in higher education. I never had to be concerned about the topics I was interested in as research topics, as Dr. Turner was always supportive. Indeed, I had several experiences with White faculty who were supportive of my development as a scholar but were not particularly fond of my research interests.

Gender played a more substantial role in creating areas of dissonance in our relationship. Given our gender differences, I often struggled with how to conceptualize our relationship, which was both professional and personal. Dr. Turner was more than a mentor. Thus, viewing her simply as an advisor or colleague seemed insufficient, almost insulting. For example, Dr. Turner was included in many of my family celebrations. During the summer prior to entering the doctoral program, I married my wife, Idara. Even though I had known Dr. Turner for only a few months at that time, I invited her to the wedding to share this experience with my family and close friends. This speaks to how close Dr. Turner and I became in such a short period of time. Furthermore, the fact that Dr. Turner attended my wedding illustrates that the feeling of closeness was mutual.

Given this closeness, I often tried to consider Dr. Turner as an aunt, mother, or grandmother, but the markers never truly fit. Possibly, this inability to mentally classify the relationship might be due to our racial/ethnic differences. However, in many ways, I did feel like Dr. Turner perceived me as a son. Indeed, her own son is also African American and nearly the same age as I am. In fact, I noted that I felt that her advice to me, at times, was given more as a member of my family rather than as a request from an advisor to student. Dr. Turner's advice always came from a place of genuine care for my personal and professional well-being; however, the power balance between us complicated matters. For example, in situations where I had choices, I felt as though I could not disagree. What made this circumstance more complex is that Dr. Turner felt that I had the flexibility to make my own decisions and that she was merely giving me a recommendation. It took some time to realize that she would accept whatever choice I made. For example, I wanted to take some additional quantitative course work after having completed my program of study. Dr. Turner cautioned me against taking focus off my dissertation and suggested that I only consider taking these courses as a no-credit audit. As a result, I audited four quantitative courses: multiple regression, analysis of variance, categorical data analysis, and survival analysis.

Dr. Turner was involved in many projects that interested me. I worked on these projects, which provided me with support in the form of a graduate assistantship. When deadlines loomed, the work required very long hours of writing and research. During these times, we would find a café in the morning and work until late in the evening, entailing working lunches and dinners. It was uncomfortable to me when other doctoral students and my noncollege friends would ask about the nature of our relationship, inquiring whether it was purely work related. Typically, such inquiries were based on a lack of understanding of cross-gendered mentoring. Possibly, the intensity of such comments and rumors are greater for Black men (in comparison to their male peers) given that they are stereotypically portrayed as hypersexualized beings in society. Of course, such questions would not have occurred had I been working with a male mentor. As such, both of us were very conscious that such perceptions could take on a life of their own, leading to erroneous assumptions from faculty and graduate students. Even the possibility of such perceptions put an extra layer of stress on our working relationship.

Our gender differences did present other points of conflict. At times, I would accompany Dr. Turner to collect interview data or to assist in coordinating a major meeting, and people would assume that I was in charge and come up to me for direction and guidance. Sometimes, they even knew Dr. Turner was in charge and, while she was literally standing next to me, would ask me questions or for permission. At first, I did not think about or recognize the gender privilege I had and would respond to their inquiries, not realizing that by doing so I was also undermining her authority. I admit that there were times when I would also act in a manner that unconsciously usurped Dr. Turner's intentions in deference to male faculty members. These actions, though unintentional, were in adherence to the norms of a male-dominated society. Dr. Turner challenged these tendencies, asking me, "If I were a male faculty member, would you respond that way?" I became more aware of my actions, and such interactions happened much less frequently as time went on. Now, our level of trust is so high that we can (and do) talk through potential conflicts.

Areas of Commonality

To suggest that our relationship is marked by differences alone would be a simplistic characterization. There are factors we have in common. First, both of us are of mixed-race heritage. As a result, we have a shared experiential knowledge of living on the margins of race. In a society where racial/ethnic categorizations are the norm, we are those who lack a perfect fit into one box or another. At times, both of us have experienced rejection or initial distrust from *some* members of our own racial/ethnic communities. This has led to an added sense of resiliency in the face of a society dominated by race and racism. Moreover, we are both frequently asked, "What are you?" or "What is your background?" Such inquiries have caused both of us to engage in self-introspection about our identities.

In addition, both of us share similar convictions toward actualizing equity in postsecondary education. Specifically, both of our bodies of work focus on the nexus of ethics, diversity, and leadership. Dr. Turner's research examines access, equity, and leadership in higher education, faculty of color, and organizational change in higher education. Her dissertation research focused on Latino students in the community college, examining achievement and transfer. My research focuses on Black (and other minority) male success (e.g., achievement, persistence, attainment, transfer, workforce outcomes) in the community college. My work also examines ethical decision-making frameworks for community college leaders. As noted previously, these shared commitments (particularly to diversity and leadership) are what led me to read Dr. Turner's scholarship as a master's student and seek her out for doctoral study in the first place.

One other way in which we share similarities is that we are both from small rural towns. Dr. Turner grew up in farm labor camps in central California, and I grew up in a logging town in the far northern area of the state. There are certain experiences or lack thereof that we believe are part of growing up in "small town" America. Namely, these include relying on community for support during good and challenging times; knowing most people in our communities; standing out as a good student of color; and having a desire to prove oneself, a sense of trust in others, and an arduous work ethic. Not to say that these virtues are not held by individuals from other locales (e.g., urban, suburban), but the manner in which they occurred for us was similar and attributed to rural life. Thus, although we had a lot of differences that caused some tension in our relationship, as described previously, we also had a lot in common. These similarities promoted a level of comfort in our relationship, areas we didn't have to explain to each other but are hard to articulate to others.

Another critical way in which we are similar is that both of us completed our doctoral education while managing family responsibilities. I (Caroline) was a single parent with two children, and Luke was married and had a daughter during his program. This commonality helped me to understand the need for Luke to spend time with family. Times were set aside strictly for him to spend with his family, and as such he was not available for doctoral-related tasks. Writing this reminds me of one evening when we were working on a project and Luke mentioned that his first wedding anniversary was the next day. I was surprised that he was working with me and not planning for his anniversary. I knew he wanted to do this, so we ceased our work immediately and turned to planning a surprise anniversary celebration. Now, he tells me that he rarely would say no to me, even when I encouraged him to do so as needed. This is no longer a problem, as we both are very honest about times when we can and cannot work together. At the time of this writing, I am visiting near Luke's home, and we have carved out some time to complete this chapter.

The Benefits of a Mentor

Although Bragg (1976) described socialization as including a wide array of competencies (e.g., behavior, actions, values, norms), his conceptualization does not fully address the benefits I (Luke) derived from being mentored by Dr. Turner. I believe a more representative list is included in Figure 3.1. From my experience as a protégé, socialization includes a wide array of proficiencies, including knowledge, skills, values, dispositions, networks, and habits of mind. I will address each one individually.

Knowledge includes the information that is foundational to the field. In my experience, *knowledge* refers to research, theories, practices, and policies relevant to postsecondary education. This information is often obtained through formal course readings and discussions (in and out of class). However, it is also obtained through direct contact with mentors who discuss their perceptions of status and trends in the field, recommend "must" readings, and ask you to summarize readings they are interested in. Dr. Turner regularly asked me to locate articles, provide her with synopses, attend conference sessions, and share my notes with her. She was committed to interrogating my knowledge base to learn of areas in need of enhancement.

Skills refer to the technical competencies needed for success in the field, including verbal communications, writing ability, use of analytic software, ability to locate "hard-to-find" resources, and other areas. For example, I entered the doctoral program believing myself to be an above-average writer. As we worked on various projects, Dr. Turner provided copious feedback for improvement, suggestions for revision, and constructive criticism. As a result, I became a much better writer.

Values involve the mentor's core convictions, as well as those commonly espoused among his or her colleagues in the field. As I am a dedicated Christian, my ability to participate in church, attend services regularly, and talk

Figure 3.1 A model of graduate student socialization.

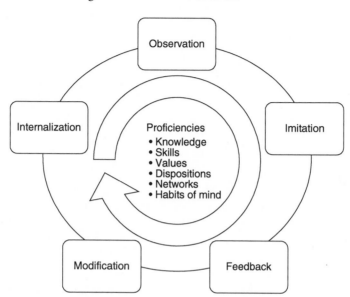

openly about my spirituality was (and is) very important to me. Dr. Turner was very supportive of my church participation. As a result, no matter what was coming up, we made an agreement that we did not work Sundays. I appreciated the space she provided me for my spiritual development.

Related to Bragg's concept of internalization, *dispositions* refers to ways of being, natural inclinations, tendencies, and temperaments. By virtue of our mentoring relationship, some of my own dispositions changed to mirror those of my mentor. I often find myself responding to others and reacting in ways that remind me of my mentor, especially in affective ways.

Developing *networks* is critical to being successful in doctoral study, transitioning to faculty, and excelling in the professoriate. Dr. Turner provided me with numerous introductions to senior scholars, emerging scholars, and up-and-coming doctoral students, which opened up incredible opportunities for me in terms of fellowships, coauthorship, leadership opportunities, and friendships.

Finally, *habits of mind* refers to one's mental processing, classification of concepts and ideas, and perspectives on issues. This concept deals with the way the world and its actors are ordered within the mind of the researcher. How I think about problems in education has definitely shifted throughout my socialization process: I am much more critical, insightful, and reflective than I was when I first entered the doctoral program.

The Benefits of Mentoring

Truthfully, I (Caroline) remain in academe primarily because of the positive interactions I have with each student with whom I work, learning much from every one. I am a scholar advocate for a diverse student and faculty body. One reason for having a diverse professoriate is, I believe, that students bring to their doctoral experience different research interests and needs for support and interaction with faculty. Faculty, in turn, have varied research interests and ways of advising and mentoring. Ideally, a match can be found. In my experience, typically, if a student's dissertation research topic is of interest to faculty, the student will have the most productive dissertation experience. Of course, there are personality traits and other ways in which faculty and students may differ, as Luke and I discussed earlier. The dissertation process is one that requires a focused and, many times, intense time of working together for professor and student. Commonalities and differences between student and professor are factors that may contribute to and shape this experience.

In my family, I am the oldest child and the first to go to college. I am the only one who never left school, completing a doctorate and becoming a professor. Several students I have chaired have become part of my academic family. Luke is one of those students. He is an exceptional person and has helped me in my career in ways in which we both could not have predicted. One day as we worked on yet another research project, Luke noticed an ad for a research award on my desk and asked why I had not won that award. I do not recall exactly what I said, but likely I indicated a lack of interest and also that I supported many who had won such awards. Several days later, after printing out all of my published papers and collecting copies of the books I had been involved in writing, Luke presented me with a large stack, stating that I needed to be nominated for several awards. Taking it upon himself, in his focused, astute, determined way, he led a nomination effort on my behalf. The outcome was that I was selected as a recipient for several awards acknowledging my lifetime research contributions.[3] Needless to say, I was honored to be so recognized. For this reason, Luke has influenced my career in ways I could not have predicted. I am fortunate to have him as a part of my academic family and to be a part of his.

Conclusion

We have discussed mentorship and socialization in light of our mentor–protégé experiences. We have done so using two frameworks: Holland's (1993) *taxonomy of faculty–student mentoring* and Bragg's (1976) *model of socialization.* To frame the discussion of mentoring and socialization, we addressed several topical areas, including (a) the origins of our relationship, (b) initial experiences in the mentor–protégé dyad, (c) opportunities for growth, (d) points of demographic distinction, (e) areas of commonality, and (f) benefits accrued for a protégé and mentor. As illustrated in this chapter, commonalities between us as mixed-race minorities from small rural towns with similar research interests and family responsibilities served to facilitate a respectful and productive professional and personal relationship. Although gender differences did, at times, create areas of dissonance, open communication and trust allowed for these challenges to turn into opportunities for greater understanding.

Notes

1. I refer to Caroline S. V. Turner as Dr. Turner throughout this chapter. To this date, I have never referred to Dr. Turner by her first name. I consciously do so in recognition of my great respect for her and her scholarship.
2. Luke is biracial, of African American and Ashkenazi descent, and identifies as African American.
3. Dr. Turner felt we did not need to name the awards, but I insisted. As a result of these efforts, she was the recipient of the following honors: 2008 Mildred Garcia Award for Exemplary Senior Scholarship from the Council on Ethnic Participation, Association for the Study of Higher Education; 2009 Carlos J. Vallejo Award for Senior Scholarship from Multicultural/Multiethnic Education, a special interest group of the American Educational Research Association (AERA); and 2009 Career Contribution Award from the AERA Scholars of Color in Education Standing Committee.

References

Arnold, J. (2006). *Moving beyond access: Institutionalizing best practices for the inclusion of underrepresented faculty and administrators* (Unpublished doctoral dissertation). University of Pennsylvania, Philadelphia.

Bragg, A. K. (1976). *The socialization process in higher education* (ASHE/AAHHE Research Report No. 7). Washington, DC: Association for the Study of Higher Education.

Cominole, M., Riccobono, J., Siegel, P., Caves, L., & Rosen, J. (2008). *National Postsecondary Student Aid Study (NPSAS:08) field test methodology report.* Retrieved from http://nces.ed.gov/pubsearch/pubsinfo.asp?pubid=200801

CSU Analytic Studies. (2006). *First-time full-time freshmen, 2000 to 2006 degree-seeking FTF campus reports.* Long Beach: California State University System Office.

Dixon-Reeves, R. (2003). Mentoring as a precursor to incorporation: An assessment of the mentoring experience of recently minted Ph.D.s. *Journal of Black Studies, 34,* 12–27.

Flowers, L. A. (2003). Investigating the representation of African American student affairs administrators: A preliminary study. *National Association of Student Affairs Professionals Journal, 6*, 35–43.

Guiffrida, D. (2005). Othermothering as a framework for understanding African American students' definitions of student-centered faculty. *The Journal of Higher Education, 76*(6), 701–723.

Holland, J. W. (1993, April). *Relationships between African American doctoral students and their major advisors.* Paper presented at the annual meeting of American Educational Research Association, Atlanta, GA.

Johnson, S. D., Kuykendall, J. A., & Laird, T. F. N. (2005, November). *An examination of workload of faculty of color by rank.* Paper presented at the annual meeting of the Association for the Study of Higher Education, Philadelphia, PA.

Kee, A. M. (1999). *Campus climate: Perceptions, policies and programs in community colleges* (AACC Research Brief). Washington, DC: American Association of Community Colleges.

Knoell, D. M. (1994). California community college faculty from historically underrepresented racial and ethnic groups. *New Directions for Community Colleges, 87*, 27–34.

Lovell, N. B., Alexander, M. L., & Kirkpatrick, L. A. (2002). *Minority faculty at community colleges: Fastback 490.* Bloomington, IN: Phi Delta Kappa Educational Foundation.

Nevarez, C., & Wood, J. L. (2010). *Community college leadership and administration: Theory, practice and change.* New York, NY: Peter Lang.

Opp, R., & Smith, A. (1994). Effective strategies for enhancing minority faculty recruitment. *Community College Journal of Research and Practice, 18*(2), 147–163.

Peterson-Hickey, M. M. (1998). *American Indian faculty experiences: Culture as a challenge and source of strength* (Unpublished doctoral dissertation). University of Minnesota, Twin Cities Campus.

Stanley, C. A. (2006). Coloring the academic landscape: Faculty of color breaking the silence in predominantly White colleges and universities. *American Educational Research Journal, 43*, 701–736.

Turner, C. S. V., González, J. C., & Wood, J. L. (2008). Faculty of color in academe: What 20 years of literature tells us. *Journal of Diversity in Higher Education, 1*(3), 139–168.

Turner, C. S. V., & Myers, S. L., Jr. (2000). *Faculty of color in academe: Bittersweet success.* Boston, MA: Allyn & Bacon.

Umbach, P. D. (2006). The contribution of faculty of color to undergraduate education. *Research in Higher Education, 47*(3), 317–345.

U.S. Census Bureau, Population Division. (2010). *Annual estimates of the resident population by sex, race, and Hispanic origin for the United States.* Retrieved from http://factfinder2.census.gov/faces/tableservices/jsf/pages/productview.xhtml

Williams, B. N., & Williams, S. M. (2006). Perceptions of African American male junior faculty on promotion and tenure: Implications for community building and social capital. *Teachers College Record, 108*(2), 287–315.

Wood, J. L. (2008). Ethical dilemmas in African American faculty representation. *eJournal of Education Policy.* Retrieved, from https://www4.nau.edu/cee/jep/journals.aspx?id=162

Wood, J. L. (2010). *African American males in the community college: Towards a model of academic success* (Unpublished doctoral dissertation). Arizona State University, Tempe.

4

BREAKING THROUGH RACIAL AND GENDER BARRIERS

Reflections on Dissertation Mentorship and Peer Support

Edward P. St. John, O. Cleveland Hill, Ontario S. Wooden, and Penny A. Pasque

Across institutions and over time, we have learned that dissertation mentorship and peer support are powerful sources of social agency in breaking through racial and gender barriers to educational opportunity. When Professor St. John took a midcareer turn to academic life after spending his early career in government and the private sector, he worked with his inner images of his own mentors and peer groups during undergraduate and graduate school to encourage and support students in completing their doctoral work. At the University of New Orleans (UNO), he worked with African American graduate students engaged in social change, including O. Cleveland Hill, an administration liaison, former principal, and retired dean at Nicholls State University (NSU); at Indiana University, he mentored students interested in educational social policy, including Ontario S. Wooden, dean at North Carolina Central University's University College; and at the University of Michigan (UM), he worked with students committed to social justice in K–16 education, including Penny A. Pasque, an associate professor at the University of Oklahoma. In this chapter, St. John, Hill, Wooden, and Pasque reflect on their graduate school experiences and how they influenced their images of education and social change.

Setting the Stage: St. John's Reflections on Racism and Sexism

The fact that sexism and racism are deeply embedded in academic culture is not a surprise, given the extensive critical literature on these subjects. Works such as Shaun Harper, Lori Patton, and Ontario Wooden's (2009) analysis using critical race theory to examine our history of racism are needed and necessary as a source of information for reflection by scholars across fields. I am glad to see such work being published. Academe has made some progress since William Tierney and Estela Bensimon published *Promotion and Tenure* in 1996, but the underlying challenges remain with us. In my view there is still a large gap between the rhetoric about diversity and the practice of fairness and student support within academic communities. In my academic travels, I find myself aligning with faculty colleagues who have an authentic understanding of race and gender and have worked with them to support students who seek to address these issues in their work. It can be especially hard for students who care about inequality and aim to address critical issues in their careers to find support, even in contemporary higher education programs. As a student, I was very fortunate to find supportive faculty advisors who were committed to promoting social justice in their practices. As a process of passing it forward, I have tried to support students facing those challenges and to help them find dissertation committees that were both rigorous and supportive.

If students seek to address critical social issues in their academic work, they will face greater scrutiny than their peers who stick to mainstream topics and methods, so they need highly rigorous standards, along with mentoring that supports them as they address these issues. I developed a framework that documents my understanding of mentorship in *College Organization and Professional Development* (St. John, 2009b). I don't restate these concepts in this chapter, which was written with former graduate students still engaged in navigating their own academic careers. Some of the understandings that have guided me in my work as a research advisor are as follows.

The dissertation is the student's work: As much as we might like to support students in their journeys to emotional maturity as graduate students preparing themselves for professional work as administrators and/or academics, we must recognize that students write their own dissertations. The dissertation is an experience that can give doctoral graduates confidence in their future endeavors, so it is crucial that the dissertation experience helps students gain confidence, an inner sense of self-efficacy, that can provide an experiential basis for their future development. I have not always been successful in meeting this goal, but I have tried to learn from experience.

It is necessary to respect the boundaries that define our roles as advisors and mentors: Not too long after I accepted my first full-time academic position at UNO, my sister gave me *Power in the Helping Professions* (Guggenbuhl-Craig, 1971/1982), a book that helped me understand my role. We had grown up in a family with multiple forms of abuse, so it was important for me to reflect on social-critical issues in mentorship as I started my second career as a professor. She had gone through advanced training in counseling, so I took her advice seriously.

Students' peer groups are vital to their academic success: On the basis of my experiences as an undergraduate student and a graduate student, I realized that having strong peer support was crucial to academic success in graduate school. My first year at UNO, a year of being the only full-time, full-year professor in the educational administration or higher education programs, I observed patterns of student interaction and worked with newly hired colleagues the next year to redesign the doctoral program to provide a strong set of core courses that helped to build peer support. I have adhered to this concept ever since, although I had trouble holding my own groups of students together at UM in 2010 after I entered a period of conflict with my faculty colleagues.[1]

The advisee–advisor relationship works best when both function as "thought partners": I discovered this as a meaningful image when I took the opportunity to reflect on my career, as I discuss later. There are many instances in which I have not been able to realize this sense of collaboration in dissertations and research projects, but I now understand that actualizing this inner and shared sense of collaboration is crucial in working relationships in academe.

My working relationships with Cleveland Hill, Ontario Wooden, and Penny Pasque meet and exemplify these criteria. So, as I read over the text that follows, I realized there was a selection bias in the framing of this chapter. We wrote about successful experiences of working together across racial and gender boundaries. Most but not all of the experiences as a dissertation advisor meet the standards I noted previously. Fortunately, I have always worked in environments in which most students have choices about dissertation advisors and committee members. I am delighted that we can share some success stories. I know we all share the hope that our reflections have value to readers.

Reflections on Mentoring and Peer Groups

St. John's Reflections

When reflecting on what to say in gratitude when I received the research achievement award from the Association for the Study of Higher Education (ASHE), I had the opportunity to recall the roles mentors and peers played in my professional and intellectual development. Like many who study higher education as a field, I am indebted to my early mentors. They were the sources of my interest in higher education policy and practice.

I remembered and thanked three of my early mentors: Mary Regan, Orville Thompson, and James Meyer, all now deceased. They each had a lasting impact. As my undergraduate advisor, Mary Regan at the University of California, Davis (UCD), was a coach for my student activism. We eventually copublished my undergraduate thesis as a monograph (St. John & Regan, 1973), and I learned a great deal about academic publishing in the process. As a master's student, I had the opportunity to work half-time as a graduate assistant on her studies of college students. Mary inspired my interest in higher education as a field of study and as a force for social change. I also worked half-time for Orville Thompson, chair of applied behavioral science. I collaborated with Orville on faculty retreats in community development, human development, and design, the core subjects in the department, and we eventually cowrote an academic plan for the department. In the process I learned a great deal about academic governance.

Also at UCD during a year of student protest against the war in Vietnam and rising education fees, I had the opportunity to serve as student assistant to Chancellor James H. Meyer. He was an insightful man, and we worked through many complicated issues that seemed crucial at the time (St. John, 1973). Jim tried to help me be realistic. He is the one who told me I (a) was destined to be a professor because I thought too much for a career in politics and policy, (b) needed to become an expert in something before I could lead or change institutions, and (c) should go to UCLA for my doctorate in higher education rather than Stanford or Harvard.

I went to Harvard. I have never been good at taking advice. At Harvard I worked with many excellent thought partners (i.e., people with whom we think collaboratively about problems involving theory, research, and action), with peers in classes, and on the editorial board of the *Harvard Educational Review*. In addition, I had the opportunity to work on a study of Title III of the Higher Education Act with George Weathersby (see Weathersby, Jackson, Jacobs, St. John, & Tingley, 1977). Involvement in George's project led to my dissertation, which was eventually published as a book on policy and management (St. John, 1981) and was the stimulus for some comparative studies on the topic (i.e., St. John & McCaig, 1983, 1984). On several occasions I enjoyed long reflective conversations with George. He, too, was interested in individual and organizational development. My third year at Harvard, about the time I was working on my dissertation, Mary Regan was a visiting professor as part of her sabbatical leave. I think we were all lucky to have time to think, talk, and reflect together on shared topics of interest.

After Harvard, I had more than a decade of real-world experience in policy before I made a midcareer shift to academe; Jim Meyer had been right about my nature. I have been lucky to develop expertise in policy and practice, but I have never lost a focus on promoting equal opportunity. After a decade in government and consulting, I took my first academic appointment, as an associate professor at UNO. My commitments to social justice, mentoring students, and encouraging peer group collaboration in classes and on projects were very high priorities for me, in addition to getting tenure.

Four ideals have had a substantial influence on my mentoring of students and my research on professional development (St. John, 2009a, 2009b).[2] First, the inner images we hold of mentors can have a huge influence on our actions as advisors. Mary Regan and Orville Thompson were deeply committed to social justice. As Caucasian scholars in the 1960s, they had built a community studies program that included Asian American Studies, Native American Studies, and Black Research and Services as research and academic concentrations. We worked together as thought partners in a diverse learning environment and shared commitments to improving diversity in the university. Second, I have come to think of research as a cocreation with thought partners. I work best with students who want to engage collaboratively in the thought process, just as I was invited to collaborate with mentors at UCD. I have more difficulty with students who want to be told what to do in research or who won't engage in discussion about research problems. Third, because I am deeply committed to working toward greater justice in education, I find it easiest to work with people who share this value. When I have worked with students who share commitments to justice in education and who are willing to engage collaboratively in critical thought about problems, I have not experienced racial or gender barriers per se. Instead, working through issues related to race and gender differences has provided us opportunities to learn and work together. Finally, I have long been interested in patterns and processes of professional development. As a mentor, I have often continued to work with students after they graduate, using collaborative projects as part of our shared professional development. I have worked best when research involves collaborative thought, a personal trait that has been true regardless of whether I am senior, junior, or peer on a project.

The University of New Orleans

St. John's Reflections

Starting out at UNO in 1989, I began to work on my early publications and to become a teacher and mentor. I found a program in shambles. In addition to being the only full-time, full-year professor in either higher education or educational administration, I served as chair of both programs. In the winter of 1990, I worked with Louis Mirón, who joined me as a full-time assistant professor in educational administration, to restructure the doctoral program in leadership, which had options in higher education and educational administration. We began by developing a cohort-based program. In addition to admitting several students from New Orleans to diversify a program that had previously served the suburbs better than the city, I reached out to students I heard about who might be interested in the revised program, which started in the fall of 1990.

One of my goals during this period was to desegregate the doctoral programs in higher education and educational leadership I chaired when I first arrived at UNO. Although there had been previous attempts to settle the federal desegregation case in Louisiana, the universities had remained mostly segregated when I arrived in 1989. The higher education program I chaired had been formed as a joint program with Southern University as part of a prior agreement, but before I arrived at UNO the agreement had broken down. The program was run by UNO with no involvement of faculty from Southern, and many of the students of color who had applied for the program were denied admission. I chose to review these cases when I started as chair of the program. As I brought cases forward, my department chair kept telling me, "No one is going to thank you for this." I could not accept that.

Cleveland Hill was one of several students formerly denied admission whom I decided to encourage to apply. Cleveland was a quiet, independent-minded African American man with great leadership potential. He had been a basketball star in college and was invited to stay on at his college as a coach, which led to an academic appointment in the education school at NSU. He had charisma but was also shy. At UNO we had developed an action research option for the EdD program that emphasized doing research in support of educational improvement. I contacted him after reviewing the application files and encouraged him to reapply; he was accepted into the first entering class in the doctoral program in 1990. Cleveland and his peers learned the meaning of working in teams as thought partners in the pursuit of social justice, a theme that ran through core courses by Louis Mirón, Alison Griffith, and Ira Bogotch, colleagues who were hired in 1990. Cleveland Hill's (1993) dissertation adapted Argyris and Schön's (1974) theories of professional effectiveness (Argyris, 1993) in the design and implementation of a summer program for youth at NSU. Cleveland was also the first of the graduate students at UNO to complete an action research dissertation, an option we had built into the doctoral program. More important, Cleveland and his peers were groundbreakers at UNO. In their graduate courses many of the students had their first open conversations about issues of race and power, topics that had not previously been openly discussed in the graduate programs at the university.

Hill's Reflections

My decision to reenter graduate school and pursue a doctoral degree was made rather late in my career; I was in my late thirties. There are two main reasons I waited. First, after completing my bachelor's degree in 1972, I spent three years on active duty in the military. After that, I returned to school for three semesters to complete requirements for teacher certification.

My decision to seek teacher certification was inspired by the late Hal Fisher. Hal was my basketball coach and mentor during my military stint. On a State Department–sponsored trip to Jordan in 1975, we were asked to teach Jordanian youth the game of American basketball. Evidently I displayed some skills and qualities teachers needed, because Hal approached me about entering the profession when I left the armed forces. My initial reaction was, "I wouldn't mind being a coach someday, but I have no desire to teach." His response was, "What the hell do you think coaching is if not good teaching?" These eloquent words of Hal Fisher, an early mentor, inspired me to become a teacher.

After certification, I taught middle school for two and a half years, at the same time working on achieving a master's degree in school-based educational administration. After completing this advanced degree in 1978, for all intents and purposes I believed my career was set. However, just one year later I received an offer to become a college basketball coach at NSU, which I accepted. I held this position for the next six years.

I looked upon this offer to coach at the college level as simply an opportunity to advance my career. On the other hand, the university at the time was under a consent decree to integrate its faculty and staff. There was an extant consensus by predominantly White higher education institutions with sports programs that for recruiting purposes it was a good strategy to have a person of color on the coaching staff. There was a mutual benefit to my being hired for this position, but the long-term impact for me was that I received very little quality mentoring.

In 1985 fate struck again. NSU and all public colleges and universities in Louisiana were still under a federal court-ordered consent decree to more actively desegregate their instructional faculty. This time I was asked to become a member of the health and physical education department at NSU. The department chair was quite honest when he stated that the department would rather *integrate* with someone they knew than bring in someone from the outside. Not knowing whether to feel complimented or insulted, I accepted the position. The year was 1985, and I had no desire to pursue any more educational opportunities.

One reason I had never entered a doctoral program was that on three occasions I believed my professional career was set. A second reason was that conducting quantitative dissertation research did not appeal to me. Several of my colleagues who held a doctorate recounted for me how they had conducted meaningless quantitative research for the sole purpose of getting their degrees. I instinctively felt that if I was going to ever engage in dissertation research, it was going to be in some area of social justice in which I had a moral and purposeful interest.

I digress here to give the reader a better understanding of my addiction to social justice issues. I am a native of the state of Mississippi, first venturing out of that state in 1968 on a college basketball scholarship. During the late 1950s and early 1960s, members of my family, persons in my community, and even I, to a lesser extent, were subjected to some of the most heinous injustices perpetuated upon African Americans in the segregated south. On one hand, some of those terrible experiences influenced me to be shy and untrusting of others. On the other hand, I was influenced to try, in some small way, to actively put an end to acts of oppression and injustice. Very simply, I came to believe that I must do more than write about oppression and injustice; I wanted to be actively engaged in their demise.

Still, my ultimate decision to enter the doctoral program was the result of several serendipitous opportunities.

Opportunity 1: I had begun taking graduate classes before some of the other members who would later form my cohort. My first semester at UNO was in 1987. Quite honestly, this initial foray into graduate school proved to be an aimless venture. There was very little support and guidance from what I characterized then as a seemingly disinterested faculty. In 1988, my initial request to enter the doctoral program then in existence was denied.

In 1990, a student enrolled in one of my classes informed me that a new graduate school coordinator named Ed St. John had been named and that he wanted to meet with me. After some procrastinating, I finally met with him, and he asked why I was not in the doctoral program at UNO. Ed St. John would eventually become my instructor for several classes and also my major professor; with his intervention, guidance, and support, I was admitted to the predoctoral program at UNO, which resulted in my being placed on the right path to ultimately be accepted into the doctoral program.

In all honesty, the influences from my youth in Mississippi, the theories in use (Argyris, Putnam, & Smith, 1985) I had witnessed as a middle school teacher, and the "real" reasons I had been hired for my first two positions at the university level made me very skeptical and untrusting of the motives of Ed St. John in 1990. The idea of having a mentor who was Caucasian was indeed a foreign concept to me. However, upon reflection, this was the beginning of doctoral mentoring for me. I personally define *mentoring* as providing sincere support and encouragement to others without any ulterior motives at all.

Opportunity 2: The doctoral program at UNO was restructured to broaden the kinds of research acceptable for dissertations. Between 1988 and 1990, the graduate faculty at UNO were almost completely new, and some expressed interest in qualitative research and social justice issues.

Another slight digression here is in order. Similar to experiences during my formative years in Mississippi through the time I was a middle school teacher and spent my summers working as the director of a school dropout prevention program, I had been concerned with a specific social justice issue that existed then and still does to this day. I wanted to know why there was a huge academic achievement gap between minority students (African, Native, and Latina and Latino Americans) and their Caucasian and Asian American counterparts. I already knew poverty played a key role, as well as racism, sexism, and other factors. Yet, most of the teachers I worked with in middle school and those I hired for my dropout prevention program seemed to be well meaning and interested in the academic achievement of all of their students. They seemed devoid of racist, sexist, and gender-based attitudes and beliefs. However, too often minority students were not achieving, and I kept asking myself, "What else is going on here? Could there be some factor or factors not addressed in the literature to explain the academic achievement gaps between ethnic groups?" These questions became the focus of my dissertation research.

However, for the purposes of this chapter and given my adversity to meaningless quantitative research, Opportunity 2 was the decision by the incoming graduate faculty at UNO to embrace qualitative research at what proved to be for me the right time.

Opportunity 3: Still, the fact remained that although I wanted to somehow address the social justice issue of the academic achievement gap in my dissertation research, I had no framework for doing so. That framework emerged for me (and, as I would learn later, for several others) when Ed St. John chose *Action Science* (see Argyris et al., 1985) as the textbook for one of our graduate classes. In this book, the authors discuss the concept of leaders who espouse one set of beliefs (as theories) but actually operate from another set, "theories in use." This concept helped me understand how a group of leaders (schoolteachers) could espouse high expectations, rigorous instruction, equity, and social justice for all students yet at the same time within the confines of their classroom expect very little from poor and minority students, provide them with subpar instruction, demonstrate subtle discrimination and bias, and practice a skewed form of social justice (meaning social justice as practiced for some was different from social justice as practiced for others). Keep in mind that many of these teachers were decent, well-meaning people who truly thought they were engaging in fair practices with poor and minority students. I remain convinced even now that most had no conscious malevolent intentions.

For example, I would later learn that sometimes teachers had low expectations for poor and minority students, but these low expectations were often grounded in sympathy. Low expectations, even those grounded in sympathy, often, for example, influenced 9th-grade English teachers to give minority students grades that promoted them to the 10th grade even though they were reading on a 4th- or 5th-grade level. Similar examples occurred in mathematics classes. I remember vividly in 1979 one African American teacher protesting to the principal at my school that she thought it was wrong to promote unprepared students. The response of the principal was, "Well, do you want those older boys back here next year to be a negative influence on 7th- and 8th-grade girls?"

Opportunity 4: The final opportunity was the stabilizing of the graduate faculty and cohort members at UNO. As mentioned earlier, there was a large turnover in faculty between 1988 and 1990; similarly, students with whom I had begun taking classes in 1987 attended UNO in a very haphazard manner. From 1990 until I completed the doctoral program in 1993, the new faculty members would remain relatively intact, and the cohort of graduate students became a stable group of candidates who had a unified objective-completion of a doctoral degree. As these opportunities came together at the right time for me, seemingly it should have been easy for our stable cohort to become mentors and mentees. However, it did not happen in a linear manner for me.

Independent mind-set: As I reflect on why I did not readily accept graduate school cohort mentoring, I think it had a lot to do with my mind-set and personal background at the time. Although Ed St. John and other members of the graduate faculty strongly encouraged us to form a cohort, I was a reluctant participant. One reason for my reluctance I now believe had to do with the experiences I had in my formative years in Mississippi, with my experiences I alluded to earlier being a middle school and college coach and teacher, and finally with geographical settings. Most of the members of our cohort were from an urban setting (mainly New Orleans and its suburbs) in close proximity to UNO, whereas I was from a rural part of Louisiana somewhat distant from UNO. Although all of us were interested in social justice issues, I believed there was a major difference. It was my position that if one lived in an urban area, one not only believed in social justice but also had an ingrained hope that the actions personally (or as a group) taken advocating for social justice would make a difference. On the other hand, when one lived and worked in a rural area for a long period of time, a sense of despair set in. So even though I advocated for social justice, I had begun to believe that no matter what actions I took, nothing would change. At least that was my dominant mind-set at the time.

A number of events influenced the values inherent in mentoring, and my gradual acceptance of them will always stand out as significant. One event involved a study group consisting of all members of our cohort, organized by the late Leetta Allen-Haynes, a strong presence and a member of our cohort. One particular Saturday morning study session (for our general exams), designed to last 4 hours, turned into an all-day event. This special session produced discussion, dialogue, laughter, emotional swings, arguments, heated debate, and tears. As I recall, the most heated discussions revolved around whether we needed to answer test questions in a unified manner or from an individual perspective.[3] At one point, when things became very contentious, it became necessary to summon Ed St. John, who was the major professor for several of us, away from his home and family to come and restore calm. I do not remember what Dr. St. John said that quieted the storm. What stayed with me is the fact that he gave up his Saturday morning to do for us what I have learned over the years is something he does naturally for all of his students. I have come to learn that acts such as these are what mentoring is about.

Upon reflection, I see this particular study session proved to be the catharsis that firmly established our cohort group as one where we comfortably became both mentors and mentees until the completion of our doctoral program and beyond. As we completed our personal doctoral programs over the next several semesters, it became routine for members of the cohort to continue to mentor those still in the program. For example, Leetta Allen-Haynes, who completed her doctorate in the summer of 1993, offered advice and read and edited dissertations for Donaldo Batiste, Louise Kaltenbaugh, and me prior to our graduation in December 1993. I did the same for another cohort member, Louise Olsen, prior to her graduation in May 1994.

The benefits of being in a cohort mentoring program during graduate school were many. The program showed that a group of disparate individuals could come together and learn to disagree without becoming disagreeable. Members could learn to discuss and dialogue and begin to appreciate rich and varied objective points of view. We also learned to genuinely guide, support, and share with each other. What many of us learned in cohort mentoring influenced us as faculty instructors and later in professional practice as administrative leaders. Two examples are worth noting here. First, when I became the education dean in 1999 at NSU, I inherited a unit that had three departments: physical education, teacher education, and psychology. The faculty of the three departments rarely engaged in research and scholarly endeavors together. One of my goals as dean was to create a positive culture and climate among the faculty of the three departments. The objective was for them to engage in scholarly work, research, and grant writing together. It took three years to achieve dividends from my efforts, but it did happen. A second example of cohort mentoring that had a lasting impact occurred in 2004. I worked very closely with Leetta Allen-Haynes, who was then the dean of the graduate school at Southern University at New Orleans (SUNO). SUNO was seeking national accreditation for its college of education programs. NSU had recently completed its reaffirmation of national accreditation, and I was able to provide Dr. Haynes with documents, support, and advice for her school's venture. Both of these examples are grounded in the cohort mentoring relationships we had developed years earlier at UNO.

Indiana University

St. John's Reflections

I left UNO in the fall of 1996. After a stimulating year at the University of Dayton, a campus I truly adored, I accepted a professorship at Indiana University starting in January 1998, where I also served as director of the Indiana Education Policy Center. My work in the policy center involved studies of reading programs (e.g., St. John, Loescher, & Bardzell, 2003), school reform (e.g., St. John & Mirón, 2003), and student financial aid (e.g., St. John, 2003). After serving my five-year term as director of the center, I began the Indiana Project on Academic Success, an initiative designed to use quantitative studies and action inquiry to inform and support campus efforts to improve retention (see St. John & Musoba, 2010).

During this time, I reflected a great deal on my UNO experience. In particular, I began to write articles with former UNO students that focused on issues of racial justice (e.g., Allen-Haynes, St. John, & Cadray, 2003; Kaltenbaugh, St. John, & Starkey, 1999; St. John & Cadray, 2004). At UNO I had learned a great deal about racial prejudice. The doctoral students had helped me overcome my prejudice about the south, as I came to understand how generations of African Americans and Caucasians had struggled with the legacy of segregation and the attitudes deeply embedded in the culture of the city. I left UNO with an even deeper commitment to social justice in education, but at Indiana University I found myself confronting entirely new challenges.

At Indiana University, I was chair of the Higher Education and Student Affairs program for several years. There was student discontent at the time. On the basis of my experience at UNO, I encouraged students to engage in action research and worked with them to navigate the doctoral program. Ontario Wooden was a master's student I encouraged to enter directly into the doctoral program. He also completed a post-master's certificate in institutional research, a program we started with support from the Association for Institutional Research and the National Center for Education Statistics. Ontario worked on projects in the Indiana Education Policy Center, including a study of state student aid programs (e.g., St. John, Simmons, Hoezee, Wooden, & Musoba, 2002). He and I collaborated with his graduate student peers on many research projects during graduate school (e.g., St. John & Wooden, 2005); he also worked and collaborated with peer groups of learning partners.

The Indiana Education Policy Center developed a strong culture of peer support while I was there. We were engaged in applied policy research projects that had potential for generating dissertation topics; many students chose to craft dissertation topics that built on their research at work. Ontario got involved in work at the center because of his interest in college access and the opportunity to engage in research on this topic. We wrote papers together that could have developed into dissertation topics (e.g., St. John & Wooden, 2005, 2006), yet Ontario also frequently reflected on his own educational experiences when he thought about access issues. Eventually he chose to conduct an ethnographic study of his own high school and returned to his home community for fieldwork. During this process I encouraged him to read about the African American education tradition and to reflect on his own experience in relation to this tradition of uplift (e.g., Walker, 1996) rather than attempt to replicate pipeline studies that focused only on students like himself who were channeled down the academic path. He discovered that his high school had tracked students in ways he had not known about, and he wrote an excellent chapter based on this work (Wooden, 2007). He entered his work as academic administrator at his alma mater with a deep personal commitment to cross-generation uplift, a tradition he benefited from and continues to deeply value.

Wooden's Reflections

Initially, my educational aspirations were to become an elementary school teacher, principal, and eventually superintendent of schools. Being a first-generation college student, I did not know how I was going to get there. However, becoming the vice president for the student body as an undergraduate changed my career trajectory (and my life). This experience gave me the opportunity to interact with my peers, as well as university administrators and leaders from the University System of Georgia. At the same time, one of my friends was in the Higher Education and Student Affairs (HESA) program at Indiana University. I had such a great experience as a student leader that after graduation I decided to give HESA a try. I enrolled in the master's program and set off on what was to be a most interesting journey. Having attended a historically Black university for my undergraduate education, Albany State University in Georgia, I had some things to get accustomed to. The greatest challenge was getting my peers to be open to the experiences of those who were different. There were times I felt my sharing in class was devalued and that, because of not having attended a mainstream, predominantly White institution, I should remain silent. I remember being enrolled in a course, Diverse College Students, where it seemed my experiences were often discounted. Students openly questioned the value of my degree and my preparation for graduate school because I had attended a historically Black university; some of my classmates clearly did not think my degree was worth the paper on which it was printed. These classmates even reported me to the program coordinator because they were "uncomfortable" with my behavior in the course. No regard was given to the faculty member, a Latina woman, who taught the course in that they totally bypassed her and went directly to the program coordinator. I had an assistantship in the Office of Student Financial Assistance, which was the bright spot of my day. Not only did I work alongside some of the best financial aid administrators in the country, but I also was passionate about helping provide students with access to higher education.

Most of my excitement during the first year of graduate school came from hanging out with the African American students in my cohort. We all had our specializations—mine was college access. I only wanted to read items related to college access and only wanted to discuss the same. This was my topic of conversation whether in or out of the classroom. I was vaguely aware there was a scholar on campus (Ed St. John) doing research on college access. After hearing of my interest in college access, my program coordinator informed me one day that Ed wanted to have a conversation with me. I did not know what the conversation was in reference to and did not know who Ed was, but I took my chances.

Upon entering the office, I figured, "This guy does quite a bit of reading," and I would later find that he does quite a bit (to put it mildly) of writing. We talked at length about our lives, both personally and professionally, in what must have been the most engaging conversation in my life. It was as if we had met before. We talked briefly about the national picture concerning college access, specifically financial access, and he shared with me a copy of a National Center for Education Statistics report (Berkner & Chavez, 1997). At the end of the conversation, we agreed to meet again.

Given that I had the report, I figured I had better start reading it because I had no idea when I would see Ed again. I shared information with my friends about Ed and the report and how excited I was that someone had taken an interest in me being not only a successful student but also a successful person. Ed became my faculty advisor and my dissertation chair. The most interesting piece was that this was coming from a White man. As an African American man from the South, I had been taken aback by the sometimes "cold" environment on the campus. There was the usual rhetoric of an appreciation for diversity and acceptance, but sometimes that was just not the case. Most of the African American students were trying to connect with faculty who looked like them because it was comfortable to do so. Meeting Ed and hearing about his experiences growing up in California and his career trajectory made me feel as if he "understood" me, and there was no need to explain things. I also felt his experiences at UNO prepared him to serve as a mentor and thought partner for me. This relationship has turned into one of the most appreciated friendships I have today.

Ed and I had another conversation to discuss the report. In this conversation, we discussed college access as it relates to academic preparation, college costs, and what eventually led to the development of the Balanced Access Model (St. John, 2002). At the end of my first year as a master's student, I gained admission to the doctoral program and was later offered an assistantship at the Indiana Education Policy Center, where I was able to work on projects related to higher education access, comprehensive school reform programs, higher education finance, and a number of new initiatives Ed was able to garner support for. Ed even convinced me I should complete the post-master's certificate in institutional research. This certificate has been extremely helpful in reviewing and managing data relative to those critical retention and graduation rates.

At the same time, I had become a part of a group of African American doctoral students who not only were serious about their pursuit of a doctorate but also all finished their degree. These friends were my peer thought partners: Shaun Harper, Brian Bridges, Lori Patton, Michelle McClure, John Kuykendall, and Carla Morelon. The group also included a peer in the School of Environmental and Public Affairs, Leah Davis. We would study, write, party, and even have a marathon editing session if someone needed to get something ready for a defense or the submission of the final copy of a dissertation. Shaun, Lori, and I published an article reviewing reforms for African Americans in higher education (Harper et al., 2009). We supported each other through a number of life challenges during and after graduate school. We all remain great friends and colleagues. These relationships were important at the time because these friends provided a safe place for me. I did not have to explain why I looked a certain way or said a certain thing—they understood. Also, each of us was working with a different faculty member, almost all across racial and gender lines. We would often discuss those experiences and share information that had been shared through our individual relationships with our faculty advisors.

My employment at the Indiana Education Policy Center allowed me to meet other colleagues who were passionate about educational issues that ran the gamut from elementary school to higher education. It was a dynamic place to work. During this time, I became a member of another, much more diverse club that consisted of Larry Hoezee, Glenda Musoba, Osman Cekic, Kim Kline, and Jesse Mendez—"The Ed Heads." This name came about because of the respect and regard that we held for Ed's commitment to developing us into the best scholars we could be. Ed is a thinker; The Ed Heads were going to be thinkers, too! These students were interested in completing degrees and supporting one another. Jesse and I shared an office and became good friends; I still look forward to receiving a Christmas card each year. Most of us still keep in touch. This was also the opportunity to interact more with Ed to learn about his upbringing, his family, and his passion for excellence. I would simply be amazed at the rate at which he could turn an article or even a book around; it seemed as if he worked day and night. However, I learned that it was a priority for him to spend time with his wife and children while he pursued his other interests.

Ed and I shared, at length, our interest in cultural context and the African American tradition (e.g., Allen-Haynes et al., 2003; Walker, 1996) as a part of the work we did during our time together. These ideas would become the foundation for my dissertation, which I was happy to allow Ed to lead; he also selected the remainder of the committee. He was always patient and understanding during the process and would give feedback that could take a while to interpret, but I would always catch on. This is not easy to put into words, but when talking with Ed, I had moments where I would follow him very closely. However, at some point in the conversation, he would remove his glasses, rub his face, and enter this phase of thinking critically that took a minute for me to grasp. He interacted with me as he did with his senior colleagues. He would challenge me in this process in ways I had never been challenged before. For example, I remember him telling me that if I was going to write this dissertation, I was going to have to get to the point where I was comfortable critiquing my community, the African American community.

That, at times, was tough because my dissertation was almost revisiting my education experiences, and on some level I wanted to think that everyone was well meaning. I later understood that even among the well meaning, there are often casualties. A number of folks I respected for doing the work they did in public schools lost my respect because I felt they were taking advantage of students to receive personal gain rather than genuinely assisting students in becoming better persons and providing them with access to information to be successful high school students and later college graduates.

There were rumors that Ed was going to be leaving the university. Interestingly enough, although I had completed my doctorate and joined the faculty and administration at my alma mater, Albany State University, I did not want Ed to leave Indiana. I wanted other students to have the great experience I had at what I thought was the best higher education program in the country. Because of my work at the Indiana Education Policy Center and the Indiana Project on Academic Success, the focus of my professional career has been centered on student success initiatives.

To this day, I feel the need to call Ed from time to time to check in with him and update him on what is going on in my life. This is likely due to my need for affirmation from him. We have completed a number of writing projects together, and he is always there when I need him. For example, every career move I have made since meeting Ed, I have shared with him. I feel a sense of connectedness to him and possess a level of respect for him that makes this a natural part of my life—Ed is family. My work with Ed guides the work I do each day to prepare the next generation of college graduates to transform their communities.

University of Michigan

St. John's Reflections

After much reflection with my wife about our life goals, I accepted a collegiate professorship at UM. I was recruited, along with an assistant professor and associate professor, as part of a cluster hire to start a new initiative on K–16 education. By the time I went to UM in January 2008, it was evident that the K–16 initiative had been a strategy by UM colleagues to hire more faculty. I labored for a few years with no support trying to encourage new program development in K–16 education, but other faculty had little interest. However, for several years I flourished in this academic engagement as a senior professor.

At UM, I avoided taking program leadership positions and instead focused on studies related to my interest in equal opportunity for preparation, access, and academic success. In truth, one of the reasons I accepted the offer from UM was that I thought there would be an opportunity to work with UM leadership to develop strategies to promote diversity on campus in the wake of the Supreme Court's *Gratz* and *Grutter* decisions. I worked with several national and local groups on interesting initiatives as an action-oriented researcher, attempting to use the method in which I was most interested: action inquiry to support social change (St. John, 2009a, 2009b). As is the case at most universities, at UM faculty were assigned new student advisees each year. When possible, I engaged my graduate students in research leading to joint publications, extending my ideas of graduate mentoring and of working with students as thought partners. For example, I am currently working with three UM graduate students (Johanna C. Masse, Kim Callahan Lijana, and Victoria Milazzo Bigelow) on *College Prep: Transforming High Schools, Overcoming Failed Public Policy, and Preparing Students for Higher Education*, a book for Johns Hopkins University Press.

One interesting feature of the UM program is the varied pockets of student engagement in research. Other students work at the National Center for Institutional Diversity, the Center for Research on Learning and Teaching, and the National Forum on Higher Education for the Public Good and on faculty research projects. Four of my first six doctoral graduates at UM had worked with the National Forum on Higher Education for the Public Good, directed by John Burkhardt, a unit that actively supported justice-oriented initiatives (www.thenationalforum.org). Most of these students share a strong commitment to advocacy in support of educational reform and social justice.

Penny Pasque was my first dissertation student; Lesley Rex, a qualitative methodologist, and I codirected Penny's dissertation. By the time I started working with Penny on her dissertation, she had completed her qualifying work, which led to the literature review for her dissertation. The first day she came in my office to talk about her topic, I invited her to lunch along with my wife.[4] My sense was that we'd be working together, and I have always wanted my students to know my wife. There weren't many faculty members who shared Penny's deep interest in and passion for social justice, so I sensed it was best to start off as friends. Penny graciously accepted the lunch invitation and picked the restaurant, and we took her out. I started the process of sharing my family with students in New Orleans, a place where students often dropped by our house or even called my wife if they struggled with the challenges I put before them. The further along I got in my career, the more I realized that if my wife knows the women and men with whom I work, it would be easier to talk about matters of the heart—and for me social justice is centered in an ethic of care (St. John, 2009a)—at home and work. By the way, Penny's dissertation was turned into an outstanding book (Pasque, 2010), now in its second printing.

Pasque's Reflections

When I met Ed, I was finishing my comprehensive examination for the PhD program in the Center for the Study of Higher and Postsecondary Education (CSHPE) at UM and was employed as a graduate assistant with the National Forum on Higher Education for the Public Good. The mission of the forum is "to significantly increase awareness, understanding, commitment, and action relative to the public service role of higher education in the United States" (National Forum on Higher Education for the Public Good, 2008, para. 1). This mission resonated with me. I had worked for 10 years after finishing my master's degree, before starting my doctoral degree, in academic and student affairs programs at Cornell University and UM. At UM I had cofounded the Michigan Community Scholars Program (MCSP), a living-learning program focused on the connections among service-learning, social identity (race, class, gender, sexual orientation, etc.), and leadership (Galura, Pasque, Schoem, & Howard, 2004). The goal of this program was to encourage critical thinking and dialogue among students, staff, community partners, and faculty about issues of community to model a just, diverse, and democratic community and make a difference in local, national, and global communities (Schoem & Pasque, 2004).

As such, MCSP and the National Forum compelled me to think more deeply about issues of community engagement and social justice. Yet, it was Ed St. John who encouraged me to connect these practical interests to my academic scholarship through my work as a PhD candidate. In this way, Ed showed me I did not have to leave my passions behind and become a stereotypical "stodgie" faculty member whose research did not intersect with real-life practice and community engagement. This may not be a revelation for some, but for me the connections among theory, practice, activism, reflexivity, and passion were relatively new. Let me explain where I was coming from a little more clearly.

Reflexivity: As a second-generation Italian on one side of my family and second-generation Sicilian born in the United States on the other side (yes, my family takes this distinction seriously), I was raised in the outskirts of Detroit by a single mom who never attended college. She literally cried when paying bills each month and worked three jobs to keep a roof over our heads and the heat turned on; I still have chilling memories of the frigid air when jumping from the bed to the shower in the mornings to get ready for high school. Michigan does get cold in the winter!

My mom did not know much about what to tell my brother, sister, and me about college life, but she did know enough to tell us that we needed to go: We would have to pay for it ourselves, but we needed to attend college. This was her way of encouraging us to do well and excel. As a first-generation college student, I attended a regional institution—Eastern Michigan University—and at first I did not understand that "room and board" on my bursar bill meant room and *food*: I could eat in the dining halls at every meal! I became involved in the residence halls through hall government, a job at the front desk, and, later, as a resident advisor. I completed my BS in communication and marketing and moved to Syracuse University, where I received an MS in interpersonal communication as I worked as a teaching assistant in the Department of Communication and Rhetorical Studies.

I vividly remember an interaction with a faculty member a few years later, when I worked full-time and took graduate classes at Cornell University. This faculty member learned where I had attended high school and knew the area through some of his former interactions with the African American community in Detroit. His response was, "Wow, you've really come a long way." There was a part of me that thought, "Yes, that's right—it has been a long road" and yet another part of me simultaneously thought, "Who are you to perpetuate judgment about my home community and the people living in this community, as though we are not expected to succeed at Cornell?" It was the complexities of social capital (Bourdieu, 1986) and academic capital (St. John, Hu, & Fisher, 2011) implicit in comments like this that propelled me to work on issues of educational inequities, community engagement, social justice, and social change. Importantly, it was Ed, among a few others, who encouraged me to combine these passions and life experiences with academic scholarship.

Ed St. John as a mentor: My first real interaction with Ed was at a national conference prior to his arrival on UM's campus. I was sitting at a table in a hotel bar with a number of graduate student colleagues, all women. We had recently learned that Ed had accepted the Algo D. Henderson Collegiate Professor position at the School of Education. We invited him to join us, at which point he received an earful of our student perspectives about the politics and processes of the program. For example, we talked about the politics of designing dissertation committees and which faculty would not work with each other. Ed handled this with grace; he listened to our perspectives, asked questions, and was supportive of our experiences. The conversation was relatively short, but it gave me a sense of his ethics of care and justice, of which I have since learned he has written about extensively (St. John, 2006).

Ed's sense of care and his academic scholarship in equal opportunity for preparation, access, and academic success led me to meet with him about cochairing my dissertation with Dr. Lesley Rex in English education. At this point, I gave him a copy of a research paper I had written, and he immediately invited me to revise it and submit it as a chapter (Pasque, 2007) in his book *Confronting Educational Inequality: Reframing, Building Understanding, and*

Making Change (St. John, 2007). With Ed, a revision is never a simple process. Each time I would meet with him about a revision on this manuscript or a dissertation chapter, his only words to me were, "Think more deeply as you revise again." Okay, this is *not* literally how it went, but these are a small number of the words he would use each time he provided me with thoughtful feedback. I share this story (in jest) with my own doctoral students in order to encourage them to think more critically as they engage in the ever-familiar "write and revise" process. In fact, it was these words that prompted me to write the word *think* on a sticky note and put it on my computer, where it remains today as an impetus to engage more deeply in critical inquiry in a way that intentionally connects with social change. In this important way, Ed has mentored me as a critical scholar. He encouraged me to go further with my own thinking; to take implicit knowledge and make it explicit; to empirically show, describe, and analyze the essential findings in a study; and to explore action-oriented research and critical inquiry. This example is representative of the "good old boys network" in academia or the "Michigan Mafia" of UM CSHPE graduates. It is an ubiquitous relationship of which you are not certain you belong, but you are extremely certain when you do not belong. Stated another way, as a woman and a first-generation college student, I cannot tell you what I do not know or what goes on in circles of which I am not a part. I can, however, clearly articulate who is in the know and that I'm not necessarily certain I want to be integrated in some of these groups. As someone often on the margins, who does not know the questions I should be asking of mentors in the academy, I find it helpful to have a mentor who is already in the know to guide and encourage. I see Ed as someone who readily shares information I might not have access to, in a way that I can hear; someone who renders academic culture and processes visible. Furthermore, he is not threatened when I raise questions that challenge the status quo or talk through the underlying politics of the situation. Ed is not afraid to give up information and power to people who might not have been born and raised in the academy, and this action is indicative of a mentor who is inclusive of people across gender and class.

As such, Ed has always been supportive of my continued involvement with the Disruptive Dialogue Project (DDP), even though these efforts lie at the fringes of the field of higher education. As graduate students, five of us from across the country developed the project to facilitate our shared interest in interrogating, interrupting, and resisting dominant (positivist and postpositivist) methodological assumptions and research practices that perpetuate the marginalization of critical inquiry within the higher education research community (Carducci, Pasque, Kuntz, & Contreras-McGavin, 2013; Gildersleeve, Kuntz, Pasque, & Carducci, 2010; Pasque, Carducci, Gildersleeve, & Kuntz, 2011; Pasque, Carducci, Kuntz, & Gildersleeve, 2012). More specifically, having recognized and experienced gaps in dialogues about methodology taking place within higher education graduate programs, scholarly journals, and professional conference sessions—gaps that serve to undermine research methodologies that challenge and transform oppressive structures and relationships via the research process itself—we seek to "inhabit the gap" (Komives, 2000) in order to contest the methodological norms that frame and constrain contemporary higher education scholarship.

The creation of the DDP speaks to our personal desire to foster an intimate forum for collaboration, learning, support, and renewal as we individually and collectively navigate our way from graduate students to assistant professor positions and further along the tenure track. Our public concerns (of equal importance and naturally overlapping with the personal) include the intention to establish a space of resistance from which we can critique, challenge, and ultimately overturn the colonizing research practices that continue to constrain the achievement of educational equity and the establishment of socially just educational institutions. It is important to note that these dialogic spaces were not created overnight; the format and nature of the DDP has evolved over time. We have moved from casual conversations at the International Congress of Qualitative Inquiry and the Association for the Study of Higher Education, to the informal exchange of relevant critical methodology references, to the formal establishment of biweekly "disruptive dialogue" teleconferences and research memos, to national and international conference research paper presentations, to guest speaking in qualitative research courses, and to publications. Each step has provided us with an opportunity to discuss and collectively address the opportunities and challenges embedded in a commitment to conducting decolonizing education research. In addition, each coauthored publication and conference presentation includes the footnote, "These authors are part of a collaborative research collective known as the Disruptive Dialogue Project. All authors contributed equally to this manuscript, but have elected an egalitarian authorship rotation order among and across different publication products," which is reflective of our thought and writing processes.

The DDP is an important form of peer mentorship. As a mentor and faculty advisor, Ed has encouraged me to create and maintain such relationships in order to deepen and further my own critical qualitative scholarship. To this day, Ed has supported the DDP by reviewing papers in progress, putting forth our work for recognition on a national level, offering advice when needed, and including relevant texts in his courses. These actions are indicative of how webs of mentoring are fostered, how they grow from and are furthered by interconnections among intergenerational scholars. In this way, Ed continues to be a thought partner of my critical qualitative inquiry work.

Mentorship as a lifelong process: I offer one final story about my relationship with Ed St. John as an example of the evolution of lifelong mentorship. Have you ever been at a crossroad in your career where potential life changes and opportunities were rolling around in your mind without a clear answer? Who do *you* call on, and why? Who calls on *you* at these moments?

I was at a crossroad point in my career very recently, unclear as to what path to follow. I was with my partner, Frank, taking off my shoes at airport security after an on-campus visit, mulling over the complexities of the decisions ahead. I looked up and saw Ed's kind and familiar eyes. A huge hug ensued. (The Italian in me just cannot help it, even if I am in the airport security line. Thankfully no one was waiting behind us!) This was such perfect timing. We had time enough for a quick coffee and for Frank and me to share our dilemmas with Ed.

It was Ed's kind eyes that glimpsed knowingly into my soul that I remember most from that day. In addition, I remember his words to *both* of us: As life partners we both need to be happy in our personal and career adventures. He shared some additional words of wisdom that can come only from a lifetime in academia and left us both with a feeling of calm and reassurance, a sense of peace that only a true mentor can elicit.

This is one example of how a mentor–mentee relationship can grow and change over time. As Ed has come to know Frank and me, as we have come to know Ed and Angie (his wife and life partner), and as we have read and reflected on each other's growing body of scholarship, there is a way in which we have come to "know" each other on a deeper level. As such, it takes less time to zero in on a problem, concern, dissonance, critical issue, or life challenge. It is this interwoven relationship that allows Ed to know just the right thing to say at just the right moment in time.

In sum: As a woman, a first-generation college student, and a scholar interested in critical qualitative inquiry, I do not have a clear pathway, trajectory, or "good old boy" network offered to me, and it is not offered to many of us, for that matter. Mentors like Ed St. John create new and innovative connections that inspire, challenge, and support us throughout our careers at whatever particular developmental point in our lives. For example, scholars and practitioners have said when we first meet, "Oh, you're Penny Pasque. Ed speaks highly of you." In this subtle and consistent way, Ed supports and encourages the reputations of his mentees even years after they graduate.

It is the seemingly little things, such as "virtually introducing" you to a colleague with similar interests, inviting you to write a chapter in a book, challenging you to "think more deeply," and supporting critical inquiry toward educational equity and social justice, that are unquantifiable yet essential to mentorship and growth within academia.

Concluding Reflections

St. John's Reflections

Fortunately, the inner images of thought partners stay with us as forces of change. Engaging students in authentic partnerships in thinking about theory, research, and social change has been one of the most enjoyable aspects of my academic career. The lessons learned in my own advocacy for diversity at UNO have stuck with me as I have worked with students at Indiana University and UM. We never know where our careers will take us, but the lessons we learn from collaborating with others on issues we think important are a great way to learn about leadership, change, and social agency. We all need guides in the discourse on research, theory, and actions. Those of us who have partners in the process have the chance to find our own ways rather than merely follow the accepted rules.

For me, mentors, students, and peers have been tremendous sources of insight and support as thought partners over the years. As an academic, I have written and cocreated with hundreds of thought partners. I am happy to have had mentors who took me seriously and students who were willing to engage openly in discussing with me the issues that matter most to them. It is through this process of discourse with thought partners that we break through barriers that constrain access to the specialized knowledge of diverse groups, a gain in academic capital (St. John et al., 2011).

At the outset of this chapter, I stated four principles I held when I returned to academe in midcareer at UNO. As a student at UCD, I learned to derive theoretical constructs from practice and to test them through research and experience. Since that time, I have learned to work with the principles formed earlier as a mentee, while working with graduate students as a mentor. Perhaps the most important lesson from experience—extending boundaries of theoretical principles formed based on my own experience as a mentee—has been the necessity of integrating the ethic of care into practice while also respecting the boundaries of mentoring relationships. Mentoring is an important aspect of academic capital formation, but it must be given without expectations of quid pro quo, a pattern more typical in social networking (Coleman, 1988). Mentoring differs from networking because of giving back across generations rather than exerting expectations through tacit social control (St. John et al., 2011).

Hill's Reflections

There are numerous values a person can learn and practice after being involved in a true mentoring program. I use the word *true* here to distinguish between those administrative leaders who advocate participatory democratic leadership (espoused theories) but in reality practice autocratic and other leadership styles (theories in use; Argyris et al., 1985). There is no intention here to deceive the reader. Although I firmly believe in and have attempted to practice participatory democratic administrative leadership, I have in different situations resorted to practicing other styles of leadership.

As a social justice advocate, I maintain all persons should have a voice in issues that concern them. As such, the first correlated value I learned as a mentor and mentee was that each member of the cohort needs to feel he or she has an equal voice. As members of the cohort, we insisted all members put their ideas on the table for discussion, no matter how outlandish. Fast-forwarding to my practice in leadership roles, this value is synonymous with listening and encouraging staff members to be actively involved in finding solutions to organizational problems. Simply put, I phrase this correlated value as *giving equal voice.*

One final thought: Incidents from my formative years in Mississippi and events surrounding my first professional positions as a teacher, college basketball coach, and university instructor all influenced me to be a skeptical and untrusting person. The mentoring I received from thought partners like Ed St. John and the members of my doctoral cohort had a profound influence on my becoming a more trusting human being. In addition to receiving the benefits mentoring produces in a doctoral program and in professional practice, I benefited by having my entire outlook on humanity change.

Wooden's Reflections

Being an African American male, first-generation college student who was able to accomplish so much at a relatively young age, I have been able to continue my journey. This journey is one that has had, and continues to have, crooks and turns, but it does continue. I am encouraged often to revisit my graduate school days, and I seek ways to support student success and to ensure that our policies and processes are supportive as well. I also, because of Ed, continue to frame this work within the context of caring and community, which has been instrumental to all of my success. I never would have thought that Ed St. John would be there to accompany me on this journey, a journey so great that a number of my mentees now have Indiana University degrees.

Pasque's Reflections

As faculty or administrators, we are not expected to take a course on mentoring. No one has ever really taught me how to be a mentor, yet people like Ed St. John *show* me how to be the thoughtful and intentional mentor I aspire to be to graduate students. As such, there is somewhat of an oral tradition (see Pasque, Franklin, & Luke, 2004) or way in which mentorship is learned through example. Within four months of defending my dissertation and two weeks of arriving as an assistant professor at the University of Oklahoma, I was chairing three dissertations for graduate students. This process is reminiscent of a medical model of education where the first time you learn, the second time you do, and the third time you teach. Currently, I serve as an associate professor and program area coordinator for adult and higher education with 10 faculty where mentoring is focused on graduate students and junior faculty. Through Ed St. John's "teaching" or modeling of mentorship, I have learned about the type of intentional mentor I hope to become.

Notes

1. I mention this because the editors have strongly encouraged us to address the negative issues we have faced, a reason for acknowledging this bit of history. At the same time, I don't feel at liberty to write about this experience at this time, so I make no further comments about these circumstances.
2. *Action, Reflection and Social Justice* (St. John, 2009a) includes two chapters examining my teaching strategies with students in the UNO doctoral program. I approached this academic work as an "action experiment" in teaching. My aim at the time was to model the types of professional responsibilities I espoused. Engaging in classroom-based action research provides one method of building this type of inner confidence as a teacher working with diverse student groups. In *College Organization and Professional Development* (St. John, 2009b), I developed a generalized framework based on my experience working in complex organizations to resolve critical-social issues.
3. St. John: My recollection is that . . . we had organized some of the core courses to be offered on Saturdays. I had set up the class so it could self-navigate, but I should have been there for this event. It turns out to have been a breakthrough session as students began to identify as peers in cross-racial groups as a result of this collective process. The conflict resolution process that followed was actually part of the course content. Students learned about reflection in action and communicative action through their own experiences. At the time, some colleagues and I worked with teams of teachers in elementary schools on conflict resolution. We had been challenged many times by racial issues in schools, and so it was not totally unexpected that our first integrated cohort at UNO would have some conflict as students learned to work together. I am glad I could respond to the crisis, and for years I have had regret I was not there at the time.
4. I frequently take graduate students to lunch. It was something Orville Thompson did frequently for me when I was a senior and graduate student. I view the lunches with my graduate students not only as payback to Orville but also as a way to get to know them better. Often I have taken my wife on social lunches, more often with women graduate students than men. To be frank, I don't want any confusion about the nature of my relationships with students, an issue that was not taken seriously by earlier generations in academe (Riggs, Murrell, & Cutting, 1993).

References

Allen-Haynes, L., St. John, E. P., & Cadray, J. (2003). Rediscovering the African American tradition: Restructuring in post-desegregation urban schools. In L. F. Mirón & E. P. St. John (Eds.), *Reinterpreting urban school reform: Have urban schools failed, or has the reform movement failed urban schools?* (pp. 249–275). Albany, NY: SUNY Press.

Argyris, C. (1993). *Knowledge for action: A guide to overcoming barriers to organizational change.* San Francisco, CA: Jossey-Bass.

Argyris, C., Putnam, R., & Smith, D. M. (1985). *Action science: Concepts, methods, and skills for research and intervention.* San Francisco, CA: Jossey-Bass.

Argyris, C., & Schön, D. A. (1974). *Theory in practice: Increasing professional effectiveness.* San Francisco, CA: Jossey-Bass.

Berkner, L., & Chavez, L. (1997). *Access to postsecondary education for the 1992 high school graduates.* Washington, DC: U.S. Department of Education, Office of Educational Research and Improvement.

Bourdieu, P. (1986). The forms of capital. In J. Richardson (Ed.), *Handbook of theory and research for the sociology of education* (pp. 241–258). Westport, CT: Greenwood Press.

Carducci, R., Pasque, P. A., Kuntz, A., & Contreras-McGavin, M. (2013). Disrupting façades of clarity in teaching and learning of qualitative research. *Qualitative Research in Education, 2*(1), 1–26.

Coleman, J. S. (1988). Social capital in the creation of human capital. *American Journal of Sociology, 94,* S95–S120.

Galura, J., Pasque, P. A., Schoem, D., & Howard, J. (Eds.). (2004). *Engaging the whole of service-learning, diversity, and learning communities.* Ann Arbor, MI: OCSL Press.

Gildersleeve, R. E., Kuntz, A., Pasque, P. A., & Carducci, R. (2010). The role of critical inquiry in (re)constructing the public agenda for higher education: Confronting the conservative modernization of the academy. *The Review of Higher Education, 34*(1), 85–121.

Guggenbuhl-Craig, A. (1982). *Power in the helping professions.* Dallas, TX: Spring Books. (Original work published 1971)

Harper, S. R., Patton, L. D., & Wooden, O. S. (2009). Access and equity for African American students in higher education: A critical race historical analysis of policy efforts. *The Journal of Higher Education, 80*(6), 245–282.

Hill, O. C. (1993). *Implementing a process of inquiry to improve a dropout prevention program* (EdD dissertation). University of New Orleans, LA.

Kaltenbaugh, L. S., St. John, E. P., & Starkey, J. B. (1999). What difference does tuition make? An analysis of ethnic differences in persistence. *Journal of Student Financial Aid, 29*(2), 21–31.

Komives, S. R. (2000). Inhabit the gap. *About Campus, 5*(5), 31–32.

National Forum on Higher Education for the Public Good. (2008). *Mission statement.* Retrieved from www.thenationalforum.org

Pasque, P. A. (2007). Seeing the educational inequities around us: Visions toward strengthening the relationships between higher education and society. In E. P. St. John (Ed.), *Readings on Equal Education: Vol. 22. Confronting educational inequality: Reframing, building understanding, and making change* (pp. 37–84). New York, NY: AMS Press.

Pasque, P. A. (2010). *American higher education, leadership, and policy: Critical issues and the public good.* New York, NY: Palgrave.

Pasque, P. A., Carducci, R., Gildersleeve, R. E., & Kuntz, A. M. (2011). Disrupting the ethical imperatives of "junior" critical qualitative scholars in the era of conservative modernization. *Qualitative Inquiry, 17*(7), 571–588.

Pasque, P., Carducci, R., Kuntz, A. K., & Gildersleeve, R. E. (2012). Qualitative inquiry for equity in higher education: Methodological innovations, implications, and interventions [Special issue]. *ASHE Higher Education Report, 37*(6).

Pasque, P. A., Franklin, S., & Luke, S. (2004). Leadership and empowerment: Working to make change. In J. Galura, P. A. Pasque, D. Schoem, & J. Howard (Eds.), *Engaging the whole of service-learning, diversity, and learning communities* (pp. 195–205). Ann Arbor, MI: OCSL Press.

Riggs, R. O., Murrell, P. H., & Cutting, J. C. (1993). *Sexual harassment in higher education from conflict to community* (ASHE-ERIC Monograph No. 2). Washington, DC: George Washington University.

Schoem, D., & Pasque, P. A. (2004). The Michigan community scholars program: Engaging the whole of service-learning, diversity, and learning communities. In J. Galura, P. A. Pasque, D. Schoem, & J. Howard (Eds.), *Engaging the whole of service-learning, diversity, and learning communities.* Ann Arbor, MI: OCSL Press.

St. John, E. P. (1973). Students work from within now to influence higher education. *California Journal, 4,* 169–171.

St. John, E. P. (1981). *Public policy and college management: Title III of the Higher Education Act.* New York, NY: Praeger Press.

St. John, E. P. (2002). *The access challenge: Rethinking the causes of the new inequality* (Policy Issue Report No. 2002-01). Bloomington: Indiana Education Policy Center.

St. John, E. P. (2003). *Refinancing the college dream: Access, equal opportunity, and justice for taxpayers.* Baltimore, MD: Johns Hopkins University Press.

St. John, E. P. (2006). *Education and the public interest: School reform, public finance, and access to higher education.* Dordrecht, the Netherlands: Springer.

St. John, E. P. (Ed.). (2007). *Readings on Equal Education: Vol. 22. Confronting educational inequality: Reframing, building understanding, and making change.* New York, NY: AMS Press.

St. John, E. P. (2009a). *Action, reflection and social justice: Integrating moral reasoning into professional education.* Cresskill, NJ: Hampton Press.

St. John, E. P. (2009b). *College organization and professional development: Integrating moral reasoning and reflective practice.* New York, NY: Routledge.

St. John, E. P., & Cadray, J. P. (2004). Justice and care in post-desegregation urban schools: Rethinking the role of teacher education programs. In V. S. Walker & J. R. Snarey (Eds.), *Race-ing moral formation: African American perspectives on care and justice* (pp. 93–110). New York, NY: Teachers College Press.

St. John, E. P., Hu, S., & Fisher, A. S. (2011). *Breaking through the access barrier: How academic capital formation can improve policy in higher education.* New York, NY: Routledge.

St. John, E. P., Loescher, S. A., & Bardzell, J. S. (2003). *Improving reading and literacy in grades 1–5: A resource guide to research-based programs.* Thousand Oaks, CA: Corwin.

St. John, E. P., Masse, J. C., Callahan Lijana, K., & Milazzo Bigelow, V. (2014). *College prep: Transforming high schools, overcoming failed public policy, and preparing students for higher education.* Manuscript in preparation.

St. John, E. P., & McCaig, R. (Eds.). (1983). *Case studies in higher education policy and management* (Monograph Series No. 1982/2). Armidale, New South Wales, Australia: University of New England, Institute for Higher Education.

St. John, E. P., & McCaig, R. (1984). Management development in Australian colleges and universities. *Higher Education, 13*(6), 619–634.

St. John, E. P., & Mirón, L. F. (2003). A critical-empirical perspective on urban school reform. In L. F. Mirón & E. P. St. John (Eds.), *Reinterpreting urban school reform: Have urban schools failed, or has the reform movement failed urban schools?* (pp. 279–298). Albany, NY: SUNY Press.

St. John, E. P., & Musoba, G. D. (2010). *Pathways to academic success: Expanding opportunity for underrepresented students.* New York, NY: Routledge.

St. John, E. P., & Regan, M. C. (1973). *Students in campus governance: Reasoning and models for student involvement* (Research Monograph No. 11). Davis: Department of Applied Behavioral Sciences, University of California, Davis.

St. John, E. P., Simmons, A. B., Hoezee, L. D., Wooden, O. S., & Musoba, G. D. (2002). *Trends in higher education finance in Indiana compared to peer states and the US: A changing context, critical issues, and strategic goals* (Policy Research Report No. 02-02). Bloomington: Indiana Education Policy Center.

St. John, E. P., & Wooden, O. S. (2005). Humanities pathways. In M. Richardson (Ed.), *Tracking changes in the humanities: Essays on finance and education* (pp. 81–112). Cambridge, MA: American Academy of Arts and Sciences.

St. John, E. P., & Wooden, O. S. (2006). Privatization and federal funding for higher education. In D. M. Priest & E. P. St. John (Eds.), *Privatization and public universities* (pp. 38–64). Bloomington: Indiana University Press.

Tierney, W. G., & Bensimon, E. M. (1996). *Promotion and tenure: Community and socialization in academe.* Albany, NY: SUNY Press.

Walker, V. S. (1996). *Their highest potential: An African American school community in the segregated south.* Chapel Hill: University of North Carolina Press.

Weathersby, G. B., Jackson, G. A., Jacobs, F., St. John, E. P., & Tingley, T. (1977). The development of institutions of higher education: Theory and assessment of four possible areas of federal intervention. In M. Guttentage (Ed.), *The evaluation studies review annual* (Vol. 2, pp. 488–546). Beverly Hills, CA: Sage.

Wooden, O. (2007). High school guidance counselors as reproductive forces in the lives of African American students: A study of a Georgia high school. In E. P. St. John (Ed.), *Readings on Equal Education: Vol. 22. Confronting educational inequality. Reframing, building understanding, and making change* (pp. 245–280). New York, NY: AMS Press.

5

LATINA FACULTY AND LATINO MALE STUDENT MENTORSHIP PROCESSES

Aprendiendo y Compartiendo Juntos

Jeanett Castellanos and Mark A. Kamimura-Jiménez

La luz de anlante es la que alumbra.

—Unknown

This quote is an old *dicho* (saying) that reminds us to take opportunities when they present themselves. Working in higher education and recognizing the role and value of opportunity and timing, we have a mentoring relationship that stresses the importance of professional opportunity, personal growth, and human connection. As a dyad, we identify different options facilitating multiple choices, maximize on promising educational and professional scenarios, and nurture a safe space to pursue them. This chapter provides an overview of Latino male representation in higher education and their challenges, the important role of mentorship, and the various elements that contribute to our personal mentorship relationship over a 10-year span. Reflecting on the authors' personal experiences of being in a mentoring relationship with each other places specific emphasis on the individual processes that facilitated the success of the dyad.

Higher education continues to demonstrate a meager trajectory for preparing Latina and Latino students to continue their education and even consider academia as a venue for their professional careers. The faculty figures in higher education for 2011 show that 84% of full-time professors were

White, 8% were Asian/Pacific Islander, 4% were Black, 3% were Hispanic, and less than 1% were American Indian/Alaska Native (U.S. Department of Education, National Center for Education Statistics [NCES], 2013a). When we examine the Latina and Latino numerical representation by sex, we see that in 2011, Latino males (hereafter referred to as Latinos) held the majority of the faculty positions (52%), with a dismal total of 16,345 Latino faculty, followed by their counterparts, with only 14,986 Latina full-time faculty. By rank, there were 5,180 Latina and Latino full professors, consisting of 3,499 Latinos and 1,681 Latinas. A total of 3,437 Latinos were associate rank, and 3,692 were assistant professors, and there were 3,133 Latino male instructors, 753 lecturers, and 1,831 other instructors. Although historically males have outnumbered females in faculty positions (and the same pattern has been evident for Latinas and Latinos), a downward statistical pattern has surfaced for Latinos since 2005 (NCES, 2013b).

Latina and Latino Educational Pathways and Degree Attainment

In an educational snapshot of Latina and Latino educational progress in the educational circuit, Latinas and Latinos earned a mere 13.5% (112,211) of the 833,337 associate degrees awarded in 2009–2010. Showing greater underrepresentation with the examination of more advanced degrees in 2009–2010, Latina and Latino students earned 8.8% (140,316) of the 1.6 million baccalaureate degrees granted, 7.1% (43,535) of the 611,693 master's degrees, and 5.8% (8,085) of the 140,505 doctoral degrees, with males earning 45% of the degrees and females earning 55% (NCES, 2012). These figures underscore the consistent "disappearing act" of Latina and Latino students highlighted in the literature and prompt practitioners to understand why Latina and Latino students start with 15% representation in kindergarten (Gándara, 2009) and lose over half of their population in their efforts to navigate the system and access higher education.

The issue of Latina and Latino representation, retention, and success in education becomes even a larger concern when we examine educational progress by class, ethnicity, and sex. When the educational trajectories are examined by ethnic groups, it becomes clear that Chicana and Chicano students (Mexican American) and Puerto Rican youth are having the most difficult time navigating the system and completing their studies (Solórzano, Villalpando, & Oseguera, 2005). Moreover, a persistent gap between both sexes underscores the multiplicity of the attrition within the Latina and Latino community and the various possible underlying factors that pull and push out Latina and Latino students (Sáenz & Ponjuán, 2009, 2011, 2012). Specifically, although Latino male enrollment in higher education has increased, female enrollment has increased even more rapidly, and educational figures suggest better educational attainment by Latinas, who are achieving greater strides than their male counterparts (Excelencia in Education, 2007; Sáenz & Ponjuán, 2012).

Theoretical Framework

The dismal number of Latina and Latino students completing their degrees underscores the necessity to examine Latina and Latino educational pathways and experiences (Castellanos & Gloria, 2007; Castellanos, Gloria, & Kamimura, 2006). Although there are a handful of established works proposing theories and models for Latina and Latino academic success (Oseguera, Locks, & Vega, 2009), the educational system often still works from a Eurocentric paradigm that minimally addresses culture and multiculturalism. Selecting a culturally grounded and context-driven perspective, in this chapter we utilize the psychosociocultural (PSC) framework (Castellanos & Gloria, 2007; Gloria & Rodriguez, 2000) to examine Latina and Latino experiences and factors that enhance their educational stay and possible long-term pursuit of graduate degrees. The PSC examines the dynamic and interdependent relationships of psychological, social, and cultural constructs in understanding educational experiences and context-specific issues of Latinas and Latinos. Empirically tested with racial and ethnic minority students in higher education, the framework suggests the integration of the three dimensions (i.e., psychological, social, and cultural factors) to examine how they work cohesively with one another while considering that the factors can be identified individually but interact collectively. Moreover, it reinforces the need to understand the "dimensionality of students as whole persons" (Gloria, Castellanos, Besson, & Clark, 2014) as well as the need to explore Latina and Latino retention complexities at its various levels.

Latino Males in Education and Mentorship: *Sembrar para Cosechar* (Sow to Harvest)

Recent literature on Latinos and Latinas highlights the varying challenges both groups encounter, the similarities across groups, and the unique barriers each sex faces in their educational journeys (Gloria, Castellanos, & Orozco, 2005; Gloria, Castellanos, Scull, & Villegas, 2009; Kamimura, 2006; Morales, 2010; Sáenz & Ponjuán, 2009). Specifically, the literature clearly delineates that Latino men espouse different masculinity ideologies than other men and report more traditional gender adherence compared to that of other groups (Abreu, Goodyear, Campos, & Newcomb, 2000; Edwards & Jones, 2010).

In general, the literature on Latino males supports that this subgroup is less encouraged and has fewer resources and social connections than their female counterparts (Fischer & Good, 1994; Gloria et al., 2005; Hernandez, Cervantes, Castellanos, & Gloria, 2004). Moreover, literature on Latino males suggests they experience greater isolation and marginalization than their female counterparts experience and also indicates a consistent downward-spiraling trend that suggests less representation in higher education, which impacts college attainment, graduate education, and the pursuit of an academic career.

Despite the difficult experiences of Latino males in higher education and the consistent repeated findings of limited college satisfaction, mentorship has proven to be an effective tool to improve the current crisis and enhance the educational journeys of Latinas and Latinos (Anaya & Cole, 2001; Morales, 2010). *Mentorship* has been defined as "the act of providing wise and friendly counsel" (Redmond, 1990, p. 188) and has been a traditional practice of academia and the development of scholars. Mentorship includes various components ranging from assisting with the development of basic scholarly skills to emotional and social support in the process where students may need assistance to navigate their education or may lack knowledge about the process (Hill, 1989; Johnson, 2007; Redmond, 1990). Moreover, when a good working relationship is developed, this dyad is also known to increase retention, student integration, academic performance, and student satisfaction (Gloria et al., 2014; Santos & Reigadas, 2002).

Johnson (2007), however, reminded us that it is uncommon for males to have opposite-sex mentors but not uncommon for females. When opposite-sex mentorship dyads form, across-sex mentorship challenges and obstacles can arise (e.g., power issues, sexual attraction, and respect issues). In particular, female faculty have been noted for providing more psychological help than their male counterparts, who focus on instrumental help (Sosik & Godshalk, 2000). Focusing on multicultural and cross-cultural dyads, Anaya and Cole (2001) emphasized that race is a salient factor to mentorship dynamics, whereas Davidson and Foster-Johnson (2001) cautioned that cross-cultural dyads potentially experience conflict with communication styles, cultural values, and subtle racial dynamics.

Examining literature on Latina and Latino mentorship by sex, Orozco (2003) highlighted the impact of mentorship on her educational advancement. Through mentorship, she learned organizational values, the key players in the process, and specific strategies on how to navigate her challenges. Similarly, Morales (2010) expressed "the legitimization of hope" for Latino males through a mentorship program and reported that mentors provided valuable social capital, academic validation, and motivation.

Examining the educational social process by sex, Vera Sanchez (2006) indicated that his mentors and peers were catalysts for his success. A positive support system reinforced the possibility of experiencing "intelligence as a masculine trait" (p. 237) and the validation that learning does not have to emasculate a male student. In a similar way, Quijada (2006) reflected on his doctoral experiences and recalled the role of his mentor, who took interest in his personal and professional goals and provided emotional support and academic guidance. Positive mentorship experiences reinforce Latino male academic identities and propel their satisfaction with the system, reinforcing their comfort with their studies while enhancing their overall satisfaction through an environment that fosters critical dialogue, academic exploration, and professional validation (Castellanos & Gloria, 2007). Although a handful of literature addresses some of the effective components to mentoring Latina and Latino students in academia with specific attention placed on the Latino male processes in certain research, minimal work has focused on the processes of the Latina faculty and Latino male student dyad and their interactions, factors that contribute to this important dyad, and ways to facilitate more of these types of relationships.

Mentee Experiences: *Navegando Juntos* (Navigating Together)

I learned about standing in line when I started kindergarten, and by the time I was about to finish college, I realized I waited in line for two reasons: out of necessity and out of desire. One of my least favorite places to wait in line is at the DMV: It's hot and stuffy from always being at maximum occupancy, you can't sit down, you wait in a line for a person to tell you which line you need to wait in, and you can even make an appointment to wait in line. I wait in this line out of necessity. Conversely, taking an hour trip from Harlem to Greenwich Village and waiting in line in the freezing cold or even in the humidity of summer just for a few moments to smell and indulge in the rich sweetness of fresh baked, warm cupcakes from Magnolia Bakery is purely desire. The summer of my senior year, I made the decision to go to graduate school, but I felt like I was at the DMV at 15 minutes before closing. I had no appointment, was outside in a line around the corner, couldn't see the front door, and didn't even know what I needed to do to get a driver's license. At the end of that summer, I met Dr. Jeanett Castellanos (I nicknamed her Dr. C), who turned, what seemed to me at the time, an insurmountable challenge of preparing and applying for graduate school into a journey of opportunity. She turned the DMV into Magnolia Bakery.

In high school, the one person I went to for advice on college (my counselor) told me I wasn't college material and I had to figure it out myself.

Four years later, I was looking at a similar situation, trying to find my way to graduate school. I was part of the Community Service Internship Program (CSIP) at the University of California, Irvine (UCI), and as a part of the program we were asked to select a mentor. I reflected on my time at UCI and thought about a few different individuals who had served as advocates for my educational experience throughout my undergraduate education. I grew up in the barrio, where learning whom to trust could mean the difference between life and death. There weren't many people I could trust at UCI. Selecting a mentor to me was about finding someone I could trust, someone who wouldn't let me fail.

During the fall quarter, I was taking a course taught by Dr. C, and we met weekly during office hours to get my graduate school applications in order. Of all the courses I had taken up to that point, she was the most demanding professor at UCI, and she challenged me to work harder than I ever had. I developed a great amount of respect for her not only because of all she had accomplished at such an early age but also, more important, because of the expectations she placed on her students. We were expected to perform academically as graduate students. Weighing all of these observations and experiences, I asked Dr. C to be my mentor as a part of CSIP. I took a lot of miscalculated risks in college; however, choosing Dr. C as my mentor was a process of thoughtful considerations.

Kram (1983, 1985) described four phases of a mentoring relationship: initiation, cultivation, separation, and redefinition. The initiation phase was a very important aspect of our relationship because in addition to the afore-mentioned factors, I also considered our shared precollege experiences, our similar experiences with ethnic identity formation, our lack of a generation gap, and the tone of our discussions. There was a lot of my life that I did not need to explain because of all our shared experiences. I mention "tone of our discussions" because I did not need to change my language; change my accent; change my vocabulary; or, most important, change who I was. Our dialogues were about my future; our shared research interests; and learning together by exploring alternative perspectives on the Latino pathway to the PhD, which was the most significant gap between us.

The cultivation phase of our relationship was strengthened as Dr. C learned how to develop my academic abilities. Together, we explored my PSC identity as I readied for graduate school. Thinking back, this was the first time I had really talked with someone, faculty or administrator, about my experiences growing up and connecting them to how and who I was as a student, as a person. Our weekly *pláticas* (conversations) became consistently a safe place for discussing the connections of complex theories with real-life situations. These intellectual *pláticas* became ground zero for building and exploring the impact of race on the educational paths of students of color, mainly Latinos.

As a mixed-race (Asian, Latino, European) student, I had not explored most aspects of my racial identities, and these dialogues were instrumental in my own development as a Chicano. I had always struggled with being accepted in a single-race group in general and was often called a "mutt" growing up. Being Latino Mexicano Chicano was no different: I was told I was not Mexican enough and didn't speak Spanish enough, and especially because I had an Okinawan surname, I was not easily categorized as Chicano by others. Dr. C, unlike other Latinos who had been role models but struggled as mentors, did not question or define me by my racial background, my grades, or my involvement on campus.

As the older brother of a sister, I grew up with the expectation that I always had to know what to do and who to be and to have all the answers. In reality, I was lost and stressed to find my way. In my path, race/ethnicity was only one aspect influencing my journey: I was also facing the challenge to mature as a partner and as a father of a three-month-old while changing majors as a fifth-year senior. Setting my goals on graduate school and possible career paths available with a graduate degree with no understanding of research compounded the situation. Gender did not play a role in the selection of Dr. C as my mentor, but it did play the role in her position of *hermana mayor* (older sister) because of our close proximity in age. This fact made it easier for me to trust that she could relate to my experience and that she had gone through it just five years earlier at UCI. Dr. C shared her own challenges and path as I experienced doubt in my abilities to achieve academically.

Coming out of high school, I was fighting against the system, trying not to become a victim of my environment and the institutional discrimination and racism practiced by counselors and teachers in our educational system. Choosing Dr. C as my mentor facilitated balance between my past and my future. Up to that point, in every way possible, others were defining my challenges and obstacles; Dr. C understood that what I needed was a way to navigate these barriers. Mentorship can be described as a relationship that maintains equilibrium between challenges and support (Sanford, 1967).

Mentee Perceptions of a Latina Mentor

In the mentorship dyad, Dr. C provided guardrails to my undergraduate experience, because of our shared experiences, and she was able to anticipate and guide my path. For example, I remember being convinced that I was going to law school. Dr. C, knowing my interests in educational equity, encouraged me to consider applying to master's programs in education. Six months later, I received an acceptance letter from Teachers College at Columbia University and knew that I had a mentor who kept me on the path. Since then she has continued to affirm her role by providing publishing opportunities, engaging in new conversations on issues facing our students and the academy, and managing our administrative roles within our various educational environments.

Many times thinking about how to describe mentorship in higher education, I had this picture of a winding road to the top of a mountain with warning signs along the path: curvy road ahead, falling rocks, slow down, or turn lights on. Mentors put up the signs or help us see them. Although not literally translated, the messages are the same: Mentors are directional. For the past 11 years, I have been on a career track and trajectory that has offered little time for reflection on the impact of this relationship. Dr. C (now Jeanett or *hermana*) and I have talked many times about getting involved in professional associations, serving the community, working with students, being a mentor while being mentored, and collaborating with colleagues. At the core of my work, mentorship has been a foundational value for success.

The scarcity of the female mentor–male protégé mentorship was described by O'Neill and Blake-Beard (2002) as a reflection of complex organizational, social, and gender power dynamics. The current demographics of higher education have provided a critical mass of females within the organizational structure to serve as mentors. While I was in college, the chancellor, dean of students, assistant vice chancellor, director of student academic advancement services (where I was a part of Summer Bridge and Student Support Services), and ombudsmen were all female. Leadership at the highest level within our institution was female and, for the time, deconstructed the power paradigm of gender within the organization.

Furthermore, I viewed college as a continuation of my K–12 education and bought into the socially constructed perception that by nature educational institutions were female dominant. Under this paradigm, I embraced the *hermana* connection to Dr. C, which in all instances sustained *respeto* (respect). It was not until after I had left for graduate school that I realized the influential nature of gender and the underrepresentation of females in leadership positions and, more specifically, women of color.

The complexity of gender within my mentoring experience is intimately connected to strong female influences in my life, namely, my mom. However, as I developed my own sense of a mixed-race identity, my mom was also learning what it meant to be a mixed-race Latina. Inevitably, given the role of culture and ethnic identity in the process, Blake-Beard (2009) reminded us, "Within mentoring relationships, understanding the difference between cultural influence and individual attributes may provide critical guidance to a mentor" (p. 17).

In many ways, my mom served as my first female mentor. Her focus was clearly on guiding and developing my individual attributes but did not provide a space to explore the complexities of multiple cultural influences while growing up. Throughout graduate school, I have had three more females serve as both academic and professional mentors: Dr. L. Lee Knefelkamp from Teachers College, Columbia University, and Dr. Sylvia Hurtado and Gloria Taylor from the University of Michigan. In each instance, these female mentors understood how to provide a space that facilitated ethnic identity exploration through theory, practice, and dialogue.

The mentorship dyad between me and Jeanett is still a foundational aspect of our relationship and continues to develop and organically redefine itself. It has matured through periods of separation (Kram, 1983, 1985) through graduate school, which opened new opportunities to be mentored by others and coincidentally by females. The aforementioned women also became a source of sustainability for me within the academy because of their own diverse backgrounds. An important similarity between all of them is that when you became a mentee, you also became a part of a larger family of students mentored by them.

One of the most impactful lessons from this mentoring relationship was the development and responsibility of being a part of an academic family: a family of mentors and mentees. This idea was passed on to me by Dr. Shirley Hune about building capacity for the academic community of color, which is an adaptation of a Jacob Miller song: "Each one, teach one; each one, reach one." The importance of mentoring others must be a constant priority and integrated into our daily practice.

Faculty Experience: *Nuestra Próxima Generación* (Our Next Generation)

Being a product of an exemplary mentorship relationship that encompassed strong family ties, established social networks, and direct guidance, I made student interactions a central component of my career in academia. As a Latina lecturer at a research-extensive institution who started in the late 1990s, I unfortunately witnessed the dismal numbers of Latinas and Latinos in the educational pipeline, and the persistent dwindling numbers of Latino males became more evident as years passed.

A Latina of Cuban descent (with a Mexican stepfather) growing up in southeast Los Angeles with close and personal encounters with oppression and marginalization, I had a clear understanding of how my gender, ethnicity, and working-class background impacted my educational experiences, opportunities, and realities. Furthermore, my mentor—an African American male (Dr. Joseph L. White) who was part of the Black movement and the early installation of Early Academic Outreach Programs in California—infused the importance of cultural awareness; cultural competence; and the recruitment, retention, and racial/ethnic minority student satisfaction in my academic blueprint early on in my career.

Working at my alma mater and having numerous social contacts across campus upon my arrival to UCI facilitated a smoother transition to create academic family—interpersonal academic relationships that parallel family social systems (Castellanos & Gloria, 2007) that would facilitate a pipeline of resources and opportunities for racial/ethnic minority students navigating the system. Having my mentor serve as an active emeritus faculty on campus and being able to rely on over four additional top administrators who had also mentored me made it easier to identify connections and key players for incoming students to solicit when they needed assistance at various levels of the campus.

As a Latina mentor, I have taken the active role to nurture, motivate, and inspire my students. Growing up in a refugee family, I developed a natural inclination for fostering positive attitudes and creating alternative solutions in life. Consequently, I often identify various solutions to my students' educational challenges and different ways to perceive their current experiences. In particular, I often serve as a life coach, helping my mentees get rid of their internal fears and internalized stereotypes while offering a safe space for open dialogue and communication. With respect and *confianza* (trust), I personally challenge their attitudes and beliefs and help them ground their values. Knowing their background, however, and understanding many of their challenges, I pace the interactions, the disclosures, and the heated dialogues step-by-step (*paso a paso*) to ensure my students are growing from the relationship and understanding their academic and personal lessons. Through these disclosures and interactions, I help them recognize their power within and eliminate the surmounting fear of approaching problems head-on.

As I was in my mid-20s and Latina and Mark was Latino, we shared similar struggles, a common language, histories, and similar oppressions. Espousing *respeto* (respect) throughout our encounters, we still shared an uncommon experience in comparison to most faculty–student interactions. Eliminating the generational gap and our cultural familiarity facilitated a space to share common stories and unique challenges, practicing our common values of *personalismo* (personalism), *confianza* (trust), *simpatia* (harmony), and *familismo* (family). Throughout our *encuentros* (encounters) we were natural, genuine, and filled with *cariño* (care) and acceptance. Viewing Mark as a younger brother, I championed for his greatest success, and I put forth every effort to facilitate his educational dream. Throughout our meetings, we discussed campus climate, discrimination, cultural relations, and the means to improve the current status of racial/ethnic minorities in higher education.

Given Mark's multiracial background and my own cultural mixed heritage (i.e., Cuban American with African roots and a Mexican male figure in my home), it was natural to address social justice for the greater whole and not just Latinas and Latinos. In my relationship with Mark, I recall hearing stories about his grandfather in the fields and his mother's journey of ethnic identity and its impression on Mark and his own identity. Moreover, it was Mark's abilities to connect his realities and struggles to those of his peers that often prompted a research question, a direction for community service, or a potential consideration for a future professional pursuit. These many positive and exploratory *momentos* (moments) ignited my passion to teach and mentor while validating and reinforcing my mentee's professional, cultural, and social identities. Furthermore, these moments reminded me that my students not only were searching for graduate school placements and jobs ("Un buen trabajo no era el *único* resultado que buscaba" ["A good job wasn't the *only* result I wanted"]) but also needed to create a professional pathway that would lead them to becoming community leaders and scholars invested in social issues with a deep understanding of *La Lucha* (historical struggles) and community responsibility.

Reflecting on my experiences within the mentorship relationship, I see there are various benefits to having Latina and Latino mentees, particularly Mark. Throughout our relationship, I often found myself addressing multicultural issues and instilling the importance of cultural awareness, learning, and understanding. In particular, I instilled the value of multicultural research and scholarship while Mark's passion and interest in our community propelled me to learn more about various racial/ethnic minority communities' needs and histories. Mentoring Mark (who identified as a Latino multicultural multiracial male) made the topic culture central to our conversations. Consequently, Mark's passion for minority communities reinforced the importance of my own interests in helping underrepresented communities, while his insights resulting from community exchanges furthered my understanding of his realities, our communities, and the value of community and culture-specific research. These exchanges underscored the notion that we had a common purpose (*Tenemos un propósito juntos*) and a collaborative task to achieve as mentee and mentor, educators, and community leaders.

Recognizing the value of mentoring racial minority students and despite my enthusiasm to mentor all, my interactions with students often reminded me that the selection of a mentee is one that happens naturally and cannot be forced. There are specific elements necessary for a working mentorship relationship. Students must reciprocate in the relationship, have a positive attitude, and respect their faculty. Working close to 16 years in academia, I have come across entitled students who believe you must do what they want and when they want it. In the past, I would simply become upset and work with these students despite their disrespect. Today, I have more respect for myself and do not tolerate bad attitudes and self-absorbed students. Therefore, part of the mentee/protégé selection is based on students' community investment, values of cultural competency, and mutual interests in areas of psychology and education. The student must demonstrate a commitment to learn and share the dream to give back to a community. Matches are not instant and automatic but develop over time and through long-term interactions.

Although the mentorship relationship with Mark has many benefits and I have found it extremely rewarding, the relationship still introduced multiple challenges. Professionally, given the time in my career, I questioned my abilities to train a young scholar and the effectiveness of my mentorship. Because I was starting my profession and Mark was one of my first mentees, there was no blueprint to follow or how-to book to instruct my mentorship. The possibility of misdirecting him occasionally stopped me in my tracks, but I would confer with his other mentors (some who were my mentors) to cross-reference our advice and perspectives. Hence, it was through the *multi-generational mentorship model* facilitated through collaboration and communication that I gained confidence in the mentorship process and learned how to most effectively guide my mentees. Moreover, I reinforced a multilayered mentorship paradigm where Mark learned various styles of mentorship by having multiple mentors (all Latino and Latina colleagues, most of whom were male in high positions at the university) and received varying viewpoints about a given matter. These practices maximized Mark's experiences, resources, and opportunities.

Another significant challenge to the mentoring dyad included having to see Mark experience a hostile campus climate and discrimination and need to prove himself or debunk stereotypes. For example, it was often that Mark came to the office sharing stories about microaggressions he encountered (e.g., being tokenized in the classroom, being questioned on commitment to his community). In fact, these experiences persisted in graduate school, where one professor actually expressed surprise once he realized Mark was the best writer in a group where he was the only minority. Consistently, I was invested in his well-being and academic success and countered these invalidations. It was emotionally challenging to witness his educational barriers and see him personally struggle with the environment. Yet, I worked by his side to motivate and remind him of his abilities and to encourage him to not lose sight of his long-term educational and professional goals. In particular, I made myself available on the phone when he left for graduate school and even saw him during holiday breaks. Understanding the role of a student's motivation in academics and the value of social support, I consistently incorporated *"como no"* (why not?) talks to debunk any internalized stereotypes of his potential and the possibility of his future. Examples of these talks encompass topics of "why not": Why not make it despite the challenges, why not show them wrong, why not exceed their expectations, why not study harder, why not include family, why not be proud of your roots, and why not stay in education?

Navigating masculine expectations and Mark's need to prove himself as an accomplished male in his community was another challenge we encountered when we explored the possibility of graduate school and not a high-paying job following graduation. The misconception of *el niño estudioso* (the studious boy) reading books and not working with his hands created cultural distress for Mark and an internal struggle that was silent but occasionally shared. As the oldest in the family with a younger sister, he felt pressure to finish his degree and make money. Moreover, the distance to attend graduate school (i.e., Michigan) only reinforced his familial obligations and surfaced feelings of guilt and abandonment from his family for considering studying out of state. The value of *familismo* (family) consistently kept family as a central part of our discussions while we explored the means of integrating their involvement in the process. Given Mark's unique circumstances as a first-generation Latino male, I often facilitated academic family for him to identify other peers with the same educational circumstances and reminded him of the long-term benefits of his advanced degree. Moreover, we problem solved his most pressing issues and identified resources or contacts to enhance his current educational experiences.

Placement in a top graduate master's degree program—and later a doctoral program—also raised unique challenges for a student who knew very little about graduate education, its demands, and academe's political culture. To prepare him for his educational journey, I suggested that Mark complete the five educational pillars (i.e., academics, research, practical experience, leadership, and community service). These experiences required Mark to do a range of activities in his field while being integrated into the UCI community and building social and leadership skills. Through the pillars, he was required to attain knowledge of his selected field while attaining practical experience through internships and field placements that expanded his understanding of his future profession and equipped him for graduate school expectations and discussions. The pillars enhanced Mark's educational self-efficacy, reinforced cocurricular involvement, and helped shape his professional and scholarship identity through research and hands-on activities that illustrated the connection between theory and practice.

Along with the pillars, constant checks and balances occurred to ensure that Mark's confidence and motivation remained strong. His other mentors and I explained the expectations of graduate school and shared our own stories for reflection and understanding. Similarly, I emphasized the importance of including family in the process and explaining the value of an advanced degree to his important social support system. Regarding culture, we discussed Mark's impressions of the existence of prejudice in the education system and ways to navigate these encounters. For example, we addressed the value of finding a mentor in his new institution, the role of maintaining respect toward others even though he often felt disrespected, and the multiple possible consequences of abrupt reactions in a hostile environment. Our discussions also centered around developing academic skills, multiple options, academic resources, and emotional support systems to help sustain him through his educational processes and difficult experiences (e.g., feeling marginalized, isolated, and undervalued). Last, a critical and underlying success factor in Mark's progress at the doctoral level was his placement in a strong program with a good Latina mentor who advocated and guided Mark throughout his doctoral education. Knowing his advisor's work and her own research on cultural integration and campus climate, I knew she would serve as an excellent mentor and advisor for Mark. Framing the placement from an academic family perspective, I feel sending Mark to work with Dr. Sylvia Hurtado was like passing down a young son or brother to a sister or *comadre*.

Though I could believe I have been an exemplary mentor with no failed mentorship encounters, this viewpoint would be naïve and shortsighted. Reflecting on various other mentees whom I have sought to train and guide, I see that not all students are open to the learning experience and the professional relationship. Clearly stated, mentorship is not a guaranteed fit. Mentorship requires time, investment, and commitment. Students must have the desire to learn and persist. It is more than weekly conversations about campus climate and family. Although we do address PSC elements of my mentees' educational journeys, my students are simultaneously responsible for their work and academic performance. I expect weekly research progress, engagement in the classroom, preparation for our meetings, leadership in the community, advocacy, and a deep understanding of existentialism. For example, my students are given readings written by other faculty of color to attain a deep understanding of the role of culture in research. They are required to do community service hours for low-income communities (e.g., painting houses for the poor, volunteering for an education conference for youth going to college, serving at a soup kitchen). The key is that students learn the needs of the community and their role in assisting the social problem while identifying their personal meaning in the process and purpose of existence. Challenging Mark to see the overlap between education and his community only propelled him.

Over the course of our relationship, I have learned that mentorship includes multiple dimensions of support that cannot be restricted to simply practical professional knowledge or emotional support. Although a combination of the two has shown to be most effective, I also learned that my mentorship with Mark did not follow the common mentorship parameters ascribed by higher education. Given that I was in a system where students were primarily numbers for some, I would often remind myself, *Son mas que estudiantes* (they are more than students); they are people with personal needs. Consequently, Mark's well-being, means of coping, social support, family, and community were always at the root of our exchanges.

Most mentoring relations are primarily established for academic progress and professional development, and this model included additional dimensions of life purpose, human connection, meaningfulness, community leadership, and service. Although the academic elements were certainly critical and central to our relationship, the existential element of Mark's realities (e.g., his life purpose) never escaped my assessment of the situation and therefore became a pivotal component of our mentorship process. In the center of our encounters, we often questioned why we are granted opportunities and what we must do with them. I challenged Mark on why he wanted the degree, what he planned to do with it, and what benefits he planned to give to others as a result of his leadership. What would be his legacy after 40 years of service?

As I developed a strong investment in Mark's academic and personal progress, the importance of maintaining contact in the process was clear. Throughout the years, it was essential to be flexible with our time; to be open to changes in the plans; and, most important, to keep informed of his personal wellness as he navigated his professional goals. Ongoing contact, although sporadic at times, was kept, and the value of "checking in" was reinforced as he moved through the system, attained his first job, and balanced his personal life demands. Clearly, mentorship takes time by both parties and involves one's energies and genuine interest in the wellness and progress of the mentee. Today, it is the *confianza*/trust, *cariño*/affection, and established rapport that have grown through the years that facilitate our professional relationship and reinforce the processes of being colleagues and feeling like *familia* while still providing mentorship.

Equally important in this Latina and Latino mentorship relationship was being able to counter colleagues' negative perceptions of my overinvestment in students. Having confidence in one's practices and recognizing that what works for one group may not work as well (*no somos todos iguales*; we are not all the same) for another is critical in establishing culturally relevant and effective mentoring relations. I recall someone asking, "Why spend so much time on these students when you can be writing an article?" Today, some of my initial mentees (who have now completed their degrees) work as colleagues with me, forwarding the vision of social progress. In my perspective, the traditional mentorship model of short exchanges or no contact after graduation would not have been as effective for Mark in his continued journey through his advanced degree and his continued progress in the profession. Moreover, the impact we are making as colleagues (and he is making as a professional) may not have been possible without the value of community responsibility established early in our professional relationship.

References

Abreu, J., Goodyear, R. K., Campos, A., & Newcomb, D. M. (2000). Ethnic belonging and traditional masculinity ideology among African Americans, European Americans, and Latinos. *Psychology of Men and Masculinity*, *1*(2), 75–86.

Anaya, G., & Cole, D. G. (2001). Latina/o student achievement: Exploring the influence of student-faculty interactions on college grades. *Journal of College Student Development*, *32*, 3–14.

Blake-Beard, S. D. (2009). Mentoring as a bridge to understanding cultural differences. *Adult Learning*, *20*(1–2), 14–18.

Castellanos, J., & Gloria, A. M. (2007). Research considerations and theoretical application for best practices in higher education: Latina/o achieving success. *Journal of Hispanic Higher Education*, *6*, 378–398. doi:10.1177/1538192707305347

Castellanos, J., Gloria, A. M., & Kamimura, M. (2006). *The Latina/o pathway to the Ph.D.: Abriendo caminos*. Sterling, VA: Stylus.

Davidson, M. N., & Foster-Johnson, L. (2001). Mentoring in the preparation of graduate researchers of color. *Review of Educational Research*, *7*(1), 575–611.

Edwards, K. E., & Jones, S. R. (2010). "Putting my man face on": A grounded theory of college men's gender identity development. *Journal of College Development*, *50*(2), 210–228.

Excelencia in Education. (2007). *Latino males in higher education*. Washington, DC: Author. Retrieved from http://www.edexcelencia.org/gateway/download/2068/1403536691

Fischer, A. R., & Good, G. E. (1994). Gender, self, and others: Perceptions of the campus environment. *Journal of Counseling Psychology*, *41*, 343–355.

Gándara, P. (2009). Progress and stagnation: 25 years of Hispanic achievement. *Diverse Issues in Higher Education*, *26*(9), 37–38.

Gloria, A. M., Castellanos, J., Besson, D., & Clark, L. O. (2014). *Cultural fit, mentorship, and college and life satisfaction of racial and ethnic minority undergraduates*. Manuscript in preparation.

Gloria, A. M., Castellanos, J., & Orozco, V. (2005). Perceived educational barriers, cultural fit, coping responses, and psychological well-being of Latina undergraduates. *Hispanic Journal of Behavioral Sciences, 27*, 161–183.

Gloria, A. M., Castellanos, J., Scull, N. C., & Villegas, F. J. (2009). Psychological coping and well-being of male Latino undergraduates: Sobreviviendo la universidad. *Hispanic Journal of Behavioral Sciences, 31*, 317–339.

Gloria, A. M., & Rodriguez, E. R. (2000). Counseling Latino university students: Psychosociocultural issues for consideration. *Journal of Counseling and Development, 78*(2), 145–154.

Hernandez, H. R., Cervantes, A. M., Castellanos, J., & Gloria, A. M. (2004, August). *Coping strategies and college experiences of Latino male undergraduates.* Paper presented at the APA Annual Convention, Honolulu, Hawaii.

Hill, S. K. (1989). Mentoring and other community support in the academic setting. *Group and Organization Studies, 14*, 355–368.

Johnson, W. B. (2007). *On being a mentor: A guide for higher education faculty.* Mahwah, NJ: Lawrence Erlbaum.

Kamimura, M. (2006). Finding my way: Enculturation to the Ph.D. In J. Castellanos, A. M. Gloria, & M. Kamimura (Eds.), *The Latina/o pathway to the Ph.D.* (pp. 191–199). Sterling, VA: Stylus.

Knapp, L. G., Kelly-Reid, J. E., & Ginder, S. A. (2010). *Employees in postsecondary institutions, Fall 2009, and salaries of full-time instructional staff, 2009–10: First look (NCES 2011-150).* National Center for Education Statistics. Retrieved from http://nces.ed.gov/pubs2011/2011150.pdf

Kram, K. E. (1983). Phases of the mentor relationship. *Academy of Management Journal, 26*, 608–625.

Kram, K. E. (1985). *Mentoring at work.* Glenview, IL: Scott, Foresman.

Morales, E. E. (2010). Legitimizing hope: An exploration of effective mentoring for Dominican American male college students. *Journal of Student Retention, 11*(3), 385–406.

O'Neill, R. M., & Blake-Beard, S. D. (2002). Gender barriers to the female mentor–male protégé relationship. *Journal of Business Ethics, 37*, 51–63.

Orozco, V. (2003). Latinas and the undergraduate experience: ¡No estamos solas! In J. Castellanos & L. Jones (Eds.), *The majority in the minority: Expanding the representation of Latina/o faculty, administrators and students in higher education* (pp. 127–138). Sterling, VA: Stylus.

Oseguera, L., Locks, A. M., & Vega, I. I. (2009). Increasing Latina/o students' baccalaureate attainment: A focus on retention. *Journal of Hispanic Higher Education, 8*(1), 23–53. doi:10.1177/1538192708326997

Quijada, D. A. (2006). Exploring one Chicano's perspective on mentoring in research and academia. In J. Castellanos, A. M. Gloria, & M. Kamimura (Eds.), *The Latina/o pathway to the Ph.D.* (pp. 255–266). Sterling, VA: Stylus.

Redmond, S. P. (1990). Mentoring and cultural diversity in academic settings. *The American Behavioral Scientist, 34*(2), 188–200.

Sáenz, V. B., & Ponjuán, L. (2009). The vanishing Latino male in higher education. *Journal of Hispanic Higher Education, 8*(1), 54–89.

Sáenz, V. B., & Ponjuán, L. (2011). Men of color: Ensuring the academic success of Latino males in higher education. Washington, DC: Institute for Higher Education Policy.

Sáenz, V. B., & Ponjuán, L. (2012). Latino males: Improving college access and degree completion: A new national imperative. *Perspectivas: Issues in Higher Education Policy and Practice, 1*, 1–12.

Sanford, N. (1967). *Where colleges fail: The study of the student as a person.* San Francisco, CA: Jossey-Bass.

Santos, S. J., & Reigadas, E. (2002). Latinos in higher education: An evaluation of a university faculty mentoring program. *Journal of Hispanic Higher Education, 1,* 40–50. doi:10.1177/1538192702001001004

Solórzano, D., Villalpando, O., & Oseguera, L. (2005). Educational inequities and Latina/o undergraduate students in the United States: A critical race analysis of their educational progress. *Journal of Hispanic Higher Education, 4*(3), 272–294.

Sosik, J. J., & Godshalk, V. M. (2000). The role of gender in mentoring: Implications for diversified and homogenous mentoring relationships. *Journal of Vocational Behavior, 57,* 102–122.

U.S. Department of Education, National Center for Education Statistics. (2012). *The condition of education 2012* (NCES 2012-045, Table A-47-2). Retrieved from http://nces.ed.gov/fastfacts/display.asp?id=72

U.S. Department of Education, National Center for Education Statistics. (2013a). *The condition of education 2013* (NCES 2013-037, Characteristics of postsecondary faculty). Retrieved from http://nces.ed.gov/fastfacts/display.asp?id=61

U.S. Department of Education, National Center for Education Statistics. (2013b). *Digest of education statistics 2012* (Table 291: Full-time instructional faculty in degree-granting postsecondary institutions, by race/ethnicity, sex, and academic rank: Fall 2007, fall 2009, and fall 2011). Retrieved from http://nces.ed.gov/programs/digest/d12/tables/dt12_291.asp

Vera Sanchez, C. G. (2006). Juggling intellectuality and Latino masculinity: La calle, mi familia, y la escuela (the streets, my family, and school). In J. Castellanos, A. M. Gloria, & M. Kamimura (Eds.), *The Latina/o pathway to the Ph.D.* (pp. 233–240). Sterling, VA: Stylus.

6

A CRITICAL RACE JOURNEY OF MENTORING

Dimpal Jain and Daniel Solórzano

There are multiple forms of mentoring within the academy between peers, younger and older students, junior and senior faculty, and senior and beginning administrators (Campbell & Campbell, 1997; Stanley, 2006). These types of mentoring relationships can be informal or formal, either supported by the institution or purposefully clandestine (Savage, Karp, & Logue, 2004). The positive benefits associated with a mentoring relationship have been well documented and vary from an increased sense of inclusion, to instilled confidence, to higher rates of academic success (Sorcinelli & Yun, 2007; Turner & Myers, 2000).

Although much has been documented regarding the mentoring process, an area that warrants further exploration is how mentoring differs across gender and race, in particular for graduate students and faculty of color (Diggs, Garrison-Wade, Estrada, & Galindo, 2009). In this chapter, Dimpal Jain, who identifies as a South Asian American woman, and Daniel Solórzano (Danny), who identifies as Chicano, will explore this concept as Dimpal traces their mentoring relationship from the onset of her entrance into the academy as a graduate student, through her dissertation journey, and eventually to her placement as an assistant professor. This mentoring relationship has been facilitated through the framework of critical race theory (CRT), which posits that race is a social construct and that racism occurs implicitly and explicitly at micro (i.e., individual) and macro (i.e., institutional) levels (Solórzano, 1998). This chapter will include key components of CRT such as counterspaces (Yosso & Lopez, 2010), transformational resistance (Solórzano & Delgado Bernal, 2001), and the utility of an interdisciplinary approach (Solórzano, 1998). Each theme will be explored in a chronological manner that supports the scholarship of mentoring. This exploration will be constructed through reflections, meeting notes, exchanges of e-mails, and conversations between Dimpal and Danny over 10 years.

Student to Professor: Engaging in Counterspaces

As one of the few graduate students of color in my doctoral program, I (Dimpal) often felt that my voice was silenced and that my past experiences as a practitioner were not viewed as legitimate. At any moment I feared that it would be found out that I had "faked" my way into being accepted into graduate school and I would be asked to leave. I now know this is what scholars have labeled as the "imposter phenomenon or syndrome," a psychological barrier to success experienced by high achievers who put themselves under constant pressure to maintain an impression of competence (Clance & Imes, 1978). This self-induced pressure often results in low self-esteem and constant academic or socially related anxiety (Chrisman, Pieper, Clance, Holland, & Glickauf-Hughes, 1995). The pressure of graduate school makes it an ideal environment for the imposter syndrome to dominate among first-generation doctoral students of color, despite their having gained entrance into an elite university with rigorous admission standards.

Although I still experience the imposter syndrome to some degree today, my anxiety was reduced when I entered Danny's Research Apprenticeship Course (RAC), Race, Racism, and U.S. Education, in 2004. That is where I was introduced to a community of scholars (past and present) who valued the contribution of lived experiences and were committed to racial justice through their research and practice. In this space, there were no dumb questions,[1] and it was safe to express any fears or doubts that one had about one's progress (or perceived lack thereof) throughout the program.

Danny's RAC met twice a month, throughout the year, and was open to any undergraduate or graduate student, faculty, or community member, often resulting in a classroom where students had to stand or sit on the floor because of a lack of seating. I attended the class up until my graduation and have come back numerous times to participate, as I've grown to miss research-based discussions centered on race and racism. This course is not a traditional class offering within UCLA and is one of the many testaments to Danny's approach to critical pedagogy and mentorship, insisting that advanced doctoral students, beginning graduate students, and undergraduates all engage in dialogue centered on scholarship and current affairs, present their own work, and solicit feedback regarding their progress.

Danny's RAC can be viewed as a counterspace within the Graduate School of Education at UCLA. According to Solórzano, Ceja, and Yosso (2000), academic and social counterspaces are established by students of color by finding people who look like themselves and establishing a space that pushes them yet is comfortable and hospitable. The essential function of a counterspace is to find refuge from microaggressions and to be in a physical or virtual space that is validating and supportive (Howard-Hamilton, 2003). In higher education, a counterspace is often a refuge from a negative and hostile campus racial climate (Patton, 2010).

By engaging in this counterspace, I was allowed to ask crucial questions related to community colleges as valid sites of learning for students of color and their intersection with CRT. I learned that by way of transfer, community colleges play a critical role in access to higher education for students of color; however, this is often overlooked in traditional research and scholarship (Rendón, 1993). In particular, in California, community colleges serve nearly 80% of all African American and Latino students enrolled in the state's three-tier public higher education system, as well as 75% of Native American students and 61% of Asian American students (California Postsecondary Education Commission, 2011). Although students of color compose the majority of enrollment, many of them are pushed out and do not transfer to four-year institutions (Crisp & Nuñez, 2014; Jain, Herrera, Bernal, & Solórzano, 2011).

These were important revelations to a graduate student of color like myself who was a former community college staff member, had feelings of guilt for leaving her undergraduate students "behind" to go back to school, and did not feel like she was aligned with the academic values of most of her professors. Not until I was attending Danny's RAC regularly and also began meeting with him one-on-one for mentoring was I exposed to a perspective that allowed for the marginalized voice to be centered. It was through RAC and Danny's conversations and scholarship that I was introduced to CRT and saw it as the "missing link" in how to frame and validate my work.

An excerpt from RAC notes on April 29, 2005, one of my first introductions to CRT, states the following:

> CRT foregrounds race and racism unapologetically, it focuses its research, curriculum, and practice on the experiences of students of color and views these experiences as sources of strength (This is a strength in your research,

not a weakness! Their experiences are central!). Our hope is that our work will have an impact on practice, on students of color that are entering the academy; we do this work knowing and hoping for this future impact.

Danny gave this definition of *CRT* to the class, and it's a definition that I often refer back to as I begin to doubt the purpose and worth of my teaching, research, and/or service. Although CRT centers on race and racism, it also recognizes its intersection with other forms of identity such as class, gender, citizenship, and sexuality (Solórzano & Yosso, 2002). This is important to note, as my research focuses on the experiences of women of color and how race and gender affect their lives in higher education. Toward this end, I have used CRT, along with womanist theory, to be able to fully explore this complex intersection (Jain & Turner, 2011/2012). CRT has been not only a theoretical framework that guides my design and analysis of research projects but also a frame of reference as I develop pedagogy; interact with students; and dialogue with colleagues regarding student success, inclusive curriculum, and student of color experiences. CRT has also aided me in facilitating relationships with those who believe that race and racism are real forces within our educational system.

The Advisee–Advisor Relationship: Transformative Resistance

After I attended Danny's RAC and enrolled in his other courses and met with him one-on-one regarding my dissertation project centered on women community college student leaders of color and their transfer preparation, he agreed to be my cochair for my dissertation. This was a cochair position because Danny was not from my home academic department. However, after four years with my advisor, numerous conversations where I left doubting my intellectual ability, and a particular disheartening e-mail exchange, I reconstituted my committee, with Danny as my sole chair and advisor.

As a woman of color, I noticed a different gender dynamic with Danny than with my previous advisor, who was a White male. I recall that my former chair made it a point to tell his female advisees that he had to leave the door to his office open when meeting with us because he did not want to arouse suspicions by having closed-door meetings with women. Nearly every time I met with him, he made this proclamation. This did not make me feel comfortable, but rather it made me feel uneasy because it led me to believe that inappropriate relationships between women graduate students and their male advisors must be common and that it must look bad in particular for a young woman of color graduate student to be alone with her White male advisor. Danny did not have this policy at all, although a majority of his advisees were also women. Leaving the door open or closed was never made a proclamation in all the years that I have met with him.

Ultimately, changing advisors was a pivotal moment in my graduate career and one that did not lack controversy. It was unorthodox in my department and school for students to disassociate with their advisors after several years; however, Danny reassured me with these words in an e-mail: "I just want to mention to you as I always have—you have my support and this is just a small bump that we will get over." After this move, my department reformed its policies, stating that the dissertation chair must come from the student's home department. I was the last student who was "allowed" to have an advisor from another department, and I had to fill out extensive paperwork and secure signatures, including one from my former advisor.

The institution saw me as someone who was creating more work for administration and was "breaking the rules." The institution did not see my choice to reconstitute my committee and to take ownership of my dissertation project as resistance, particularly transformative resistance (Solórzano & Delgado Bernal, 2001). The term *resistance* can often have a negative connotation; however, within educational settings it can be seen as a strategic tool for survival if applied correctly. Theories of resistance are important in schooling, as they acknowledge the role of human agency and one's ability to navigate structures and relationships on one's own behalf (Solórzano & Delgado Bernal, 2001).

In the process of reconstituting my dissertation committee, I recognized my agency and resisted institutional structures. I viewed my research, through the lens of CRT, as forwarding a social justice agenda by giving voice to a group of students who have largely been silenced or unexplored in higher education literature—women of color community college students (Jain, 2010). In addition, I was interested in the intersection between race and gender for community college student leaders and how these intersecting identities impacted their academic trajectory. I viewed the linkage between activism and academics, and holding steadfast in my commitment to this as my research agenda, as resisting the university's attempt to hold me to traditional conventions of an advisor-advisee relationship.

Influenced by the work of Paulo Freire (1970a, 1970b), Solórzano and Delgado Bernal (2001) defined *resistance* as the oppositional behavior of students who meet one of two intersecting criteria: (a) Students have a critique of social oppression (liberating ideology) and (b) students are interested in working toward social justice (liberating practice). Accordingly, there are four forms of oppositional behavior based on these two criteria: (a) reactionary behavior, (b) self-defeating resistance, (c) conformist resistance, and (d) transformative resistance (see Figure 6.1). Thus, the resistance that I described was transformative, rather than reactionary, self-defeating, or conformist.

Figure 6.1 Defining the concept of resistance.

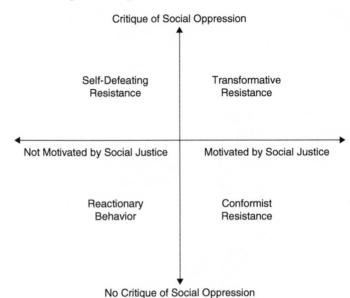

Note. Adapted from "Examining Transformational Resistance Through a Critical Race and LatCrit Theory Framework: Chicana and Chicano Students in an Urban Context," by D. Solórzano & D. Delgado Bernal, 2001, *Urban Education*, 36(3), pp. 308–342.

Transformative resistance, unlike the other forms of resistance, has a critique of social oppression and a desire for social justice. If students engage in reactionary resistance, they hold no critique of oppression and no desire for social justice. A third type of resistance, self-defeating resistance, occurs when students have some form of critique but no interest in social justice. Last, conformist resistance "refers to the oppositional behavior of students who are motivated by a need for social justice yet hold no critique of the systems of oppression" (Solórzano & Delgado Bernal, 2001, p. 318). Each form of resistance serves as an explanatory framework of students' behavior and how they respond to social and institutional structures within their environment.

Transformational resistance can further be divided between internal and external resistance. Internal resistance "appears to conform to institutional or cultural norms and expectations, however individuals are consciously engaged in a critique of oppression. . . . One example is the Student of Color who holds a critique of cultural and economic oppression and is motivated to go to graduate school by a desire to engage in a social justice struggle against this oppression" (Solórzano & Delgado Bernal, 2001, p. 324). On the surface, this student might appear to conform to societal norms by pursuing graduate school to receive a higher degree; however, in this example he or she is not motivated by personal advancement or monetary gain but rather driven to return and contribute to the community through service and learning.

External transformative resistance "involves a more conspicuous and overt type of behavior, and the behavior does not conform to institutional or cultural norms and expectations. . . . [It] differs from internal transformational resistance because it is openly visible and overtly operates outside the traditional system" (Solórzano & Delgado Bernal, 2001, pp. 325–326). Solórzano and Delgado Bernal (2001) argued that external transformative resistance is often easier to recognize because of its explicit and visible actions and that internal resistance can often go ignored or misidentified because of its introverted nature. They further asserted that although they are constructing transformative resistance as dichotomous, there is indeed overlap and fluidity between the internal and the external and that students can engage in both simultaneously or at different points in time.

On the surface, by reconstituting my dissertation committee and drastically altering my scholarly trajectory, it may appear that I engaged in conformist resistance rather than transformational resistance by still participating within the formal structures of a dissertation process. However, I see this as an example of internal transformative resistance. My desire to work with Danny and to have him serve as my sole chair was not to capitalize on his scholarly prominence but rather to feel secure that he would not challenge my belief that the experiences of women of color was a valid subject to explore and would represent a contribution to scholarship. In addition, as a former student leader myself, I felt that Danny was able to connect to my activist past because of his critical race lens and his own experiences working with undergraduate student groups such as MEChA (Movimiento Estudiantil Chicana/o de Aztlan).

In general, the culture of graduate school can be seen as oppressive and dehumanizing for students of color (Gildersleeve, Croom, & Vasquez, 2011). It can often lead to students engaging with the question "Am I going crazy?," which represents a narrative of "tentativeness, insecurity, and doubt that can be projected onto doctoral students of color. It also represents the active engagement with struggle and resiliency required by doctoral students of color" (Gildersleeve et al., 2011, p. 100). By resisting the structures of the university, by honoring my cultural intuition as a woman of color (Calderón, Delgado Bernal, Pérez Huber, Malagón, & Vélez, 2012), and by practicing transformative resistance during my dissertation journey, the question "Am I going crazy?" often came up, yet Danny repeatedly reassured me that I was not; however, he also warned me that this question would resurface as I continued my journey through the academy as faculty. He was right.

Colleague to Colleague: Interdisciplinary Mentoring

When you enter Danny's office, you feel a sense of peace and calm that hangs in the air: the open windows that look over the sunny green lawn and bricked courtyard; the mahogany wraparound desk; the bookcase with his students' dissertations and seminal readings on CRT; his boxes of files, his souvenirs, and the pictures on his desk from his students; and his small round table, where he often directs you to sit down after giving you a warm hug upon entry. There is no pretense upon entering of making sure that gender dynamics are made apparent. Danny's office is a safe haven for most of those who enter—you can almost hear students exhale as they get ready to sit down and talk to a professor who "gets it."

I have taken many cues from the way Danny mentors his students, even taking note of the physical structure of his office. He purposefully asks you to sit at the round table, rather than his desk, so he can sit next to you to share readings and view a computer screen side by side. This breaks down the distanced power barrier if he was on one side of the desk and the student on the other. To the left of this table is a clock whose time has stopped, making students feel unrushed as they confide in Danny or share their recent work. However, more important than the setup of Danny's office is how he makes you feel as soon as you sit down to speak with him. The first question that Danny asks is how you've been and how your family is.

This is important to note because he does not start the meeting asking where your draft is, if you've completed your fellowship or job application, how you're doing in your classes, or what the status is of your dissertation progress. He begins by asking about your and your family's well-being. To this day, I've never had another mentor consistently begin with this question. As a first-generation student who comes from a low-income family with immigrant parents, I instantly feel at ease by this welcome question. This is a clear example of Danny's praxis and the importance he puts on the inclusion of family and community.

In alignment with CRT and his work with two of his former students, noted CRT scholars Tara Yosso and Delores Delgado Bernal, his question of family is in concordance with *community cultural wealth* (Yosso, 2005) and *pedagogies of the home* (Delgado Bernal, 2001). Community cultural wealth highlights different forms of capital, including *familial capital*, which can be defined as "those cultural knowledges nurtured among familia (kin) that carry a sense of community history, memory and cultural intuition" (Yosso, 2005, p. 79). Danny recognizes this familial capital among his students and encourages me to do the same with the students that I interact with.

With Danny's mentorship approach as my guidepost, I've been able to interact with my own students in a way that considers their familial background, how their career intersects with their education, and their raced and gendered experiences in the classroom. I often encourage them to see me not as an authoritative professor but more like their colleague, and when it comes to their dissertation work, I echo one of Danny's most common phrases: "You are the expert. No one will know this subject better than you, and I will turn to you for advice on this topic." This sentiment has become my mantra while working with students and something that I often repeat to them as they begin to doubt their own academic capabilities such as research and writing.

This self-doubt is especially manifested in my educational leadership students, as they are typically working professionals and older adults who have spent a significant time away from higher education prior to their admission into the program. Terms such as *theory* and *methodology* are often met with fear and suspicion as these students begin to adjust to the scholarly rigors of graduate school. In addition to self-doubt, there is some external doubt as they find themselves being mentored by someone who is of a younger age than them, a different gender, and most often a different race and/or ethnicity. This is not something that they, or I, expected, but it is somewhat common in the field of educational leadership, which has been historically dominated by older White male faculty (Quezada & Louque, 2004).

When I took my first tenure-track position at a former institution, Danny was clear in informing me that I was not a typical faculty member for educational leadership. Besides being younger and a woman of color, the fact that I have a PhD and not an EdD was, at the time, uncommon for educational leadership faculty. Traditionally, educational leadership faculty are current or retired practitioners from within the field of K–12 or higher education leadership. This means that students are accustomed to being taught by former principals, superintendents, and high-ranking higher education officials who have EdDs (Quezada & Louque, 2004).

My being trained at a research-intensive university and having a PhD made me starkly different from other faculty within most educational leadership departments across the country. Suddenly, I found myself in a new field, and Danny and I found ourselves once again in an interdisciplinary educational mentorship, he in race and ethnic studies in education, and I in educational leadership. These two disciplines hold vastly different philosophical approaches to the practice of education, with educational leadership being much more resistant to the utility of a CRT analysis of schooling (Parker & Villalpando, 2007). As a field that prepares school leaders to interact with students, staff, families, and community members from vast cultural backgrounds and differing levels of socioeconomic status, educational leadership has been largely silent on issues of race and gender within its preparation programs (Parker & Villalpando, 2007).

Unsafe in the Classroom

One of the key mentoring moments that stands out between Danny and me was when I informed him, on the brink of tears, about my student evaluations from my Introduction to Leadership course. When discussing the syllabus with Danny months ago, he was excited that I was incorporating CRT into my curriculum and was looking forward to having a conversation about the process and outcome. This was not a conversation that I wanted to have with him, almost feeling ashamed to let him know not only that I received poor evaluations but also that a group of students conspired against me and wrote their own independent evaluations prior to the last day of the course. These hostile evaluations centered on my pedagogy and the use of CRT in the curriculum. Their narrative comments totaled over six pages, and they slipped it into the formal evaluation packet so that it became part of my official teaching record. I was surprised and hurt by this, especially because I attempted to include CRT as just one component to the course and not central to the entire curriculum design.

Knowing that I was hired partially for my attention to the intersection between race and racism in education, I attempted to design a leadership course that would include perspectives that often go ignored in the traditional curriculum. The course was divided into the following sections: demography and school culture, leadership for social justice, race and urban youth, CRT, and higher education leadership. The main texts for the course were *The Color of Success: Race and High-Achieving Urban Youth* (Conchas, 2006), *Shaping School Culture: The Heart of Leadership* (Deal & Peterson, 1999), *Critical Race Theory: An Introduction* (Delgado & Stefancic, 2001), and *Leadership for Social Justice: Making Revolutions in Education* (Marshall & Oliva, 2009). There were 27 students in the class, with 16 men and 11 women, with men being overrepresented—something that does not often occur in education classrooms (Bradley, 2000). The student composition of the course was diverse and consisted of the following: 4% African American, 18% Asian American, 18% Latina/Latino, 12% mixed race, and 48% White. In addition, the students were primarily seeking their master's, with a handful of students who were in the doctoral educational leadership program.

The narrative component of the formal evaluation provided by the department asked the students to comment on how their instructor fared on the following categories: (a) evidence of content expertise; (b) effective classroom instruction; (c) regular, systematic assessment of student learning; (d) positive learning environment; and (e) student learning. The following are comments that students made within these categories and also within their independent evaluations:

"I feel like I am constantly defending my [White] race."

"She needs to prove how pioneering she is."

"Next time you teach a class, create course learning objectives that reflect the title & description."

"Leadership through a social justice lens quickly became a class about race relations with very little application to practice."

These initial comments expressed how students felt about the course, my career at the university, and me. The following comments went deeper and were related to issues of race and social justice within the curriculum:

"I don't know what she knows about educational leadership. Clearly an expert on social justice and people of color."

"There seems to be no attempt on Professor Jain's part to hide the fact that this is not a leadership course, this is a course on social justice and people of color. . . . I fundamentally feel cheated by this experience."

"Many students are leaving the class with the belief that CRT is a radical school of thought that reduces every person to a racist."

Here we see how strongly the students resisted the idea that social justice and race can be components of effective educational leadership and felt dissatisfied with CRT.

Finally, the last two evaluation comments point out my fit with the university and my perceived sense of dress and appearance:

"Any new hire at an institution needs to learn the institutional culture and what is expected. I feel that Dimpal has not done so and brought her personal values into an institution that may not quite be compatible."

"Pointing out a situation regarding a male sitting down in class creates a division of labor during a presentation of women in leadership. However, in a contradictory position [she] wears mini-dresses to class, wearing a backpack, chewing gum in class, gives the class a perception that [she is] a traditional age college student."

These were the most hurtful comments, as they were a direct attack on my credibility and body. Although I attempted to respect the students' right to freely express themselves, many of these comments were baseless and noncredible. With that said, however, it did not stop the power that these words had on my tenure portfolio at this institution, my pedagogy, and my emotional psyche.

Luckily, a concerned student called me the day before the final class to warn me that the students were "going to throw [me] under the bus," yet at that point it was too late to address the students' misperceptions. For the first time, I felt unsafe in my own classroom. It was a horrible feeling, and it was something that I recall Danny saying he experienced just a few years prior to my own incident. In 2006, a conservative UCLA alumni association student group targeted Danny by offering to pay students to take notes and turn over course materials of what the group deemed as "radical" professors (Jaschik, 2006). Danny was part of this group called the "Dirty 30," which consisted of a list of 30 professors on UCLA's campus whose curriculum included things such as a critique of the Iraq War, use of race and ethnicity in their scholarship, or pro–affirmative action views (Mosqueda, 2006). In RAC Danny shared with us his reactions to being on the list, how his family was concerned for his welfare at the university, and how it was an awful feeling to feel unsafe in the classroom and to have a culture of mistrust between students and professors.

I recalled all of this as I was sitting with Danny in Pike Place Market in Seattle, on the pier, with the sunshine and water all around us. I wanted to tell him of my reviews earlier, but I was embarrassed. I didn't know how to do it over e-mail or phone, so I waited until we met in person. I brought with me my first-year evaluation from my prior department and some notes about the student evaluations. Danny quietly listened, and when I was done he said, "I knew something like this would happen to you over the course of your career. I'm not surprised; I'm just sorry that this had to happen to you so soon."

This was definitely a critical race mentoring moment. Danny, who had over 40 years of teaching experience; who had taught Chicano studies, sociology, and education-related courses; and who was often the lone voice among senior faculty to bring up issues of race and racism, was telling me that this was normal, even expected. To receive scathing teaching evaluations from your students when you challenge them on issues of race and social justice can be anticipated (Delgado Bernal & Villalpando, 2002); however, their covert form of organizing was appalling, especially when the leadership in that institution was reluctant to name it as racism and/or sexism but rather labeled it as hazing.

Danny and I discussed how the impact of these evaluations was different for me than for him—regardless of rank and university, these evaluations carried a different weight because I am a woman. These students attacked me on my dress and appearance, something that male faculty often do not have to be conscious of. If I were teaching the same subject matter but identified as a White man, would the students' reactions have been the same? Would they have exerted such hostility and entitlement? Most likely not.

It felt good to divulge this incident to Danny, and his words were comforting. Danny has never tried to represent the academy for what it's not, a hospitable and welcoming environment for faculty of color. He's always been honest with his mentees regarding the challenges we can, and most likely will, face as we enter tenure-track appointments. Yet, when I received these evaluations, I once again began to internalize the imposter syndrome, believing that I did not belong as faculty and that these students were exposing my insecurities regarding my pedagogy and knowledge of CRT. Since I've shared this story with Danny, he has encouraged me to share it with others, to not be ashamed, and to make sure to stay connected to my community and family that support me. Danny is able to offer me this mentorship because of the foundation that he has built through problem-posing mentoring. Next, Danny will share his method of mentoring and his own journey through the academy.

Danny's Reflections on Freirean Problem-Posing Mentoring

In our many conversations leading up to this chapter, Dimpal and I have discussed the people, readings, and other influences on our life trajectories. As I wrote this section, I focused on the issues that Dimpal felt were an important part of our comentoring experience. And so, I share thoughts on someone who has influenced my work and on what I am now calling *Freirean problem-posing mentoring*. Forty years ago I was exposed to the work of educator and philosopher Paulo Freire. His book *Pedagogy of the Oppressed* (1970b) has guided my teaching and mentoring practices ever since.

For instance, according to Freire (1970a, 1970b), schools use the "banking method" to domesticate students. When this approach is taken, students are viewed as passive receptacles waiting for knowledge to be deposited to them by the teacher. They are taught in a narrative format whereby the teacher communicates with the students in one-way monologues and therefore limits dialogic learning. This approach can lead students to feel that their thoughts and ideas are not important enough to warrant a two-way dialogue with the teacher. Students also become dependent on the teacher for their acquisition of knowledge, and their critical thinking process is silenced. In the banking approach, teachers are seen as conduits through which the ideology and values of the dominant social class are transmitted to the students. Mentoring in this hierarchical and one-dimensional fashion reproduces the banking pedagogy and takes it from the classroom to the office and other spaces where we engage with and mentor students.

On the other hand, when educational settings promote emancipatory learning, students are viewed as subjects willing and able to act in and on their world. To create a liberating education, Freire developed the "problem-posing method," in which a two-way dialogue of cooperation between the student and the teacher is the focus, content, and pedagogy of the classroom.

Freire's method includes three general phases: (a) identifying and naming the problem, (b) analyzing the causes of the problem, and (c) finding solutions to the problem (Freire, 1970a, 1970b). This process of reflecting and acting on one's reality by describing and defining a problem clearly, analyzing its causes, and acting to resolve it is a key element of the problem-posing method.

Students are encouraged to view issues as problems that can be resolved, not as a reality to be accepted. Hence, students feel that their ideas are recognized as legitimate and that the problem posed can be resolved in a constructive manner, promoting an active participant role in their various communities. In addition, students and teachers become dependent on each other for knowledge. Mentoring in this nonhierarchical, multidimensional, and problem-posing fashion creates a climate where students' ideas are important and central to their intellectual growth and in challenging dominant paradigms in their field.

I've been learning my pedagogical and mentoring craft for the past 40 years. I began at the Los Angeles Central Juvenile Hall as a secondary social studies teacher in 1972. From there I taught sociology and Chicano studies at two very different Southern California community colleges—Santa Monica and East Los Angeles—beginning in 1975. I also taught in the same fields at two California state universities: California State University, Northridge, and California State University, Bakersfield. Since 1990, I've been at the UCLA Graduate School of Education and Information Studies. It has been both an honor and a unique and rich experience teaching in all three segments of California's postsecondary education system. Indeed, these varied experiences, with both the challenges and the rewards, are foundational to the educator I am today.

Teaching and mentoring are essential parts of my identity as a scholar. I see mentoring as the core of my teaching. It enters into my classroom, office, hallways, conferences, and other settings where I engage others. Teaching and mentoring are also linked to my research and service. I am constantly trying to improve my teaching and mentoring skills.

An essential part of my role as an educator is the training of future scholars. In 25 years at UCLA, I have chaired (or cochaired) 46 PhD and 2 EdD dissertations and served on more than 160 dissertation committees in education, history, psychology, sociology, information studies, urban planning, and film and television. Over the years I have served as a sponsor or mentor for 10 postdoctoral fellows from the Ford Foundation, UC/ ACCORD, and UC Presidents. Also, I have advised 33 students through the Master of Arts program and sat on 10 master thesis committees across departments at UCLA. Many of my students have gone on to faculty positions at different levels all over the country, and others have become institutional researchers, community leaders, and advocates.

Another significant area of teaching is individualized research training with students. My preference is to engage one-on-one or in small groups with students on a research project from start to finish. I use these opportunities to help students develop skills in conceptualizing, implementing, writing, and presenting research for different audiences. In this context I spend additional time helping students develop writing skills through coauthorship. To date, I have published (or have in press) 26 research articles, 26 book chapters, and 15 policy briefs or research reports with 30 of my former and current students.

Another important way students are engaged in learning is my yearlong RAC on Race, Racism, and U.S. Education, which Dimpal mentioned earlier. The RAC is an intellectual space where the students and I work collaboratively on research projects on the road to advancing the field of *race, racism, and education* generally and *critical race theory in education* in particular. It is a unique intellectual space where we discuss both the research and the pedagogy on race and racism throughout the educational pipeline. Students in this course have gone on to teach courses on critical race issues in education across the country. They often return to share with the current group of RAC students their experiences in the classrooms and communities they serve.

Students from this group also develop proposals for their dissertations and submissions to major professional conferences around the country in many fields (i.e., education, ethnic studies, sociology, and law). We encourage this and work to get the papers submitted to journals and edited books for publication. Over the years the RAC has been an intellectual incubator for ideas that lead to research, publications, and teaching on CRT in education (along with tribal CRT, Asian American CRT, Latino critical theory, critical race information theory, and critical deaf theory) and has been recognized as such. As mentioned earlier we have published many research articles, book chapters, and policy briefs and research reports with students from the RAC.

As an educator, mentor, and scholar, I feel strongly about an interdisciplinary approach to studying educational issues. For instance, I am an educational sociologist by training, but a sociological question related to education can be simultaneously addressed from a historical perspective, in literary works, in films and photographs, or in the readings of philosophy and law. For me, an interdisciplinary education takes place in a setting where ideas know no disciplinary boundaries, where the pursuit of an answer is as important as the answer itself, where learning is both a solitary and a collective experience, and where the empowerment of students is a primary concern. In the various educational spaces where I work, I try to foster a community of scholars and educators who conduct high-quality work and who respect, look after, and take care of one another. In the end, I hope my student colleagues carry this legacy forward to other pedagogical spaces around the country and the world. This is what I mean by Freirean problem-posing mentoring.

Conclusion

Danny and I have been able to trace our mentoring relationship through many stages within the academy: student to professor, advisee to advisor, and colleague to colleague. At each step, CRT and its various tools (i.e., transformational resistance, community cultural wealth, racial microaggressions) have facilitated our relationship and helped redefine and reevaluate how to mitigate the power structures within academia. I was first exposed to CRT as a student in Danny's RAC, a powerful counterspace (Howard-Hamilton, 2003) within UCLA's Graduate School of Education and Information Studies. This led me to engage in transformative resistance (Solórzano & Delgado Bernal, 2001) as I parted ways with my former advisor and reconstituted my dissertation committee with Danny as my sole chair.

As I persist throughout the academy as faculty, I have come to further value mentoring as I experience new terrain and find myself to be vulnerable as a woman of color junior faculty member. Through Danny's explanation of Freirean problem-posing mentoring and his extensive mentoring and publishing record, I see now how I am a beneficiary of his many years of labor as an educator. Although we are in a cross-racial and cross-gender mentoring relationship, CRT has helped us connect on many different levels, including the ability to speak openly and unapologetically about race, racism, and sexism within higher education. Through Danny's mentoring I have learned how to mentor others with humility and respect and to remember that family always comes first, whether it be your family within academia, family at home, or family within your community. After 10 years of guidance and mentorship, Danny has become a part of my family.

Note

1. Actually, the only dumb question is the one not asked.

References

Bradley, K. (2000). The incorporation of women into higher education: Paradoxical outcomes? *Sociology of Education, 73*(1), 1–18.

Calderón, D., Delgado Bernal, D., Pérez Huber, L., Malagón, M. C., & Vélez, V. N. (2012). A Chicana feminist epistemology revisited: Cultivating ideas a generation later. *Harvard Educational Review, 82*(4), 513–539.

California Postsecondary Education Commission. (2011). *Custom data reports.* Retrieved from http://www.cpec.ca.gov/OnLineData/OnLineData.asp

Campbell, T. A., & Campbell, D. E. (1997). Faculty/student mentor program: Effects on academic performance and retention. *Research in Higher Education, 38*(6), 727–742.

Chrisman, S. M., Pieper, W. A., Clance, P. R., Holland, C. L., & Glickauf-Hughes, C. (1995). Validation of the Clance imposter phenomenon scale. *Journal of Personality Assessment, 65*(3), 456–467.

Clance, P. R., & Imes, S. A. (1978). The imposter phenomenon in high achieving women: Dynamics and therapeutic intervention. *Psychotherapy: Theory, Research, and Practice, 15*(3), 241–247.

Conchas, G. Q. (2006). *The color of success: Race and high-achieving urban youth.* New York, NY: Teachers College Press.

Crisp, G., & Nuñez, A.-M. (2014). Understanding the racial transfer gap: Modeling underrepresented minority and nonminority students' pathways from two- to four-year institutions. *The Review of Higher Education, 37*(3), 291–320.

Deal, T. E., & Peterson, K. D. (1999). *Shaping school culture: The heart of leadership.* San Francisco, CA: Jossey-Bass.

Delgado Bernal, D. (2001). Learning and living pedagogies of the home: The Mestiza consciousness of Chicana students. *International Journal of Qualitative Studies in Education, 14*(5), 623–639.

Delgado Bernal, D., & Villalpando, O. (2002). An apartheid of knowledge in academia: The struggle over the "legitimate knowledge" of faculty of color. *Equity and Excellence in Education, 35*(2), 169–180.

Delgado, R., & Stefancic, J. (2001). *Critical race theory: An introduction.* New York, NY: New York University Press.

Diggs, G. A., Garrison-Wade, D. F., Estrada, D., & Galindo, R. (2009). Smiling faces and colored spaces: The experiences of faculty of color pursing tenure in the academy. *Urban Review, 41*, 312–333.

Freire, P. (1970a). *Cultural action for freedom.* Cambridge, MA: Harvard Educational Review Monographs.

Freire, P. (1970b). *Pedagogy of the oppressed.* New York, NY: Continuum.

Gildersleeve, R. E., Croom, N. N., & Vasquez, P. L. (2011). "Am I going crazy?!" A critical race analysis of doctoral education. *Equity and Excellence in Education, 44*(1), 93–114.

Howard-Hamilton, M. F. (2003). Theoretical frameworks for African American women. *New Directions for Student Services, 104*, 19–27.

Jain, D. (2010). Critical race theory and community colleges: Through the eyes of women student leaders of color. *Community College Journal of Research and Practice, 34*(1), 78–91.

Jain, D., Herrera, A., Bernal, S., & Solórzano, D. (2011). Critical race theory and the transfer function: Introducing a transfer receptive culture. *Community College Journal of Research and Practice, 35*(2), 252–266.

Jain, D., & Turner, C. S. (2011/2012). Purple is to lavender: Womanism, resistance, and the politics of naming. *Negro Educational Review, 62*(4), 67–88.

Jaschik, S. (2006). *The new class monitors*. Retrieved from http://www.insidehighered
.com/news/2006/01/18/ucla
Marshall, C., & Oliva, M. (Eds.). (2009). *Leadership for social justice: Making revolutions in education*. Boston, MA: Allyn & Bacon.
Mosqueda, C. (2006). *Academic witch-hunt*. Retrieved from http://loteriachicana.
net/2006/01/19/academic-witch-hunt
Parker, L., & Villalpando, O. (2007). A race(cialized) perspective on education leadership: Critical race theory in educational administration. *Educational Administration Quarterly, 43*(5), 519–524.
Patton, L. (Ed.). (2010). *Culture centers in higher education: Perspectives on identity, theory, and practice*. Sterling, VA: Stylus.
Quezada, R. L., & Louque, A. (2004). The absence of diversity in the academy: Faculty of color in educational administration programs. *Education, 125*(2), 213–221.
Rendón, L. I. (1993). Eyes on the prize: Students of color and the bachelor's degree. *Community College Review, 21*(2), 3–13.
Savage, H. E., Karp, R. S., & Logue, R. (2004). Faculty mentorship at colleges and universities. *College Teaching, 52*(1), 21–24.
Solórzano, D., Ceja, M., & Yosso, T. (2000). Critical race theory, racial microaggressions, and campus racial climate: The experiences of African American college students. *Journal of Negro Education, 69*(1–2), 60–73.
Solórzano, D., & Delgado Bernal, D. (2001). Examining transformational resistance through a critical race and LatCrit theory framework: Chicana and Chicano students in an urban context. *Urban Education, 36*(3), 308–342.
Solórzano, D. G. (1998). Critical race theory, race and gender microaggressions, and the experience of Chicana and Chicano scholars. *Qualitative Studies in Education, 11*(1), 121–136.
Solórzano, D. G., & Yosso, T. (2002). Critical race methodology: Counter-storytelling as an analytical framework for education research. *Qualitative Inquiry, 8*(1), 23–44.
Sorcinelli, M. D., & Yun, J. (2007). From mentor to mentoring networks: Mentoring in the new academy. *The Magazine of Higher Learning, 39*(6), 58–61.
Stanley, C. A. (2006). Coloring the academic landscape: Faculty of color breaking the silence in predominantly White colleges and universities. *American Educational Research Journal, 43*(4), 701–736.
Turner, C. S., & Myers, S. L., Jr. (2000). *Faculty of color in academe: Bittersweet success*. Needham Heights, MA: Allyn & Bacon.
Yosso, T. J. (2005). Whose culture has capital? A critical race theory discussion of community cultural wealth. *Race Ethnicity and Education, 8*(1), 69–91.
Yosso, T. J., & Lopez, C. B. (2010). Counterspaces in a hostile place: A critical race theory analysis of campus culture centers. In L. Patton (Ed.), *Culture centers in higher education: Perspectives on identity, theory, and practice* (pp. 83–105). Sterling, VA: Stylus.

7

CROSS-GENDER MENTORING FROM A CARIBBEAN PERSPECTIVE

Christine A. Stanley and Dave A. Louis

M entoring for us, from the perspective of two individuals born and raised in the Caribbean, is fundamentally about relationships. Cafarella (1992) stated that it is "an intense caring relationship in which persons with more experience work with less experienced persons to promote both professional and personal development" (p. 38). Our mentoring relationship spans almost 12 years, and it began in the academic setting. It began and evolved as a relationship between an academic working with a less experienced academic professional. The relationship at the outset, and to an observer, is different in terms of gender. However, when additional ingredients such as class and culture are added, the relationship can take on a different flavor. This is the essence of what we will share in this chapter: our experiences with cross-gender mentoring from a Caribbean perspective. Before we began sharing our experiences, we combed the research literature on mentoring, with a keen eye to see what we could find on the subject as it relates to gender differences. Although there is quite a bit of literature emerging on cross-gender mentoring relationships, there was less in terms of how class and culture intersect with gender in a mentoring relationship. Cross-gender mentoring is addressed in the literature (Bowen, 1986; Brass, 1985; Clawson & Kram, 1984; Fitt & Newton, 1981; Kram, 1985; Lean, 1983; Ragins, 1990; Ragins & Cotton, 1999; Ragins & McFarlin, 1990);

however, it is almost always from the point of view of the corporate sector and rarely in academic settings (Chandler, 1996; Chesler & Chesler, 2002). Moreover, as we suspected, we did not find much from the perspective of a mentor–protégé relationship deeply rooted within cultural traditions and class norms (Morgan & Davidson, 2008). Cross-gender mentoring suggests one layer of intersecting identities; however, when layers of culture and class are added, it opens up additional areas of commonalities for introspection (Morgan & Davidson, 2008) and discussion such as education, family values, background and expectations, institutional expectations, cross-cultural conflict, status, and respect for role and authority. So, we decided that this chapter could accomplish two things: (a) share our cross-gender mentoring relationship from a Caribbean perspective, and (b) open up new avenues for further research and writing on what we feel is an important and compelling topic to add to the virtually nonexistent literature.

Writing a chapter on this topic not only was delightful for us but also was, as you will see, based on openness, a great deal of reflection, and truth. In fact, in many instances we had to reexamine past wounds and "deal with them" openly before we could actually begin the task of writing. What proved to also be a challenge was finding a voice that would tell our story and in a way that is true to our Caribbean heritage and culture. In essence, our experience is really a story. Like many stories, there are many ways to weave in and out of details and incidents. So, what you will also see in this chapter is sometimes we will use a collective voice of "we," and at other times, we will revert to the voice of the "other." In this way, we hope you will get a flavor for our cross-gender mentoring experiences.

Commonalities

We share a plethora of experiences, ideologies, and interests, and we believe it was these commonalities that resulted in a mutually respectful and honest mentor–protégé relationship, which could have been tenuous otherwise. We entered an academic department in the same semester, fall 1999. Dr. Stanley at that time was an assistant professor and was gearing up for the tenure process. Dr. Louis was a generally motivated doctoral student, even though he did not have concrete ideas on his career direction. Although it was unspoken, we were highly driven individuals who possessed lofty goals, and this created a level of respect for one another. Our overlapping interest in diversity issues in higher education made Dr. Louis's journey through the program and dissertation defense tremendously pleasurable, unlike many horror stories he heard from other doctoral student peers. This intellectual common ground fostered smoother communication in our relationship. In fact, we both randomly shared articles and news clips on a variety of issues in higher education, which we discussed. Consequently, yet unconsciously, we learned of each other's philosophies and leanings within the field of higher education administration. From Dr. Louis's perspective, this aided the advising that he initially received. It was customized to meet his needs, and hence he felt comfortable with the materials and adding himself to the dialogue in his research. He believed that this was important for a doctoral student, as it nurtures a sense of ownership in the mentoring process, especially in terms of finding one's voice in dissertation writing.

We consider our Caribbean background the most significant commonality in our mentor–protégé relationship. Dr. Stanley was born and raised in Jamaica, and Dr. Louis in Trinidad. Our cultures are very similar, and the social modus operandi is almost identical. Having this acute understanding made hierarchical struggles nonexistent. In our cultures, authority and rank are staples and are taken very seriously. Therefore, as a graduate student, Dr. Louis was "subordinate," and Dr. Stanley was the "boss" in no uncertain terms. For Dr. Louis, it was a return to his roots, as it were, because all of his previous supervisors, as he was an immigrant, were American.

Beyond the hierarchical understanding lay a common experience in social adjustment, viewpoints as immigrants to America, and the dichotomy of not being African American and yet being Black in America. Although not researched heavily, the experience of Black Caribbean immigrants is unique compared to that of African Americans. For Dr. Louis, having a mentor who understood those specific outlooks, needs, and struggles made the experience less burdensome. It was a kind of support he had not experienced at any other educational level in his higher education. To this day, beyond the doctoral experience, he has never had another Caribbean peer, supervisor, or mentor. There is a marked difference in his experience.

The Black experience in America, coupled with our Caribbean background and culture, was further enhanced by the fact that we are both graduates of historically Black colleges and universities (HBCUs) (she attended Prairie View A&M University in Texas, and he attended Morehouse College in Georgia) and members of affiliated Black Greek letter organizations (she is a member of Delta Sigma Theta Sorority, Inc., and he is a member of Omega Psi Phi Fraternity, Inc.). The banter surrounding college rivalries and behaviors within our sorority and fraternity organizations started almost immediately. As a consequence, we spoke of the pride we possessed about our alma maters. We joked that Prairie View A&M was a better institution than Morehouse and vice versa. In actuality, it instilled a sense of pride in our work that we wanted to show the quality output from our schools. We also discussed the organizational and social nuances and stereotypes of our Greek affiliations. Dr. Stanley would say, "You know how you Ques [Omegas] are!" hinting that our rough-and-tumble demeanor translated into shoddy work.

However, both of us knowing these stereotypes were untrue yet attempting not to live up to them resulted in a higher standard or product. It created a friendly atmosphere without becoming overly personal. Over time, these exchanges increased the comfort with which we interacted and communicated. It was a language all our own, which incorporated the HBCU experience and the Caribbean experience. Anyone down the hall would have no idea of what we spoke and how it impacted our approach to work and research. These multiple platforms of understanding resulted in fluid communication at an early stage.

Dr. Louis believes the HBCU experience prepared us for a predominantly White research university environment, which was often filled with hidden forms of racism, sexism, and xenophobia. The Black Greek leadership experiences engrained in us the knowledge that through American history Blacks have struggled and overcame obstacles placed specifically for their impediment; our membership in these organizations aligned us with these heroes of Black history and gave us the courage to forge on in our respective arenas regardless of the obstacles. Of course, all this intertwined with our ancestry, similarity in the field, and personal determination and made our mentor–protégé circumstance positively unique.

These two aforementioned elements undoubtedly influenced the perspective we had of being minorities at a predominantly White research institution. They gave us a common lens through which we viewed the operation and culture of the department; the university atmosphere; our colleagues' interactions; and even the expectations, or lack thereof, that peers had of us. In a much unheralded way, we "had each other's back." Dr. Stanley would disaggregate the meanings of discussions that faculty and other students would have with me. She gave insight into the implicit messages. When faculty were tactful in not being overly critical of a Black doctoral student, she would share what the sometimes lower expectations were and say that I had to rise above them, to redouble my efforts as a Black student. I too provided greater quality assistance as a graduate research assistant, knowing that she could be in the firing line with other faculty because she is a Black female professor. We were not the "typical" faculty member or student in our department, and our acknowledgment of that made us work harder to ensure the safety of one another. We had to look out for each other because there was no one else who understood us beyond the superficial level. We had to support each other in an environment that was not always supportive or welcoming to individuals of color.

We are both Black immigrants striving to excel in our given fields and live up to high family expectations. From Dr. Louis's perspective, it gave him the strength to be a bit more forward and confident in his interactions with other faculty and students. For Dr. Stanley, it made her want to see Dr. Louis not only meet these expectations but also raise the bar for expectations and be mindful of the fact that there were few graduate students of color in the department and only two Black faculty members in the department during that time. This was a concern to her because she knew the research and lived experiences regarding institutional racism and how it plays out in a variety of forms, including the lack of high expectations and quality mentoring for graduate students and faculty of color (Stanley, 2006; Turner, González, & Wood, 2008; Wheeler, 1992).

When Dr. Louis left Trinidad, he knew that the bachelor's degree would not be sufficient for him. He was determined to attain the highest possible degree, and his parents encouraged him fully. At seven years old, he told his mother he would get his doctorate; what that meant to him at that early age one can only imagine. Maybe it was the fact that he was cognizant of his father's studies, or his mother's teaching, or his grandfather's legacy that reinforced the value of attaining an education. But he knew from his upbringing that education was valuable and attainable. It was an indication that education was of the utmost importance in his household. Being Black in post-Independence Trinidad meant that acquiring an education was critical. It was the manner in which power and status were acquired, especially because vacancies were now present via the exit of the colonists. His mother was an elementary teacher for 46 years, and his paternal grandfather was one of the first Black pre-Independence school principals in Trinidad. His father graduated from one of the top Catholic high schools in Trinidad, studied briefly at the University of the West Indies, and became an official in the Trinidad and Tobago public services sector. He attributes the bulk of his "rootedness" in education to those three individuals. Excelling in an academic setting was engrained in him.

For Dr. Stanley, she too came from a household that valued education: Her father is a professor and department chair at Prairie View A&M University, her mother is a retired administrator with the Jamaican government, and her brother is a chiropractor in private practice. While she was growing up in Jamaica, in an upper-middle-class family, the question was not whether you were going to college but where you would go to college. Dr. Stanley's parents sacrificed a lot for their two children. Both of her parents grew up poor. A single mother raised her father, and her mother's parents did not have access to resources for an education beyond high school. Her father went to study at Tuskegee University for his baccalaureate degree and later at Iowa State University for his master's degree while she and her mother were in Jamaica. Dr. Stanley was only a few months old when her father left to study for his baccalaureate degree. Her mother relied on her parents to help her with child care and other support as needed. Dr. Stanley's parents wanted to carve out a better life for their children than they themselves had growing up.

Having these formative foundations of excellence in academic pursuits influenced our approach to academic work. Our work ethic, to some observers, may have seemed impeccable and borderline neurotic; however, the standards that we placed on one another, for example, in the quality and presentation of our work, were extremely high. Our work was a reflection of our Caribbean identity; our parents; and, maybe unconsciously, our culture. Often, we found ourselves being the voice and the representatives for Blacks and Caribbean immigrants in the department.

Like most families from the Caribbean, when members of the family discover or meet anyone from the islands, it is only a matter of time before they get together for fellowship. So, Dr. Louis became acquainted with Dr. Stanley's parents. Quite naturally as well, conversations ranged from food, family, politics, education, cricket (a game that only a few countries in the world enjoy), and *more* politics! After speaking with Dr. Stanley's father on numerous occasions, Dr. Louis also picked up on the fact that the path he developed for his children was quite similar to his upbringing in Trinidad, in which education *will* be obtained, and there is no other result *but excellence*. The path Dr. Louis developed for his children was quite similar to his own parents' outlook. The attainment of education was critical, not because it was a Jamaican or Trinidadian sentiment but because of the time in which the two nations found themselves, the post-Colonial era. Blacks, who were the major ethnic group at the time and had some political power, instilled the idea that hard work will result in social status and monetary gain. Both of our parents aspired for greatness from their offspring.

The striving for academic excellence is also part of a class structure of which both of our parents are products. The post-Colonial West Indies brought about the development of education for the masses, independent thought, and a system that attempted to reward those who attained the highest level of scholarship (Williams, 1993). During the Independence Movement in the West Indies, from 1950 through the late 1960s, many countries sought to educate their populace, and many of the government agencies and private sectors provided opportunities for people who had acquired certain educational credentials. This birthed a mind-set that the youth should educate themselves. Consequently, once education is attained, those individuals who reaped the benefits must maximize and secure educational opportunities for their offspring. Education was the cornerstone of success and propagation of the successful family. Our parents were part of that paradigm shift in Jamaica and Trinidad. Coupled with the immigrant ethic of success via immigration, we both possessed the educational foundation, family support, and personal drive to be successful.

Thus, pursuing a terminal degree at Texas A&M University was a "given" step for Dr. Stanley; it was a familial expectation. Her motivation to attain the degree was obvious. Dr. Stanley, after completing high school in Jamaica, applied to several colleges and universities in the United States. At the same time, her father, employed with the Ministry of Agriculture in Jamaica, was being courted for a faculty position at Prairie View A&M University as an assistant professor of poultry science and also to direct the poultry science farm activities there. He was of the opinion that it would be much less expensive if his daughter attended Prairie View. So, Dr. Stanley went there and was always under the watchful eye of her father. She remembers her father telling her on several occasions, "You are an asset to your mother and me. When you have limited resources, you plan carefully. We want the best for you." This sentiment is a reflection of how her parents were raised, the context in which they lived, the types of and access to resources that were available to them while growing up, and the life they had carved out for their children.

Dr. Stanley was also very driven. Fresh from her faculty position at Ohio State, she was poised to come in "hitting the ground running," garnering momentum for tenure and beyond. She came to the position with a strong publication record and extensive teaching and administrative experience and was quickly earning a national reputation, which was unusual for an assistant professor. Dr. Stanley immediately began to conduct research and write articles feverishly; for me, her graduate assistant, it seemed that the demand for gathering articles was monumental, and almost every other day there was a new or slightly alternative search for me to conduct pertaining to her articles. She was determined, and her graduate assistant had to be as thorough, precise, and quick as she was in turning out products. Her no-nonsense disposition toward publishing and teaching was obvious. It was an education. Many times I thought, "Am I cut out for this? Could I be a professor one day?" I learned from the mentoring experience. It taught me, via modeling, how to direct my energies on making projects successful. Time management, research integrity, and professional posture are aspects that I learned as a protégé—not always via spoken word but by observation. Dr. Stanley showed me how to reach for goals as a faculty member. Even though my aspirations at the time were not to be faculty, it taught me how to navigate the nuances of the higher education environment.

The fact that we were both driven individuals, combined with Dr. Louis's desire to learn, made the relationship from his perspective very beneficial. Again, the common element—having strong professional aspirations—made the mentor–protégé bond strong. It is these unspoken commonalities that make a mentor–protégé relationship rare, which goes beyond storefront unities. It is simply beyond obvious public displays of amiability. When values, belief systems, cultural vestiges, family traditions, and personal enterprise are common threads in a mentor–protégé relationship, it becomes a partnership.

On a more academic level, we also shared research interest in our field—higher education administration. Sharing a research interest added to the harmonious mentor–protégé relationship. Departments will often attempt to pair faculty with graduate students who have similar research interests. We are still unsure if that was the reason we were paired, but it happened that we shared interests. Dr. Stanley studied and published on faculty professional development and the experiences of faculty of color in predominantly White colleges and universities, and Dr. Louis was interested in the Black student experience. Dr. Louis was specifically interested in their experiences at HBCUs. This allowed us to have open conversations about current research, conference proposals and presentations, and developments in the field. This common ground was particularly fertile with respect to research and the development of Dr. Louis's dissertation. Sometimes the articles he secured for her publications became articles he used for his own edification. Dr. Stanley researches minority faculty issues, and the articles Dr. Louis pulled all pertained to the topic. Dr. Louis's research strand is the HBCU experience; it was through reading her reference articles that he decided to focus on faculty issues at HBCUs for his dissertation. Our discussions were honest, well informed, and strewn with our personal experiences and became an ongoing dialogue that became even richer over time.

As a doctoral student, Dr. Louis reflected that it was wonderful to have an advisor who had a keen point of reference for his research. He felt free to express, explore, and inherently discover within his subject area. Dr. Stanley observed that he evolved from an unsure, somewhat unsettled, and nonnavigated student with much potential to a professional and directed educator. Dr. Louis possessed the ability to research a plethora of topics, but getting him to focus on a specific subject area in which he would eventually become an expert proved to be the task at hand. Having a common research interest made that fluidity possible: Differentiating areas may have easily resulted in conflict of topic choice, research direction, and even research methodology. Dr. Stanley's ability to mold and influence, with a sometimes firm but more often very subtle fashion, Dr. Louis as a doctoral student was simply a result of his viewing her as an expert in the field in which he was hoping to become a part of in the future.

Humility of graduate students is crucial to a positive mentor–protégé relationship because it allows the molding process to take place. The doctoral student has to be confident enough to have a grasp of the material and manner in which the program works. However, he or she must also be able to listen to and observe his or her mentor in order to develop the skills necessary for the field. Listening to Dr. Stanley and observing how she navigated faculty meetings or handled off-color comments in a tactful manner taught Dr. Louis how to have more poise in professional situations. A faculty member once commented, "This side of the department sure is getting dark!" which was a reference to Dr. Stanley and another faculty member of color having two offices next to each other. Although shocked and possibly offended, she dealt with the situation in a cordial fashion. This taught Dr. Louis much more beyond the articles and the research; it taught him how to navigate micro- and macroaggressions, difficult situations and dialogues, and the field. Humility is one factor that enables this nonverbal exchange to take place. Concurrently, faculty mentors should be open to listen to the viewpoints of their protégés. Having a greater comprehension of their passions and aspirations makes the communication relevant and in the end beneficial to both parties in the mentoring relationship.

Differences

Even the best mentor–protégé relationships have their rough spots; we were no exception. One difference was gender. An aspect of the relationship that was new, and required Dr. Louis's adjustment, was that Dr. Stanley is a woman. In Trinidad, Dr. Louis attended Queen's Royal College, a high school for young men. Subsequently, he attended Morehouse College, a historically Black college for men. His previous mentors, supervisors, and influences were mostly male. This created an extremely male dominant platform from which he launched into academia. Dr. Stanley, on the other hand, attended St. Hugh's High School, a high school for young women, ran by the Anglican Diocese of Jamaica. Subsequently, she spent her senior year of high school at Campion College, a coeducational school in Jamaica, before migrating to the United States. These experiences, coupled with being raised by a strong mother and even stronger maternal and paternal grandmothers, instilled in her a positive sense of self. In addition, she grew up in a close-knit family with a younger brother and five male cousins. Furthermore, she experienced positive male role models in her father, uncles, and maternal grandfather. In essence, she is assertive, strong, and confident around and with men.

Therefore, working and studying with Dr. Stanley was undeniably significant uncharted territory for Dr. Louis. The few studies that do examine cross-gender mentoring relationships in the academic setting seem to support Dr. Louis's experience (Chandler, 1996; Cronan-Hillix, Gensheimer, Cronan-Hillix, & Davidson, 1986). For example, in a study of psychology graduate students' perceptions of their mentoring relationships, "male graduate students tended to avoid female mentors disproportionately after controlling for the number of female faculty" (Chandler, 1996, p. 85). Several reasons are cited for this, including the notion that women and also women faculty of color are present in small numbers (particularly so in male-dominated fields) and also they are perceived as having "a real lack of power and influence in their department" (Chesler & Chesler, 2002, p. 51).

Dr. Louis reflects on the issues of power and influence and questions if he unintentionally listened less or with a more skeptical ear because Dr. Stanley is a woman. He does acknowledge, however, that he made decisions contrary to her counsel more than he did with his male mentors. He fought against teaching and the entire professoriate career, insisting he wanted to be an administrator; he fought against attending certain professional conferences for the same reason; and he fought against not maintaining his 100% student status and pursued a college-level position in student affairs during his dissertation phase, while she had fears of him not completing the doctoral program. Dr. Stanley recalled one experience where Dr. Louis turned in what he thought at the time was the first and only draft of his dissertation. She gave him specific feedback on the changes required. Dr. Louis flipped through the pages and seemed surprised by the feedback. He was also further taken aback when he had to go through subsequent edits before it was ready to go for full review with his dissertation committee. Dr. Stanley wondered if he would have reacted this way if she were male. Nonetheless, Dr. Louis recalled, she listened, she "rolled her eyes," she disagreed, but more than anything, she supported him. They had robust conversations about nonverbal behavior and how it can impact power, communication, and relationships, as well as its roots in culture, particularly the Caribbean culture.

Although gender may not have consciously made a distinctive difference in our cross-gender mentoring relationship, our Caribbean cultures came into play once again. In the British West Indies, there still exists an imbalance in gender equity (World Economic Forum, 2010). This is indicated by perceptions and acquisition of positions of power and influence. It is often seen and heard in the interactions and sentiments of males in the Caribbean. According to the World Economic Forum's *The Global Gender Gap Report 2010*, Trinidad and Tobago ranked higher than the United States with respect to equity between genders. Jamaica ranked below. Interestingly, only two Caribbean countries ranked higher than the United States. This, however, gives a snapshot of the social environment in which both our parents were raised and we were consequently raised. Men had, and still do have, an advantage over women with respect to access to education, resources, and opportunities. Thus, from Dr. Louis's standpoint of the relationship, he may possess unconscious vestiges that were male dominant. Being an advocate for diversity, he works tirelessly to minimize his biases, but his actions and subsequent reactions may reveal that some still exist. He is conscious of Dr. Stanley's position of power and influence in the mentoring relationship and respects it. Furthermore, it has allowed him to witness directly the obstacles, criticisms, sacrifices, and hardships she has endured, and continues to endure, as a Black woman (Chandler, 1996) to remain a successful and prominent figure on a large public research-intensive university campus. This is a lesson he probably could not have learned in another situation and setting.

Protégé Section: Dr. Louis's Reflections

When I first entered the higher education doctoral program at Texas A&M University, Dr. Stanley was not my faculty advisor; however, I was assigned to her as a graduate research assistant. So, I found myself discussing the graduate education process with one faculty member and research with another. This arrangement seemed awkward and disjointed, although I presumed that this may be more common than not. However, once I began retrieving articles for Dr. Stanley and realized her focus was aligned with mine, I opted for her to be my advisor. "Pulling articles" was a major portion of my role and responsibilities at the time, and it was not done blindly. When I saw the titles of the articles and started to skim the content of them, I began to discuss them with Dr. Stanley. Soon I started to discuss what I wanted to pursue as a research topic, not just for the dissertation but also for life. She encouraged me to pursue what I was passionate about and not the "buzz topic" of the time. It was through this interaction that I decided to ask her to be my advisor and chair my dissertation committee.

The aspect that I look back most fondly on, and maybe with a little more maturity today, is the ability to speak freely about difficult issues with Dr. Stanley. Whether it was a course I was taking, another faculty member with whom I had a difference in opinion, professional development decisions, my father's illness, or even a choice to move to a new city and get married when I was "all but dissertation," she was ready and receptive. Dr. Stanley was a straight shooter and gave me the truth on a platter. She did this always with the opening, "Dave, you have to think about this and make your own decision, but . . ." It was after that "but" the heavy truth came out. That brutal honesty bred my trust in her. I always knew I may not like the response, but I knew it was the truth, and it was said with my best interest in mind.

Being open to learning from a mentor is essential to a successful doctoral student. This did not mean I never resisted Dr. Stanley's tutelage; in fact, it is within the resistance that I learned some of my most valuable lessons. It was here that she and I engaged in heated discussions about the profession. We were divided on faculty life and an administrative career, and we disagreed on approaches to life, but more than anything I gained new perspectives, which I use today. I viewed administration as the manner in which I could have an impact on students in higher education, and Dr. Stanley consistently told me, "That is all well and good, but you can also make great inroads through your research. You can inform or change the direction of the field with approaches. It doesn't mean you can't be an administrator, but the scholarly portion is a vehicle to create and inform change." I listened to her, but I continued on my journey. However, through all my experiences I heard her voice and it brought new perspectives. I viewed higher education from more than my myopic student affairs lens. It was not until years later that I completely understood what she was trying to tell me, and at that juncture I had been teaching for seven years in an adjunct capacity and realized that my classroom interaction and my theoretical beliefs became valuable to student development. I saw through the eyes of my mentor, yet I did not lose myself. These experiences bleed into my advising of master's and doctoral students; I have openness to their perspectives, yet I have the tenacity to state mine. This benefits me more as I engage in challenging dialogues with faculty. It enables me to be receptive yet strong in my views and not be obstinate. My wanting to learn from my mentor was the key that made the relationship from my perspective very beneficial.

Dr. Stanley was and continues to be a model for me in two very specific ways. First, she is a strong, Caribbean woman who had entered higher education and attained her doctorate. Second, even though at the time I was bent on becoming an administrator, Dr. Stanley represented the goal I set for myself academically and the path that I wanted to pursue. Today, I see her as a model for my new adventure as a tenure-track assistant professor. I examine her journey and her progress and utilize it as the blueprint for what I am about to embark upon. She, in many ways, gave credence to my aspirations as a Caribbean immigrant and as a faculty member.

Mentor Section: Dr. Stanley's Reflections

When I was heavily recruited from The Ohio State University to Texas A&M University in 1999, I knew what I wanted to accomplish. My goal was to get tenure. However, this was not that easy, because I came with time on the tenure clock and also had administrative responsibilities as associate director of the Center for Teaching Excellence. So, one of the keys to success was having a mature and sophisticated graduate student who could assist me with my research. In addition, I needed someone who could be independent and follow through on assignments with little nudging. Dr. Louis is correct. It was pure coincidence that he was assigned to me as a graduate research assistant.

Dr. Louis proved to be a delight to work with. He not only assisted me with my research program but also helped me to prepare for teaching classes each week. Having someone with his skills and maturity level made my life on the tenure track easier, and the mentoring relationship seemed natural given our Caribbean background and culture. One of the elements of our mentor–protégé relationship that would surface now and then was our relationship outside of the department and how he addressed me. The issue was his calling me by my first name. There was no specific incident or experience where this came up; however, we did notice that some of the faculty in the department and the college as a whole encouraged their students to call them by their first name. Is this gender related? Several of my female colleagues have shared this phenomenon with me. For example, in their examination of gender-informed mentoring strategies for women engineering scholars, Chesler and Chesler (2002) discussed interpersonally and institutionally generated gender roles and dynamics that make the construction and maintenance of mentoring relationships difficult for women in male-dominated fields. Too often in the academy we observe these gender roles and dynamics, and they are rarely discussed. The dominant mentoring style is still based on a traditional model of male socialization (Chesler & Chesler, 2002).

Although some of my colleagues had no qualms about accompanying or inviting graduate students out to socialize or allowing them to address them by their first name, this was not something that I either wanted to encourage or felt comfortable doing. I saw this as a way to maintain boundaries and respect for position and authority. Dr. Louis, however, did not assume anything. I attribute this to our Caribbean culture. In fact, I remember telling Dr. Louis that I cannot be a friend *and* an advisor. While he was working on his degree with me, it had to be the latter. In addition, I assured him, as I do all my graduate students, that the day he walked across the stage, the relationship would proceed to a different level, and he could call me Christine. It is a rare occasion when he addresses me by my first name. I still address my former dissertation advisor as Dr. Johnson.

The educational system in Jamaica is patterned after the British system. Teachers, elders, and anyone in a position of authority or power are respected and in many instances emulated or revered. I could not imagine a situation wherein I would address a teacher or professor by his or her first name. In addition, I certainly would not expect to socialize with him or her. Although there were no explicit boundaries drawn between teachers and students, it was clearly unspoken and understood.

Our mentoring relationship almost came to a halt when Dr. Louis decided that he was leaving to take a full-time administrative position having not yet completed his doctorate. However, he assured me that he would finish. In fact, he made every effort to stay in touch and would schedule meetings to discuss his data analysis and his drafts. Upon reflection, I will say that much of my reaction to his leaving for the position without finishing his dissertation came from a place of fear that (a) he would not finish the program, (b) he would have lived up to yet another stereotype, and (c) I had failed in my role as an advisor and mentor. A stereotype that often plagues many talented graduate students of color is that they are perceived as not being able to complete dissertation course work or the dissertation. However, he proved me wrong. When it came time for his dissertation defense, not only was he ready, but he also delivered on his defense superbly. The committee remarked on the quality of the dissertation writing and the sophistication of his data analysis, findings, and implications for further research.

Conclusion: Lessons Learned From Each Other

From Dr. Louis

As in any mentor–protégé relationship, each individual enters with his or her own expectations about the experience. Looking back, I started the doctoral program not well focused, and I was seeking guidance and help in learning about my intended field because my undergraduate degree was not in education, and I was not privy to courses that dealt with the philosophy of education or pedagogy. I believe if I had had more insight into education as a major or minor, I would have had a greater context for higher education. I had to learn about the context in my master's program and through my experiences at Columbia. Therefore, having a sounding board and someone I could have discussions with about school issues or life in general was of the utmost importance. I wanted the experience to prepare me and shape me into a professional. As a result of Dr. Stanley's insights, experiences, counsel, and mentoring, my personality and view of the field has drastically changed. In retrospect, I realize we approached the same field from different angles: she from faculty life to administration and me from administration to faculty life. Regardless, the lessons I learned about being Black and an immigrant in American higher education have become invaluable, lessons such as having tactfulness in professional settings, being thorough in my research and presentations, and knowing regardless of proficiency that there is always an undercurrent of "otherness." This otherness is that of being both Black in

America and an immigrant: You become the perpetual outsider. Understanding and addressing this personally and in context is important to my career. Thus, my expectations and the impact her mentoring has had on me for my career have been fulfilled.

The pivotal lesson for me as I enter my faculty appointment is that doctoral students at times may not know what they truly want out of their schooling and life. Dr. Stanley taught me three key things from our mentoring relationship: (a) Always be open and listen to your students and protégés; (b) be very honest in your interactions and advice; and (c) even if your protégés do the complete opposite of what you advise, be there to support, because what they need more than anything else is the knowledge that their mentor cares. I learned the bulk of these lessons after I was no longer Dr. Stanley's graduate assistant. I was not able to grasp some of these lessons then, but I am now. Thus, the mentoring process is not simply, if at all, formalized by station. In fact, once yoked, the mentoring process and relationship developed, if positive, lasts a lifetime. Regardless of how far I venture in my career, I believe I will always value her opinion, and I am even more certain that I will seek her counsel from afar.

An understanding of the nuances, expectations, and stress of faculty life is another great lesson I have learned from my interactions with Dr. Stanley. I have observed her scholarly works, journeys, and collaborative efforts with colleagues and students. I have had the opportunity to examine the faculty life from a very intimate perspective: contributing to the expectations that come with teaching, research, and service at a major research university; balancing the personal life with the professional life while on the tenure track; developing a research agenda; negotiating and navigating local, state, national, and international networks; being a good citizen; participating in faculty governance; meeting deadlines associated with a variety of professional activities; developing and practicing effective time management; and adjusting to life as a senior-level university administrator. Utilizing these lessons and integrating them into my own professional career is and will continue to be priceless!

From Dr. Stanley

Dr. Louis has now come "full circle" in terms of actualizing his career goals. Although he thought the faculty life was not for him during and after graduate school, it is amazing to see how much he has stretched himself over the years. It is now five years since he completed his dissertation. Prior to his current tenure-track faculty appointment, he established himself as a very capable administrator, having held several administrative positions and taught courses, off and on, for the higher education and student affairs program. Now, he is more focused as a faculty member. He will be able to rely on and use his administrative experiences to complement theoretical research, especially when teaching in the classroom setting. There are very few junior faculty in higher education administration who have this background.

We continue to visit from time to time, and after working diligently and strategically he became a tenure-track assistant professor in August 2011. I have learned a great deal from him over our 12-year mentoring relationship, as it should be. The mentor–protégé relationship is reciprocal. He has taught me to be more patient and to allow others to make their own meaning out of life and career goals. Sharing a common culture is unique, as you have learned from our story here in this chapter. However, sharing a common culture does not mean that everyone from Jamaica or Trinidad or other Caribbean islands will have similar experiences. Again, the interacting layers of gender, class, and culture make for a different yet interesting tapestry. We simply need more stories from other Caribbean scholars to either add to or counter our own experiences.

The role of a mentor is complex, and there are different types of mentor–protégé relationships. I have learned that protégés have different needs, goals, and expectations. Dr. Louis made and explored his own path. My role was and continues to be to (a) support, (b) challenge, and (c) be honest. Constructive feedback is critical to any mentoring relationship. There were times I had to tell him what he *needed to hear* as opposed to what he *wanted to hear*. The essence of any meaningful mentoring relationship, regardless of gender, class, or culture, as we have shared from our own personal experiences in this chapter, is built on honesty and trust.

References

Bowen, D. D. (1986). The role of identification in mentoring female protégés. *Group and Organization Studies, 11,* 61–74.

Brass, D. J. (1985). Men's and women's networks: A study of interaction patterns and influence in an organization. *Academy of Management Journal, 28,* 327–343.

Cafarella, R. S. (1992). *Psychosocial development of women: Linkages to teaching and leadership in adult education* (Information Series No. 350; ERIC Document Reproduction Service No. ED 354386). Columbus: ERIC Clearinghouse on Adult, Career, and Vocational Education, Center on Education and Training for Employment, The Ohio State University.

Chandler, C. (1996). Mentoring and women in academia: Reevaluating the traditional model. *National Women's Studies Association Journal, 8*(3), 79–100.

Chesler, N. C., & Chesler, M. A. (2002). Gender-informed mentoring strategies for women engineering scholars: On establishing a caring community. *Journal of Engineering Education, 91*(1), 49–55.

Clawson, J. G., & Kram, K. E. (1984). Managing cross-gender mentoring. *Business Horizons, 27*(3), 22–32.

Cronan-Hillix, T., Gensheimer, L. K., Cronan-Hillix, W. A., & Davidson, W. S. (1986). Students' views of mentors in psychology graduate training. *Teaching of Psychology, 13*(3), 123–127.

Fitt, L. W., & Newton, D. A. (1981). When the mentor is a man and the protégé is a woman. *Harvard Business Review, 59,* 56–60.

Kram, K. E. (1985). *Mentoring at work: Developmental relationships in organizational life.* Glenview, IL: Scott Foresman.

Lean, E. (1983). Cross-gender mentoring: Downright upright and good for productivity. *Training and Development Journal, 37*(5), 61–65.

Morgan, L. M., & Davidson, M. J. (2008, March). Sexual dynamics in mentoring relationships: A critical review. *British Journal of Management, 19*(S1), S120–S129.

Ragins, B. R. (1990). A role theory approach to gender and mentorship. In *Working Paper No. 9-90.* Milwaukee, WI: Marquette Business School.

Ragins, B. R., & Cotton, J. (1999). Mentor functions and outcomes: A comparison of men and women in formal and informal mentoring relationships. *Journal of Applied Psychology, 84*(4), 529–550.

Ragins, B. R., & McFarlin, D. B. (1990). Perceptions of mentor roles in cross-gender mentoring relationships. *Journal of Vocational Behavior, 37*(3), 321–339.

Stanley, C. A. (2006). *Faculty of color: Teaching in predominantly White colleges and universities.* Bolton, MA: Anker.

Turner, C. S., González, J. C., & Wood, J. L. (2008). Faculty of color in academe: What 20 years of literature tells us. *Journal of Diversity in Higher Education, 1*(3), 139–168.

Wheeler, P. H. (1992). Fallacies about recruiting and retaining people of color into doctoral programs of study. *Black Issues in Higher Education, 9*(10), 96.

Williams, E. (1993). *Education in the British West Indies.* New York, NY: A&B Distributors.

World Economic Forum. (2010). *The Global Gender Gap Report 2010.* Retrieved from http://www.weforum.org/issues/global-gender-gap

8

AUTOETHNOGRAPHY, INSIDER *TESTIMONIOS*, COMMON SENSE RACISM, AND THE POLITICS OF CROSS-GENDER MENTORING

Elvia Ramirez and Alfredo Mirandé

Existing research has made great strides in analyzing the challenges and opportunities associated with faculty–student mentoring relationships. However, research on same-race, cross-gender mentoring relationships in academia, particularly those involving Chicano and Chicana faculty and students, is still relatively scarce. In addition, few studies on student-faculty mentoring relationships have been grounded in critical race theory (CRT) and intersectional frameworks.

This chapter examines the importance of mentorship for women, people of color, and women of color in higher education. Drawing from CRT and intersectional and women-of-color feminist frameworks, we describe, via the use of personal narrative and *testimonio*, the cross-gender mentee–mentor relationship and experiences of two social scientists, a Chicano professor and a Chicana graduate student.

We begin by providing a brief overview of empirical research on mentoring before turning to a discussion of the development of new race-based and intersectional theoretical approaches in the social sciences. We then describe, using personal *testimonios*, how a highly unequal and politicized academic milieu shaped our mentoring relationship.

Research on Mentoring Relationships

According to Campbell and Campbell (2007), *mentoring* refers to "any situation in which a more-experienced member of an organization maintains a relationship with a less-experienced, often new, member and provides information, support, and guidance for the purpose of enhancing the latter's chances of organizational success" (p. 136). Within the context of academia, mentoring refers to the process by which an experienced faculty member acts as a guide, role model, and teacher and sponsor of a graduate student or junior faculty member (Harden, Clark, Johnson, & Larson, 2009). Scholars typically differentiate between two types of mentoring functions: career/instrumental and emotional/psychosocial support (Kram, 1985). Career/instrumental support refers to mentorship that helps advance a mentee's career (e.g., via sponsorship, exposure, coaching), whereas emotional/psychosocial support consists of counseling, friendship, acceptance, and confirmation.

Because the overwhelming majority of professors in U.S. doctoral institutions are White and male, the most prevalent faculty–student relationships consist of White and male faculty mentoring not only Whites but also students of color and women (Schlosser & Foley, 2008). Mixed-race and mixed-gender mentor–protégé dyads are thus ostensibly quite common in academia. Still, several studies have reported that women and students of color typically have less access to faculty mentors than White males do (Bizzari, 1995; Ragins & Cotton, 1991).

According to some scholars, mixed-race and mixed-gender faculty–student mentoring relationships are no less effective than race- and gender-matched mentoring relationships, and some researchers (e.g., Cole & Barber, 2003) have contended that race and gender are of little import in the mentoring relationship. Other scholars, however, have maintained that race and gender do matter. Ragins (1997), for example, argued, "The degree of diversity in the mentoring relationship should be inversely related with the provision of psychosocial and role modeling functions" (p. 503). In other words, individuals often identify and feel most comfortable with those with whom they share a common identity (e.g., same gender or race) and relate the least to those they perceive as different (Sosik & Godshalk, 2005). Consistent with this perspective, Allen et al. (2002) found that minority faculty presence is an important predictor of Black professional and educational attainment and that the mere presence of Black faculty is a source of validation and support for Black students.

Regardless of mentor–mentee racial/ethnic and gender background, ethical issues can emerge in faculty–student mentoring relationships, particularly in light of the inherent power differentials embedded in such relationships. According to Schlosser and Foley (2008), some of these ethical concerns include issues of power, inappropriate relationships, boundary problems, and mentor competence. Potential ethical issues emerging from cross-gender mentoring dyads, specifically, consist of male mentor insensitivity toward female mentee roles (e.g., child care, elder care) and dual-career couples, inappropriate sexual relationships, and female mentees not being seen as serious about their academic careers (Schlosser & Foley, 2008). Harden et al. (2009) asserted that sexist stereotypes about women (e.g., that they lack drive and commitment to their career; that they will leave graduate school because of familial obligations; and that they lack the personality traits deemed essential to career success, such as assertiveness and competitiveness) can also negatively shape their experiences with cross-gender mentoring relationships. Male professors may also feel discomfort mentoring women because they fear public perceptions of their relationships with female mentees and/or because they may genuinely feel uncomfortable with nonsexual relationships with women.

Notwithstanding the insights of the extant mentoring literature, significant gaps exist in our knowledge of mentoring relationships involving Chicano and Chicana faculty and students. To fill in this gap in the literature, we analyze our mentoring relationship via the lenses of CRT and intersectionality frameworks and through the use of personal *testimonios*.

Critical Race Theory, Intersectionality, and *Testimonios*

One of the most significant and challenging changes that occurred in the social sciences over the past 40 years or so has been the emergence of a number of new and critical-race-based theoretical paradigms and perspectives. CRT, for example, is a movement in law that emerged in the 1980s, and it positioned race at the center of legal analysis. Although its origins are in law (Mirandé, 2000), CRT was expanded and applied in education, sociology, and other social sciences. Valdes, Culp, and Harris (2002) noted that CRT challenges three basic beliefs about racial justice in the United States. The first and most persistent is that "race blindness" will eliminate racism. The second is that racism is a matter of individual prejudice rather than of systemic oppression. The third and final belief is that one can fight racism while ignoring sexism, homophobia, and other forms of oppression.

With the emergence of CRT, intersectionality, and other new theories, the tenets of scientism have been openly challenged and seriously undermined. Rosaldo (1989), for example, noted that a sea of change in the social sciences in recent years has eroded once-dominant absolute, timeless, and universal conceptions of truth and objectivity, so that "the social sciences agenda has shifted from a search for universal truths and law-like generalizations to political processes, social changes, and human differences" (p. 21). Today, terms such as *objectivity, neutrality,* and *impartiality* refer to "subject positions" and are arguably no more or less valid than those proposed by researchers who are more engaged and knowledgeable and no less perceptive social actors (p. 21). There has been a parallel concern with developing new methods such as autoethnography, *testimonios,* and outsider narratives.

Because of the impact of CRT and cultural studies, the narratives of previously excluded groups have been slowly incorporated into law and the social sciences. As part of the movement to incorporate the voices of excluded groups, new methodologies and research tools have been introduced. In a classic article on legal education, Montoya (1994) used her personal story and the concepts of *Trenzas y Greñas* (braids and disheveled hair) to weave together a narrative about the challenges and obstacles she faced at Harvard Law School as a working-class Chicana from New Mexico. Chávez (2012) similarly employed autoethnography—that is, a research methodology that "uses one's own experience in a culture to look at our culture" (p. 341)— as the research and methodological tool of choice for Chicanas and other marginalized groups. She argued, "*Testimonios,* autobiographical educational experiences, must be used as valid ethnographic research to contribute to existing knowledge around issues of educational equity" (p. 334).

This chapter uses the narrative style of CRT and autoethnography to elaborate on the mentor–mentee relationship of two Chicano and Chicana academics. Subscribing to the theoretical tenets of CRT, we challenge the prevalent assumptions in academia that "race blindness" will eliminate racism and that race is a matter of individual prejudice rather than of systemic racism. We also adopt an intersectional feminist framework (Baca Zinn & Thornton Dill, 1996; Crenshaw, 1998) that posits that you cannot eliminate racism without at the same time addressing sexism, homophobia, classism, and other forms of oppression. We hope that sharing our experiences will help to elucidate the benefits of, isolate the obstacles we faced in, and describe how we were able to transcend challenges peculiar to our same-race, cross-gender mentoring experience.

Cross-Gender Mentor–Mentee Relationship: Our *Testimonios*

Mentee Statement: Elvia's Testimonio

I am a first-generation Chicana college graduate from a working-class background. I grew up in a poor, segregated, and historically Mexican barrio in Southern California. Though my parents had very little formal schooling, did not speak English, and could not read or write (in either English or Spanish), they placed a very high premium on education and instilled a love for learning in me. My dad, in particular, was very supportive of my educational endeavors and had very high expectations for me. While I was growing up, for example, he would always proudly proclaim to friends and relatives, "Mi'ja va ser una abogada o inginiera" ("My daughter will one day be an attorney or an engineer"). My family's support and high expectations thus provided me with the motivation, determination, and *ganas* (desire) to excel in school.

With the unwavering support of my parents, and with the guidance of counselors from the Early Academic Outreach Program (a University of California college outreach program), I enrolled as an undergraduate student at University of California, Riverside (UCR). It was while taking sociology and ethnic studies courses at UCR that I first met Alfredo. I had heard many great things about him from other students, so I decided to enroll in one of his upper-division courses, Law and Subordination. His class was undoubtedly among the best courses I took as an undergraduate student. Given my positive experience in his class and the great rapport I had established with him, I asked Alfredo to be my faculty mentor for both the university and the Sociology Honors programs. I had been invited to participate in these two programs based on my GPA and thought it would look great on my résumé and serve as excellent preparation for graduate school. As a participant in these programs, I was expected to conduct research on a topic of my choosing and write a thesis. I chose to write my honors thesis on a labor union and *mutualista* (mutual aid society) founded by my great-grandfather in the early 1900s. Alfredo guided me through the various research and writing phases and even attended the conference where I presented my research findings before fellow students and faculty.

After graduating with my bachelor's degree, I enrolled in the sociology doctorate program at UCR. I entered graduate school with much enthusiasm and was hopeful that it would be a positive and intellectually stimulating experience. Graduate school, however, turned out to be an incredibly difficult experience for me. Though I felt, and was, prepared academically, I was not prepared for the politics and inequalities embedded in the graduate schooling process. As Alfredo explains in his *testimonio*, the graduate program I attended has a long history of racialized ideological divisions and conflicts. Though these departmental conflicts flared up and became publicly manifest only after I had completed my course work and exams and moved out of the area, they nonetheless surfaced in subtle (and not so subtle) ways while I was there and negatively impinged on my experiences as a graduate student.

Though most faculty in my graduate program were friendly, a few denigrated my research interests and perspectives, questioned my presence in the program, and were otherwise hostile toward me. For example, one faculty member was openly hostile toward me because I had stated in class that as a Chicana I felt obliged to not only study issues concerning discrimination and social inequality processes impacting Chicano, Chicana, Latina, and Latino communities but also *do* something about it. In response to my comment, the professor pounded his fist on the table for what seemed like half an hour and admonished us that if we desired to be "political activists" we did not belong in graduate school. I felt this professor was extremely intolerant of competing perspectives in the classroom and created a hostile classroom environment; a few students and I even approached the department chair to raise concerns about this professor's behavior in class. Still another faculty member stated that students from low-income and working-class backgrounds did not belong in graduate school and were unfit for academic careers. This professor also suggested that graduate students were only "ghettoizing" themselves if they specialized in fields like race, class, and gender studies. All in all, the main socializing message I received in several of my courses was that only White-, middle-class-, and male-centric perspectives were legitimate and that people like me (i.e., a working-class Chicana) were not welcome in academia.

What made the graduate school experience much more difficult was the lack of substantive faculty and student diversity in the department. Though UCR boasts of a substantial representation of Chicanos, Chicanas, Latinas, and Latinos at the undergraduate level, the graduate student and faculty populations on campus are predominantly White. The lack of diversity at the graduate student and faculty levels translated into a lack of a support network within the department, as well as a lack of intellectual and personal validation from peers and faculty. Were it not for the support of family, friends, and mentors like Alfredo, it is likely that I would have left my doctoral program.

Alfredo's mentorship and support were crucial to my survival in graduate school. Unlike mainstream faculty, Alfredo validated my scholarly interests and perspectives. He also supported me at every step of the graduate schooling process. For example, he supplied me with data for my master's thesis and helped establish a writing group, *Onda Chicana*, in order to provide me and other students with critical feedback on our work. He was also instrumental in helping me complete my written and oral qualifying exams. I still vividly recall that he took sparkling cider and *pan dulce* (Mexican sweet bread) to my oral qualifying exams in order to celebrate my successful transition to ABD (all but dissertation) status. It was these and other gestures that demonstrated Alfredo's unwavering support for me and commitment to helping me succeed in the program.

Being a student in Alfredo's graduate-level courses was also an intellectually exhilarating experience. It was because of his courses that I became conversant in Chicano and Chicana social science theories and paradigms and learned to appreciate the importance of organic and subaltern epistemologies. Moreover, Alfredo appreciated my contributions to classroom discussion and was open to competing perspectives. On some occasions I expressed disagreement with his views, but he never responded with hostility or belittlement. Alfredo also has a great sense of humor, which made his classes all the more enjoyable and exciting.

Alfredo was also extremely supportive during the dissertation and academic job search phases. He always promptly gave me feedback on my dissertation, despite the geographical distance between us. After completing my qualifying exams, I moved to Sacramento in order to be closer to my husband, who had been offered a tenure-track position at California State University, Sacramento. I was thus commuting back and forth between Sacramento and Southern California to visit family and maintain contact with my faculty advisors. Alfredo always made time for me to discuss my dissertation while I was in town. Moreover, when it came time to navigate the academic job market, he wrote very strong letters for me, helped prepare me for my job interviews, and helped me negotiate competing job offers. I had been offered three different tenure-track positions, and he advised me on how to strategically negotiate for things like research start-up funds, teaching load, and salary.

In addition to providing me with career-related support, Alfredo provided me with psychosocial support, particularly during times of familial crises. For example, my brother (my only sibling) developed a terminal illness and passed away while I was in graduate school. While my brother was hospitalized, and even after his death, Alfredo, who is also a lawyer, offered to represent him in court and help resolve a legal dispute of his. Alfredo provided us with his legal expertise and services for free (pro bono); this kind and supportive gesture meant one less source of stress for my family during a time of extreme emotional turmoil. Despite the various familial obligations and difficulties that I experienced during my graduate schooling years, Alfredo was extremely supportive, always maintained high expectations for me, and never questioned my commitment to an academic career.

Overall, Alfredo has proven to be a wonderful mentor, advisor, and professor. Nevertheless, there were some challenges associated with our cross-gender mentoring relationship. For example, I believe that we could have had a much closer relationship if we had been of the same gender. Other female graduate students in the department appeared to have much closer relationships with their female faculty mentors. For example, some of my female classmates would meet with their female faculty mentor for lunch on a weekly basis and/or play sports together; they also confided their personal troubles and struggles (e.g., with boyfriends, spouses) to their mentors.

Although Alfredo and I had a strong mentor–protégé relationship, I did not have the same degree of intimacy with Alfredo that some of my female classmates appeared to share with their female mentors. Moreover, though Alfredo and I did interact with each other outside the classroom setting, these interactions were not of the same frequency or intensity as those involving my female classmates and their female faculty mentors. This relative lack of closeness with my faculty mentor created additional stress for me, because I felt I could not confide my personal struggles as a Chicana/Latina woman to someone in my department.

I believe Alfredo and I did not forge a much closer relationship because of the greater public scrutiny that cross-gender mentoring relationships elicit. Unlike same-gender mentoring relationships, there exists the potential for damaging gossip and innuendo about possible nonprofessional (intimate) involvement in heterosexual cross-gender mentoring relationships. This was made painfully clear when a male professor remarked, "I'm jealous!" when he saw Alfredo and I having lunch at a restaurant close to campus. I felt that professor was insinuating that Alfredo and I had an intimate, unprofessional relationship and that he was "jealous" that he did not have one with me (or with some other female graduate student). A student also once "jokingly" intimated that Alfredo and I had an unprofessional intimate relationship. I was extremely offended by these sexist comments and realized then that there were some disadvantages associated with cross-gender mentoring relationships. However, I did not let these sexist comments discourage me from seeking mentorship and support from Alfredo or any other faculty member on campus. The support my husband provided me as I confided these issues to him also helped me navigate and recover from these negative, oppressive experiences.

Another challenge associated with our mentor–mentee relationship revolved around issues concerning intellectual mentorship. Although Alfredo is an amazing scholar and mentor, I feel that a Chicana professor would have been able to provide me with stronger intellectual mentorship in the field of Chicana/Latina feminisms. I do not feel I received sufficient mentorship in this area, given the lack of representation of Chicana/Latina feminist scholars on campus. In fact, during my undergraduate and graduate schooling years, Chicana/Latina professors were scarcely represented on campus. Prior to my graduation from UCR, my department had never had a Chicana/Latina in its tenure-track or tenured faculty ranks. Thus, I always felt a void in my intellectual mentorship, and it was a void that neither Alfredo nor other non-Chicana/Latina faculty members in the department could fill. I attempted to overcome this challenge by forming peer support networks with Chicana/Latina graduate students in other disciplines. We shared and discussed readings, engaged in conversations about Chicana/Latina feminisms, presented at women's studies conferences together (e.g., the annual *Mujeres Activas en Letras y Cambio Social* summer institute), and validated each other's research interests and academic work. The intellectual exchanges and interactions I had with fellow Chicana/Latina graduate students validated and solidified my interest in Chicana/Latina feminist frameworks and epistemologies, as well as helped sustain my enthusiasm for graduate school.

I also established successful mentor–protégé relationships with female faculty in the department. For example, with Joan Edwards,[1] I presented scholarly papers at academic conferences and submitted manuscripts for review and publication. Joan was instrumental in helping demystify the academic publication process for me and helped me prepare for the academic job market. I also established a successful mentoring relationship with Eliza Cohen, a remarkable and renowned scholar, critical pedagogue, and social justice advocate. Thus, despite the many inequities and barriers I encountered in graduate school, I had access to exceptional, genuinely supportive mentors who provided me with institutional support and helped me succeed in my doctorate program.

Overall, these experiences have taught me valuable lessons concerning mentorship and academic life. One of the most critical lessons is the importance of establishing mutually respectful, nonhierarchical, and genuinely supportive relationships between mentors and mentees. Although the professor-student relationship is inherently imbued with power differentials, Alfredo was nonelitist and nonhierarchical in his relationship with me and treated me as a colleague and emergent scholar rather than as a subordinate. For example, he recognized and appreciated my intellectual talents and abilities, did not exploit me as a student (as some faculty are known to do), and never treated me in a condescending manner. These were some of the major reasons that I gravitated toward Alfredo and sought his mentorship. Now that I am a professor, I also attempt to minimize the hierarchy between students and myself, particularly because I want students to feel they can approach me for mentorship and support. For example, rather than maintain an elitist, distanced relationship with my students, I try to be as accessible to them as possible and try to get to know them on a more personal level. In particular, I attempt to develop meaningful relationships with my students both inside *and* outside the classroom setting.

Another key lesson I have learned is the importance of mentoring historically underrepresented students. As a substantial body of scholarly literature has patently demonstrated, the educational system is rife with inequalities and barriers that complicate these students' successful transitions through the educational pipeline. Consequently, racial/ethnic minority students, particularly

Chicanos, Chicanas, Latinas, and Latinos, are dramatically underrepresented at the highest level of the educational hierarchy: doctoral education. Given the dearth of historically underrepresented minorities in graduate school and academia, I feel it is imperative that we mentor underrepresented students and see it as our mission that they complete their undergraduate education and successfully transition into graduate school so that they can also one day occupy a position as faculty member in our nation's colleges and universities. Though graduate school and academia are undoubtedly difficult (and often oppressive) spaces to navigate, I believe it is much easier to challenge racial (and other) hierarchies in academia when there is a critical mass of minority students and faculty present in higher education, particularly one that is willing to speak truth to power and struggle for positive social change and equity within (and beyond) the university system. Faculty in research universities thus need to be especially attentive to historically underrepresented doctoral students' well-being and make sure they receive *both* instrumental support and psychosocial support and successfully transition into academia. As my experiences with Alfredo's mentorship clearly demonstrate, these "best mentoring practices" can make a world of difference for historically underrepresented students.

Mentor Statement: Alfredo's Testimonio

I was born in Mexico City as the youngest of three sons and migrated to the United States with my father and two brothers at the age of nine. My initial goal was to become a lawyer, but I changed my focus in high school when I decided that I wanted to be a high school social studies teacher and enrolled at Illinois State University and graduated with a BS. I subsequently earned a PhD from the University of Nebraska and a JD from Stanford and embarked on a career as a college professor. You could say that I never had a mentor until I entered law school after a long and successful academic career. I had my first Chicano/a teacher and mentor when I was in law school.

I remember meeting Elvia after returning to UCR from Stanford at the library and then running into her when I would walk back and forth between the library and my office. She later enrolled in one of my undergraduate classes, Law and Subordination, where I quickly saw that she was always prepared, had excellent analytical skills, and wrote very well. She had selected a topic that she was passionate about for her undergraduate honors thesis and asked me to supervise it. I was immediately blown away when I read her written work not only because her writing was excellent and seamless but also because her scholarship was as well. It was extraordinary to find an undergraduate student who had such advanced conceptual, analytical, and writing skills.

I also recall that I was on the Graduate Admissions Committee when Elvia applied to the doctoral program. She had a stellar GPA, good GRE scores, and excellent letters, including one from me, but there was considerable resistance to providing her with fellowship support. Some of the Anglo faculty felt that her GRE scores were not that high and were reluctant to support her for a prestigious university fellowship. One member of the committee stated that he didn't believe that she needed financial support because her husband was a graduate student in the department. This was very frustrating and puzzling to me, because we had just finished discussing and voting to recommend several White students who had comparable or lower credentials and were not particularly gifted writers for fellowship support. I recall arguing vigorously for her admission and for fellowship support and pointing to the double standard in the department where Anglo students with comparable credentials, especially males, were readily supported and Latina, Latino, and African American candidates with comparable credentials were deemed to be less qualified.

I do not know whether Elvia picked me as a mentor or I picked her as a mentee, but I expect that it was a mutual decision. I certainly was predisposed to work with her because I saw her as a very talented and deserving student. One of the benefits of working with Elvia was that she not only was intelligent and highly motivated but also came into graduate school with good study habits and excellent verbal and writing skills. I did not have to work to make her, unlike many students, into a better writer. In that sense, she has always been a joy to work with. Another benefit is that she has always been very supportive of me. Yet, perhaps the greatest benefit is that she has gone on to become an excellent teacher and a successful academic and mentor.

When I recently visited the campus where she is teaching, I saw firsthand how Elvia has become a wonderful mentor herself and a role model, especially for Latinas. I should note that even as a graduate student she mentored a large number of undergraduate students and was selected to be the keynote speaker at the Raza Graduation Awards ceremony. I also know that wherever she is and wherever she goes she will continue to work with students and serve as an important mentor and role model for Latina and Latino students.

I think that one of the major obstacles Elvia has faced is a lack of appreciation of her abilities and talents, as well as a lack of support by the department. I vividly recall that in a required core class, a senior faculty member in the department berated Elvia, a first-year graduate student, in front of the class, but she ably and bravely defended herself during class discussion. Elvia was hurt and taken aback by the comments and lack of support by other faculty, but she stood her ground and went on to distinguish herself as a graduate student.

Once Elvia settled on a topic for her dissertation, she worked rapidly and independently. Most of the suggestions I made on the dissertation revolved around its organization, not the writing. She was able to work with little or no supervision and finished quickly. Other problems that she encountered were related to gender and her role as a wife and, eventually, mother. She and her husband are both in the same field; he finished his degree and accepted a position before her studies were completed. The job market proved to be more difficult when she began a job search, because it was important for Elvia to be near her husband. I know that she had to forgo several excellent job opportunities because accepting those positions would have separated her from her family.

Elvia also had some personal family problems in her life, which impacted her. While she was working on her dissertation, her brother developed a terminal illness and passed away. This was incredibly difficult and painful not only because she lost her brother but also because she had to assume many responsibilities at home and spent a lot of time traveling between Northern California and her hometown. Thus, not unlike many other Chicanas, she had to simultaneously assume a lot of family obligations and responsibilities while completing her graduate work, and this was definitely an obstacle to her rapid completion of the PhD.

I take a lot of pride in my mentoring relationship with Elvia not only because of her unique talents but also because it proved to be a very successful cross-gender relationship. I have mentored a number of students over the years, but most of my mentees, particularly at the graduate level, have been men. I have often reflected on and pondered my tendency to work more closely with my male students. It is somehow always easier to develop close mentoring relationships that extend beyond the classroom with members of one's gender. For example, I would often invite students whom I worked closely with to go out for a drink at the Pub, which is the local watering hole on campus; to attend meetings or protests off campus; or to go to a local sporting event. I have generally been more reserved in socializing with my female students, and I have worked hard to break down these barriers.

I believe that one of the factors that facilitated the development of a successful mentor–mentee relationship with Elvia is that a group of Chicano and Chicana graduate students and faculty developed an informal reading and research group where we would meet weekly or bimonthly to discuss various issues and topics. We called the group *Onda Chicana*, and it func- tioned successfully for several years. We would discuss someone's master's thesis, professional paper, or PhD topic. We also shared, commented on, and critiqued works in progress and explored possible cooperative projects. The group involved women and men and faculty and graduate students in various disciplines in the humanities, social sciences, and education and proved to be a great vehicle for informal mentoring and socializing.

Although Elvia represents a high point in my career as a mentor, unfortunately, I have had some mentoring relationships that have failed. As painful as it is, I will discuss one of these briefly in order to contextualize her experience and the departmental climate. However, I would first like to provide some background on my experiences in the department at UCR as a context for understanding these failed relationships.

Historically, the department has had a dearth of both faculty and students of color. When I first arrived there was one African American faculty member, and I was the only Chicano faculty. The department currently has two Chicano faculty, one Chicana faculty, and no African American or Asian American faculty, but there were no Chicana faculty during Elvia's tenure as a student. It is also a department that has had a great deal of conflict historically between the predominantly White male senior faculty and the faculty of color. This conflict has been reflected in relations among graduate students. The period when Elvia was close to finishing her doctorate proved to be an especially contentious one.

Lessons Learned: Failed Mentor–Mentee Relationships

One of my more memorable failed mentor–mentee relationships involved a White student who had been in an undergraduate gender class that I taught. He was not one of the best students, but he was enthusiastic and very personable, spoke a great deal in class, and was somewhat controversial because he often took positions in the class that were politically incorrect. There were a number of feminist students who frequently attacked him because he took unpopular views, which were perceived as sexist, if not misogynist. Although I disagreed with him, I admired the fact that he was not afraid to speak up in class and take unpopular positions, and he struck me as decent and sincere. During the course of the quarter, he would come to my office regularly and talk to me about the class, graduate school, and other matters. In his senior year, I allowed him to enroll in my graduate seminar, and he asked me to write him a letter of recommendation for graduate school. I wrote him a very good letter, and he was admitted into the graduate program. I was also on the Graduate Admissions Committee at the time, and I lobbied for his admission because I felt that he had potential, which was not reflected in his grades or test scores.

Once admitted into the program, he never took another class from me and also refused to talk to me or even acknowledge me in the hallways. The reasons for his behavior are unclear to me, and I can only speculate about them. He came into the program at a particularly difficult time during which there was a great deal of conflict between the more progressive faculty and students and the senior predominantly White faculty. One thing is clear, and that is that once admitted he aligned himself with some of the mainstream faculty and students, people who were politically at odds with me and other faculty and students. The fact that there was a major split in the department at the time was unfortunate, because the division involved both faculty and graduate students. Once in the graduate program, he was accused of being not only sexist but also racist by some students, including several students of color. It seems that once aware of the split in the department, he opted to align himself with those whom he perceived had more power and control. Even though I was baffled by his bizarre actions and didn't understand why he refused to even look at me or acknowledge me in the hallways, it became clear that mentoring is not always a two-way street.

I have learned some important lessons from this and other failed mentoring experiences. One lesson is that mentoring relationships should be reciprocal. Also, my support of this student was premature, because we obviously failed in establishing a mentor–mentee relationship based on a solid foundation of mutual trust, commitment, respect, and support. I believe all of these elements are needed for a successful mentoring relationship.

Another important lesson learned is that, particularly in a highly conflicted or politicized environment, it is imperative to enter mentoring relationships with caution, recognizing that mentor–mentee relationships do not exist in a vacuum and always occur within a social and political, racial and gender context. Unfortunately, in a highly contested academic environment, too often students are forced to choose among faculty mentors, and there are political costs and benefits associated with these choices. Students who opt to work with mainstream faculty are more likely to receive more support from the department, such as fellowships, research assistantships, and teaching assistantships. Under these circumstances, students may come to the realization that it is in their best interests to work with and be mentored by mainstream faculty in the department. Those who opted to work with me, although receiving my full commitment, support, and loyalty, might receive less support from some of the faculty who were in the opposing camp.

In reflecting on Elvia's experience in the department, it is clear that race, class, and gender matter a great deal. She was a stellar student, one of the best students whom I have had in a long career. Yet, because she was a woman, working class, and of Mexican descent, she did not receive the support that she so richly deserved. Others, particularly male, middle-class, and White students, were far more likely to be identified as exceptional and strongly supported. They are endorsed for the more prestigious and lucrative university-wide fellowships, are given priority in assistantship allocations and lecturer assignments, and are more likely to be strongly supported in the job market.

Conclusion

Drawing on CRT, intersectionality, and autoethnography, this chapter presented personal *testimonios* to elucidate the mentor–mentee relationship of two academics, a Chicano professor and a Chicana graduate student, at a major research university. Although the relationship was mutually fulfilling and rewarding, it was not without major challenges and pitfalls.

Intersectionality theory (Baca Zinn & Thornton Dill, 1996; Crenshaw, 1998) cautions against a common tendency in the social sciences to essentialize race and gender and either assume that all people of color are the same or ignore racial differences among women. As applied to mentoring, an essentialist perspective would assume either that this experience is the same for Chicanos and Chicanas or that all women have comparable experiences, regardless of race or class.

Perhaps the major challenge and pitfall faced was that we had a cross-gender mentoring relationship that involved a Chicano faculty member and a Chicana mentee. Keenly aware of the obstacles and limitations of cross-gender relationships, we actively sought to overcome them. Alfredo realized that he was prone to develop intimate personal relationships and socialize less often with his female students than with his male students. Elvia was similarly aware of this tendency and felt offended when a faculty member remarked that he was "jealous" when he saw Elvia and Alfredo eating at a local restaurant near campus, implying something sexual or inappropriate in the relationship. But Elvia's concern extended beyond socializing. She also lamented that there was something substantively lacking in her mentee experience because she was not mentored by a Chicana and believed that a Chicana mentor would have provided her with a better grounding in feminist and intersectional theories. However, because both the mentor and the mentee worked to address and to transcend their gender differences, they were able to establish a successful mentoring relationship.

These experiences underscore the importance of autobiography and the personal *testimonios* and narratives of subordinated groups. Mirandé (2000), a CRT scholar, maintained not only that there is a need to incorporate the voices of excluded minorities but also that "the subordination of racial minorities is shaped more by shared understandings which define their subordination as normal than by overt racism" (p. 154). Paredes (1977) similarly argued that Chicanos and Chicanas are justified in being critical of social science, specifically anthropological, distorted depictions of Chicano and Chicana groups, but rejected the charge of racism, arguing that most anthropologists who conduct research on Chicanos and Chicanas are liberal and not racist or overtly anti-Chicano or anti-Chicana. We concur and believe that most faculty are also politically liberal and not overtly racist.

The behavior of liberal faculty relative to their treatment of racial minorities and women is paradoxical and best understood as being the result not of overt racism but of what CRT theorist Ian F. Haney López (2003) termed *common sense racism*. For example, when one looks more carefully, it is clear that the behavior of mainstream academics noted in this chapter is strikingly similar to that exhibited by superior court judges in nominating people to the Los Angeles grand jury. Haney López (2003) used the concept of common sense racism to explain the behavior of superior court judges' nominations because they ostensibly had liberal political beliefs and certainly did not intentionally exclude Mexicans from the grand jury. They did not, in other words, get up in the morning and say, "I am not going to submit any Mexican names today" (Haney López, 2003, p. 110). In fact, they insisted that they would love to have Mexicans on the grand jury, just as faculty in our program would readily say that they would love to have "qualified" students of color in their graduate program.

Each judge was asked to nominate two persons and knew that the grand jury was to be composed of a cross section of the population and that jurors had to have "sufficient knowledge of the English language" and "were to be of ordinary intelligence" (Haney López, 2003, p. 113). Although the judges acted independently, their nominations were incredibly uniform. In essence, they nominated people like themselves—relatively affluent White males. Nominees included their friends, acquaintances, and family members. Oscar Zeta Acosta, the attorney for the East LA 13, subpoenaed the judges to show that the grand jury was biased and racist. When Acosta confronted the judges about the absence of Mexicans and other minorities on the grand jury, the judges pulled the "meritocracy" card, insisting that all jurors had to be "qualified." They implicitly and unconsciously assumed that when they nominated people like them—White, male, and affluent—they were nominating people who were "qualified," but when they nominated Mexicans, they were nominating people who were "not qualified." Similarly, many White male faculty associated being qualified with people who are like themselves: White, male, and middle class.

In conclusion, we hope that the insights gleaned from our *testimonios* will help others develop mentoring relationships that will enhance the experiences and success of women, students of color, and women of color.

Realizing that the findings presented here are based on the personal *testimonios* of one mentor–mentee relationship, we invite other scholars to add to the research on the mentoring experiences of women, people of color, and women of color in order to further enhance our understanding of mentoring relationships as they facilitate the entrance of these groups into the academy.

Note

1. Except for the authors of this chapter and of the works referenced herein, we use pseudonyms for all of the individuals identified in this chapter.

References

Allen, W. R., Epps, E. G., Guillory, E. A., Suh, S. A., Bonous-Mammarth, M., & Stassen, M. (2002). Outsiders within: Race, gender, and faculty status in US higher education. In W. A. Smith, P. G. Altbach, & K. Lomotey (Eds.), *The racial crisis in American higher education: Continuing challenges for the twenty-first century* (pp. 189–220). Albany: State University of New York Press.

Baca Zinn, M., & Thornton Dill, B. (1996). Theorizing difference from multiracial feminism. *Feminist Studies, 2,* 321–331.

Bizzari, J. (1995). Women: Role models, mentors, and careers. *Educational Horizons, 73,* 145–152.

Campbell, T. A., & Campbell, D. E. (2007). Outcomes of mentoring at-risk college students: Gender and ethnic matching effects. *Mentoring and Tutoring, 15,* 135–148.

Chávez, M. S. (2012). Autoethnography, a Chicana's methodological research tool: The role of storytelling for those who have no choice but to do critical race theory. *Equity and Excellence in Higher Education, 45,* 334–348.

Cole, S., & Barber, E. (2003). *Increasing faculty diversity: The occupational choices of high-achieving minority students.* Cambridge, MA: Harvard University Press.

Crenshaw, K. (1998). A Black feminist critique of antidiscrimination law and politics. In D. Kaireys (Ed.), *The politics of law* (pp. 356–380). New York, NY: Basic Books.

Haney López, I. (2003). *Racism on trial: The Chicano fight for social justice.* Cambridge, MA: Harvard University Press.

Harden, S. L., Clark, R., Johnson, W. B., & Larson, J. (2009). Cross-gender mentorship in clinical psychology doctoral programs: An exploratory survey study. *Mentoring and Tutoring: Partnership in Learning, 17,* 277–290.

Kram, K. E. (1985). *Mentoring at work: Developmental relationships in organizational life.* Lanham, MD: University Press of America.

Mirandé, A. (2000). Revenge of the nerds, or postmodern "colored folk": Critical race theory and the chronicles of Rodrigo. *Harvard Latino Law Review, 4,* 153–197.

Montoya, M. E. (1994). Mascaras, trenzas, y greñas: Un/masking the self while un/braiding Latina stories and legal discourse. *Chicano-Latino Law Review, 15,* 1–37.

Paredes, A. (1977). On ethnographic work among minority groups: A folklorist's perspective. *New Scholar, 6,* 1–33.

Ragins, B. R. (1997). Diversified mentoring relationships in organizations: A power perspective. *Academy of Management Review, 22,* 482–521.

Ragins, B. R., & Cotton, J. L. (1991). Easier said than done: Gender differences in perceived barriers to gaining a mentor. *Academy of Management Journal, 19,* 97–111.

Rosaldo, R. (1989). *Culture and truth.* Boston, MA: Beacon Press.

Schlosser, L. Z., & Foley, P. (2008). Ethical issues in multicultural student-faculty mentoring relationships in higher education. *Mentoring and Tutoring: Partnership in Learning, 16,* 63–75.

Sosik, J. J., & Godshalk, V. M. (2005). Examining gender similarity and mentor's supervisory status in mentoring relationships. *Mentoring and Tutoring, 13,* 39–52.

Valdes, F., Culp, J. M., & Harris, A. P. (2002). *Crossroads, directions, and a new critical race theory.* Philadelphia, PA: Temple University Press.

9

ANALYSIS OF THE MENTOR–PROTÉGÉ NARRATIVES

Reflecting the Literature

Juan Carlos González and Caroline Sotello Viernes Turner

This chapter provides an analysis of the coauthored mentor–protégé narratives, comparing the resulting themes to the themes emerging from the literature review (chapter 1). This will be done in two sections. The first section provides a brief overview of the cross-race/ethnicity and cross-gender mentoring literature. In chapter 1, the literature was split into two parts: one that provided evidence that had a direct application to cross-race/ethnicity and cross-gender relationships, and another that provided evidence where scholars mentioned the direct–indirect relationship between mentoring and cross-race/ethnicity and cross-gender relationships. This first section will provide a theoretical model that integrates all pathways and challenges of both parts from chapter 1. This integration was necessary in order to create a unifying model including all the themes from the literature by which to compare to the narratives.

The second section will provide a comparison between the integrated literature model and the narratives. Only the themes from the literature that were also supported in the narratives will be addressed.

Summarizing the Cross-Race/Ethnicity and Cross-Gender Mentoring Literature

In reviewing the literature pertaining to mentoring opportunities and challenges across race/ethnicity and gender, we identified not only the work of scholars who directly addressed cross-race/ethnicity and cross-gender relationships but also scholarship that made indirect references to cross-race/ethnicity and cross-gender mentorships. Most of the scholarship reviewed addressed either cross-race/ethnicity or cross-gender mentorship; rarely did scholarship address both. Also, most scholarship either was singular in its focus on pathways for success in cross-race/ethnicity or cross-gender mentorships or specifically addressed the challenges encountered in mentorships that are not of the same race/ethnicity or gender. Figure 9.1 presents unique concepts encountered in the literature. Although Figures 1.1 and 1.2 in chapter 1 provided a more nuanced analysis on direct and indirect successful pathways and challenges, Figure 9.1 provides an integration of all these

Figure 9.1 Literature review of theoretical model encompassing successful pathways and challenges in cross-race and cross-gender mentoring relationships.

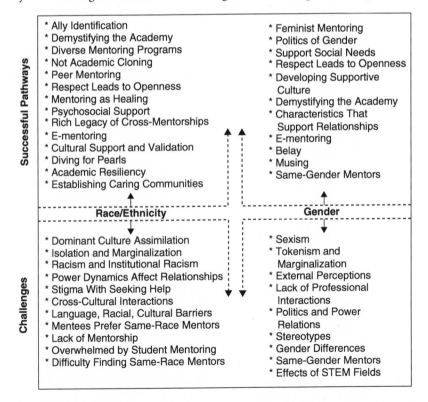

concepts for the purpose of comparing them to the themes that emerged from the coauthored narratives.

Figure 9.1 presents the overview of findings from the literature in four quadrants: (a) the top-left quadrant addresses cross-race/ethnicity successful pathways, (b) the top-right quadrant addresses cross-gender successful pathways, (c) the bottom-left quadrant addresses cross-race/ethnicity challenges, and (d) the bottom-right quadrant addresses cross-gender challenges.

In general, as shown in the top-left quadrant, authors mentioned that if cross-race/ethnicity mentorships are to be successful, scholars of color need not only different-race mentors but also mentoring from outside of their departments by scholars who may be of the same race. The authors of this literature indicated that same-race mentors can help them *demystify the academy* from the perspective of their race and culture. Faculty of color stated the importance of mentoring programs that address their cultural needs. In addition, faculty of color reported that they do not want to be paired with faculty mentors who are interested in *cloning* them. Some faculty of color indicated that they value *respect* by their mentors and appreciate mentors who provide them professional and social mentoring. *E-mentoring* was also found to be successful, along with mentorship models that provide *cultural support and validation*. For example, one article presented the idea of *diving for pearls*, which requires that the mentorship relationship, to be successful, will need to begin with significant commonalities, such as race or scholarly discipline. Building on commonalities, in order to attain *academic resiliency*, the mentor provides positive mentorship at the beginning of the relationship so that mentees have a sufficient foundation on which to build networks and knowledge to overcome potential challenges as their academic careers progress. Last, faculty of color talk about their success when paired with mentors who truly *care* about their overall development and engage them intellectually.

The top-right quadrant of Figure 9.1 documents factors contributing to successful career pathways for women. *Feminist mentorship* is identified as one factor, because it is guided by feminist theory, which values nonhierarchical relationships. For women mentees, it is also important that mentors help them navigate the *politics of gender* that marginalizes contributions by women, constraining their opportunities. *Supporting the social need* to balance career and personal and family life and *respecting* their scholarship are also identified as important to the success of women academics. To ensure the success of female academics, this literature recommends the *development of institutional cultures that are supportive* of women. Women faculty and women of color faculty also need help with *demystifying the academy*. Although women faculty do not need women mentors to be successful, research shows that they do need mentors who are good listeners, honest, nonjudgmental, persistent, and patient and who appreciate diversity. *E-mentoring* can also be beneficial in mentoring women and women of color. One program beneficial to women is called *belay*. This term refers to a concept where women are supported through institutional learning opportunities, psychosocial interventions that provide increased self-awareness and self-confidence, and encouragement to attain individual achievement. *Musing* is also noted for promoting success with women in academe. Musing includes mentorship that is peer based and given the opportunity to develop naturally. Last, research shows that providing *same-gendered mentorship* opportunities (when available) is important for the academic success of many women faculty.

In the bottom-left quadrant, scholarship on challenges rooted in race/ethnicity addresses how those mentoring scholars of color must not aim to *assimilate them to the dominant culture*, its values, and its methods of interacting within the academy. Such practices detract from success for scholars of color. *Isolation* and *marginalization* are experiences usually felt by faculty of color in predominantly White institutions. Facing *racism* and *institutional racism* also occurs for faculty of color, and mentors need to understand and mitigate such circumstances. Faculty of color also face challenges in mentoring relationships when their mentors use their power to consistently dominate their relationships so that the mentee does not develop his or her own academic identity. Also, literature indicates that faculty of color are less likely to *ask their mentors for assistance* if they are not of the same racial/ethnic group. Authors find that to mentor faculty of color, it is critical to *understand their cultural backgrounds and cultural assumptions and the types of barriers* they may face in the academy because of their language, race, and/or culture. Although some research shows that mentees of color are successful with cross-race mentors, most of the research cited in this literature suggests that *mentees of color prefer same-race mentors*, which can be difficult to achieve at institutions that *lack critical masses of faculty of color*. Last, if faculty of color are to be successful in the academy, it is important that institutions not *overburden them with the responsibility* to mentor all the students of color.

In the bottom-right quadrant are the major themes from the literature that address challenges in cross-gender mentorships. When men serve as mentors to women, the literature finds that women sometimes experience *sexism, tokenism,* and *marginalization.* The literature also reports that when women have male mentors, *they become more cautious about how other peers and colleagues may view their relationship* if they are seen together in public. Men also are *less likely to connect women with the professional contacts they need* in order to succeed in academe. Similar to what is experienced by faculty of color, women are negatively affected when their male mentors use their *political influence and power* to dominate the mentorship relationship. *Stereotypes* (by men) of women, such as specified roles for women in the academy, also provide women with challenges. Belief in the *inherent differences* that exist between males and females is also a potential cause for cross-gender mentoring challenges. In general, the literature shows that *women prefer women mentors*. Last, the *male-dominant culture inherent in the STEM fields* causes challenges for women faculty in those fields.

This section provides a summary of the themes from the integrated model based on the literature presented in chapter 1. This summary of themes will be used as a foundation for analysis of the narratives.

Comparing the Literature to the Coauthored Narratives

Themes emerging from the coauthored narratives (chapters 2–8) were compared to all the themes found in the cross-race/ethnicity and cross-gender literature. The narratives reflected 14 (out of 25) of the themes related to successful pathways, and 12 (out of 20) of the themes related to challenges. In this section, successful pathways in the narratives are presented, followed by the challenges.

Comparing Successful Pathways in the Literature to the Coauthored Narratives

As shown in Table 9.1, no single theme in the literature (chapter 1) was found in all seven of the narratives (chapters 2–8). *Respect leads to openness* was the primary theme that cut across six of the narratives. This is the idea where scholars of color and women have a fundamental understanding of each other's identity, culture, and mentorship needs. Of the narratives that exemplified this idea, Turner, in chapter 2, stated, "Juan Carlos and I both have learned to have respect and patience with each other's point of view and, bottom line, we value the colleagueship and friendship that we have developed over the years" (p. 49). González and Turner have learned that to achieve excellence in their scholarly work, it is important to have respect for each other's perspectives, ideas, and generational differences. Respect for racial difference was shared by Wooden in chapter 4:

> I shared information with my friends about Ed . . . and how excited I was that someone had taken an interest in me being not only a successful student but also a successful person. . . . The most interesting piece was that this was coming from a White man. (p. 91)

TABLE 9.1

Successful Pathways and Challenges Across Race/Ethnicity and Gender: Comparison Between Literature and Narratives

		a	b	c	d	e	f	g
Successful pathways	1 Respect leads to openness	a	b	c	d	e	f	
	2 Demystifying the academy	a	b	c	d	e		
	3 Cultural support and validation		b	c	d		f	g
	4 Ally identification	a		c		e		
	5 Psychosocial support		b	c		e		
	6 Characteristics that support relationships	a	b	c				
	7 Peer mentoring			c		e		g
	8 Diving for pearls			c	d			
	9 Academic resiliency			c	d			
	10 Establishing caring communities			c	d			
	11 Politics of gender			c	d			
	12 Mentoring as healing					e		
	13 Support social needs							g
	14 Developing supportive culture							g
Challenges	1 Gender differences	a	b		d	e		g
	2 Politics and power relations	a	b	c			f	g
	3 Sexism		b			e	f	g
	4 Dominant culture assimilation	a		c		e		
	5 Racism and institutional racism			c			f	
	6 External perceptions		b					g
	7 Power dynamics affect relationships		b					
	8 Stigma with seeking help	a						
	9 Cross-cultural interactions					e		
	10 Language, racial, cultural barriers					e		
	11 Mentees prefer same-race mentors			c				
	12 Lack of professional interactions							g

Note. a: chapter 2 (González & Turner); b: chapter 3 (Wood & Turner); c: chapter 4 (St. John, Hill, Wooden, & Pasque); d: chapter 5 (Castellanos & Kamimura-Jiménez); e: chapter 6 (Jain & Solórzano); f: chapter 7 (Stanley & Louis); g: chapter 8 (Ramirez & Mirandé).

It is these types of respectful relationships, for example, how Ed St. John's students emulate the mentorship they learned, that further advance the diversification of the faculty.

The second theme, *demystifying the academy*, was noted in five narratives. In one example, Luke stated in chapter 3, "I . . . received support in . . . navigating the politics of doctoral education and continual encouragement for my research endeavors. On the basis of discussions with other doctoral students, I realize this kind of commitment is rare" (p. 60). In chapter 4, St. John shared a similar sentiment about his relationship with his students, stating, "Engaging students in authentic partnerships in thinking about theory, research, and social change has been one of the most enjoyable aspects of my academic career" (p. 100). In helping his students use theory and research for social change in the community and in the university, St. John helped students demystify and change the academy.

The third theme, *cultural support and validation*, was also expressed in five of the narratives. Coauthors shared experiences with being of the same cultural/racial background as a benefit to building and expanding their mentorship. In one example, Kamimura-Jiménez stated (in chapter 5),

> There was a lot of my life that I did not need to explain because of all our shared experiences. . . . I did not need to change my language; change my accent; change my vocabulary; or, most important, change who I was. (p. 112)

With Castellanos as his mentor, Kamimura-Jiménez saw himself as her younger brother and never had to worry about having to conform to non-Latino ways of being an academic. He also mentioned that his time as the mentee of Castellanos was similar to home experiences where he learned from the Latinas in his family.

The fourth concept, *ally identification*, addresses the methods by which being involved in mentoring leads to access to networks of scholars of similar culture, race, or ideology. Three of the narratives addressed this concept. In one example, Hill (chapter 4) stated,

> Our cohort group [was] one where we comfortably became both mentors and mentees until the completion of our doctoral program and beyond. As we completed our personal doctoral programs over the next several semesters, it became routine for members of the cohort to continue to mentor those still in the program. (p. 87)

These cohorts of students of color, where the advanced doctoral students mentor the new ones, was made possible by the relationships that St. John forged with his students individually and as research teams. In another similar example, Jain (chapter 6) stated, "Not until I was attending Danny's RAC [Research Apprenticeship Course] regularly and also began meeting with him one-on-one for mentoring was I exposed to a perspective that allowed for the marginalized voice to be centered" (p. 127). The RAC at UCLA is a course where many of Solórzano's students meet, learn how to use critical race theory in educational policy, and validate each other's experiences and place within the academy.

Fifth, in three of the narratives mentees addressed the *psychosocial support* they received from their mentors as vital to having a successful mentorship. In chapter 3, Wood stated,

> As I am a dedicated Christian, my ability to participate in church, attend services regularly, and talk openly about my spirituality was (and is) very important to me. Dr. Turner was very supportive of my church participation. As a result, no matter what was coming up, we made an agreement that we did not work Sundays. I appreciated the space she provided me for my spiritual development. (pp. 70–71)

Hill (chapter 4) also mentioned similar psychosocial support from St. John as vital to his model of mentorship as a faculty member. He stated,

> At one point . . . it became necessary to summon Ed St. John . . . away from his home and family. . . . What stayed with me is the fact that he gave up his Saturday morning to do for us what I have learned over the years is something he does naturally for all of his students. I have come to learn that acts such as these are what mentoring is about. (p. 87)

According to Hill, part of the success of St. John in mentoring was that he viewed mentoring as an extension of life and as central to the development of mentees as scholars, professionals, and people. Mentoring for St. John was about understanding the relationship and responsibility that scholars have to their colleagues, families, and communities.

The sixth theme, *characteristics that support relationships*, was described in three of the narratives. This theme is best exemplified by González and Turner's narrative (chapter 2). After 14 years of presenting together at academic conferences, their friendship continues to grow. In their narrative, González stated, "Caroline and I have a stronger friendship than ever, even though our communication is complicated by our busy schedules, our distinct research interests, and our commitment to be student focused" (p. 56). In another example, St. John et al. talk about their commitment to the ethics of care and justice as a glue in their relationship and as something to rely on during difficult times.

The seventh theme, *peer mentoring*, was mentioned in three of the narratives. In one example, Pasque (in chapter 4) stated that as a mechanism for her success, cohort mentoring was important because of the peer mentoring that it provided:

> The benefits of being in a cohort mentoring program during graduate school were many. The program showed that a group of disparate individuals could come together and learn to disagree without becoming disagreeable. Members could learn to discuss and dialogue and begin to appreciate rich and varied objective points of view. We also learned to genuinely guide, support, and share with each other. (p. 87)

Jain and Ramirez also talked about peer mentoring that began during their doctoral programs and continues as faculty. For Jain it was a class taught by her mentor, where she met other peer mentors. For Ramirez it was a writing group supported by her chair and led by doctoral students.

The eighth theme, *diving for pearls,* is present in two of the narratives. This was the idea that if mentoring relationships begin with sufficient similarities, it is easier to take the relationship to a deeper, next level. For example, if two scholars specialize in understanding African American male college students, it is likely they will already understand the issues and quickly develop a shared research agenda based on shared understandings. From the narratives, in chapter 4, Pasque eloquently talks about a situation in which she and St. John shared these similarities of kindness and social justice. She recalls a situation where she needed St. John to come to the university after hours to resolve an academic dispute among doctoral students. St. John not only resolved the dispute but also contextualized academia as a lifelong journey, restored calm, and reassured his doctoral students of their place in the academy. After several of these mentoring learning moments, Pasque was convinced that she and St. John approached life and academia from the same social justice framework, and the difficult work that followed became a lot easier. Kamimura-Jiménez (in chapter 5) also wrote about his mentor, Jeanett Castellanos, in a similar fashion, detailing their deep relationship based on sharing a Latino background and on having the same work ethic and high expectations for themselves and others whom they mentor.

Academic resiliency was the ninth successful pathway theme. Similar to the previous theme, Pasque's and Kamimura-Jiménez's narratives addressed this theme. Pasque wrote,

As a woman, a first-generation college student, and a scholar interested in critical qualitative inquiry, I do not have a clear pathway, trajectory, or "good old boy" network offered to me, and it is not offered to many of us, for that matter. Mentors like Ed St. John create new and innovative connections that inspire, challenge, and support us throughout our careers at whatever particular developmental point in our lives. For example, scholars and practitioners have said when we first meet, "Oh, you're Penny Pasque. Ed speaks highly of you." (p. 99)

Clearly, Pasque sees St. John's mentorship as offering pathways to success that she would not normally have as a woman academic. Kamimura-Jiménez similarly talked about his mentorship with Dr. C (Jeanett Castellanos) as building his knowledge about himself and gaining the confidence to pursue doctoral education (chapter 5):

The cultivation phase of our relationship was strengthened as Dr. C learned how to develop my academic abilities. . . . Thinking back, this was the first time I had really talked with someone . . . about my experiences growing up and connecting them to how and who I was as a student, as a person. Our weekly *pláticas* (conversations) became consistently a safe place for discussing the connections of complex theories with real-life situations. These intellectual *pláticas* became ground zero for building and exploring the impact of race on the educational paths of students of color, mainly Latinos. (pp. 112–113)

Through their *pláticas*, Kamimura-Jiménez developed *academic resiliency*, the ninth theme, by understanding more deeply who he was, based on theory, and how he could and would make a contribution in higher education.

The tenth theme, *establishing caring communities*, was mentioned by Hill (chapter 4) and Kamimura-Jiménez. Hill wrote about how St. John's mentoring helped him become not only a better academic but also a better person:

The mentoring I received from thought partners like Ed St. John and the members of my doctoral cohort had a profound influence on my becoming a more trusting human being. In addition to receiving the benefits mentoring produces in a doctoral program and in professional practice, I benefited by having my entire outlook on humanity change. (p. 101)

Similarly, Kamimura-Jiménez (chapter 5) talked about the profound change initiated through mentorship. He wrote, "When you became a mentee [of Dr. C], you also became a part of a larger family" (p. 115). He talked about this family as not only having the responsibility of taking mentoring lessons to advance their academic careers but also using those lessons to teach others the ropes of academia.

The eleventh theme, *politics of gender*, addresses how mentors often lack gender-specific training to address mentoring needs of women mentees. Because of this lack of training, mentors of women make critical mistakes that lead to women distrusting the mentoring relationship. For example, Casto, Caldwell, and Salazar (2005) stated how female mentors are not introduced to other scholars at academic conferences by their male mentors, which often leads to distrust in the mentoring relationship. To address the politics of gender, those who mentor women need to be recognized for their work, and when these recognitions are apparent, successful cross-gendered mentorships occur. Pasque (chapter 4) was one of two authors who addressed this theme in her narrative, stating,

> As a woman and a first-generation college student, I cannot tell you what I do not know or what goes on in circles of which I am not a part. I can, however, clearly articulate who is in the know and that I'm not necessarily certain I want to be integrated in some of these groups. As someone often on the margins, who does not know the questions that I should be asking of mentors in the academy, I find it helpful to have a mentor who is already in the know to guide and encourage. I see Ed as someone who readily shares information I might not have access to, in a way that I can hear; someone who renders academic culture and processes visible. Furthermore, he is not threatened when I raise questions that challenge the status quo or talk through the underlying politics of the situation. Ed is not afraid to give up information and power to people who might not have been born and raised in the academy, and this action is indicative of a mentor who is inclusive of people across gender and class. (p. 97)

This quote indicates that although gender politics usually exclude females in higher education, St. John used his knowledge and influence as a White male to open doors of opportunity for women faculty and faculty of color.

The last three literature themes (*mentoring as healing, support social needs*, and *developing a supportive culture*) were each addressed in one of the narratives. Jain (chapter 6) alluded to mentoring as healing, in her mentoring relationship with Solórzano, stating, "Danny's office is a safe haven for most of those who enter—you can almost hear students exhale as they get ready to sit down and talk to a professor who 'gets it'" (p. 132).

The theme of supporting social needs was pointed to in Ramirez's (chapter 8) narrative in her explication of her relationship with Mirandé. She explained that Mirandé was not only her academic advisor and friend but also a friend of the family:

In addition to providing me with career-related support, Alfredo provided me with psychosocial support, particularly during times of familial crises. For example, my brother (my only sibling) developed a terminal illness and passed away while I was in graduate school. While my brother was hospitalized, and even after his death, Alfredo, who is also a lawyer, offered to represent him in court and help resolve a legal dispute of his. Alfredo provided us with his legal expertise and services for free (pro bono); this kind and supportive gesture meant one less source of stress for my family during a time of extreme emotional turmoil. Despite the various familial obligations and difficulties that I experienced during my graduate schooling years, Alfredo was extremely supportive, always maintained high expectations for me, and never questioned my commitment to an academic career. (p. 167)

The literature theme *developing a supportive culture* was described by Ramirez:

Alfredo's mentorship and support were crucial to my survival in graduate school. Unlike mainstream faculty, Alfredo validated my scholarly interests and perspectives. He also supported me at every step of the graduate schooling process. For example, he supplied me with data for my master's thesis and helped establish a writing group, *Onda Chicana*, in order to provide me and other students with critical feedback on our work. He was also instrumental in helping me complete my written and oral qualifying exams. I still vividly recall that he took sparkling cider and *pan dulce* (Mexican sweet bread) to my oral qualifying exams in order to celebrate my successful transition to ABD (all but dissertation) status. It was these and other gestures that demonstrated Alfredo's unwavering support for me and commitment to helping me succeed in the program. (p. 166)

In addition, Ramirez explicated that Mirandé was extremely supportive of her, as he was for all the students that he mentored. In a similar fashion, many of the other narratives talk about the support of their mentors, but Mirandé also supported the families of his graduate students and cushioned them from an institutional culture that was largely hostile to Latino students and faculty.

Comparing Challenges in the Literature to the Coauthored Narratives

As shown in Table 9.1, there were 12 literature themes that detailed faculty mentoring challenges across race/ethnicity and gender: (a) gender differences; (b) politics and power relations; (c) sexism; (d) dominant culture assimilation; (e) racism and institutional racism; (f) external perceptions; (g) power dynamics affect relationships; (h) stigma with seeking help; (i) cross-cultural interactions; (j) language, racial, cultural barriers; (k) mentees prefer same-race mentors; and (l) lack of professional interactions. None of these 12 challenges was found in every narrative. Gender differences and politics and power relations were the two most common challenges, found in five of the seven narratives. Sexism was addressed in four of the narratives. Dominant culture assimilation was found in three of the narratives. Racism and institutional racism and external perceptions were both themes found in two of the narratives. The remaining six themes each were supported by one of the seven narratives. The following explication will provide examples of these themes from the narratives.

First, *gender differences* were reported in five of the narratives. For example, Castellanos (chapter 5) described her gender mentoring challenges, as her colleagues perceived her as spending too much time with students, which was something her male colleagues were not willing to do:

> Equally important in this Latina and Latino mentorship relationship was being able to counter colleagues' negative perceptions of my overinvestment in students. Having confidence in one's practices and recognizing that what works for one group may not work as well (*no somos todos iguales*; we are not all the same) for another is critical in establishing culturally relevant and effective mentoring relations. (p. 121)

Ramirez (chapter 8) also mentioned gender differences, stating that her male mentor was not able to provide intellectual mentorship on women-centered theories:

> Although Alfredo is an amazing scholar and mentor, I feel that a Chicana professor would have been able to provide me with stronger intellectual mentorship in the field of Chicana/Latina feminisms. I do not feel I received sufficient mentorship in this area. (p. 168)

The second most common challenge was understanding *politics and power relations*. Five narratives addressed this issue. González (chapter 2) provided one example where he wanted to assert and vocalize his ideas to his mentor but did not feel confident doing this because he understood that the mentor was the dissertation chair with the power to prevent him from successfully defending his dissertation:

> Because she had power over me as my dissertation chair, and I knew this as a student wanting to graduate, trying to disrupt our relationship could affect the ultimate goal of graduating. Developing the ability to successfully

and strategically navigate and understand power relations and still not compromise your vision and values is, I believe, one of the most important lessons there is to learn to be successful in higher education. (p. 53)

Another of Turner's past doctoral students, Wood (chapter 3), had a similar experience. He wrote that he felt Turner, as his mentor, had the power to steer his decisions, regardless of what he really wanted:

The power balance between us complicated matters. For example, in situations where I had choices, I felt as though I could not disagree. What made this circumstance more complex is that Dr. Turner felt that I had the flexibility to make my own decisions and that she was merely giving me a recommendation. It took some time to realize that she would accept whatever choice I made. (pp. 67–68)

Although González and Wood both felt they had limited choices in working with Turner, part of it had to do with not understanding the politics and power relations of mentorships, as Turner wrote that she often encouraged her doctoral students to make their own choices. She stated, "[Luke Wood] tells me that he rarely would say no to me, even when I encouraged him to do so."

Louis (chapter 7), on the other hand, seemed to have a different experience in being mentored by Stanley. In Stanley's reflection of Louis, she wrote,

Dr. Louis reflects on the issues of power and influence and questions if he unintentionally listened less or with a more skeptical ear because Dr. Stanley is a woman. He does acknowledge, however, that he made decisions contrary to her counsel more than he did with his male mentors. (p. 152)

Stanley wondered if Louis's decisions were made in part because of the Caribbean culture they both shared, in which men are generally the leaders. Such situations could have had a negative effect but did not, as possibly trust and respect for one another worked to overcome these challenges.

Third, *sexism* is mentioned in four of the narratives. Wood and Turner (chapter 3) talked about their work on national projects. For example, when they were working together, people always assumed he was in charge, likely because he was a male, and would defer to his authority even when they knew she was in charge. Luke wrote,

[When we worked together] people would assume that I was in charge and come up to me for direction and guidance. . . . At first, I did not think about or recognize the gender privilege I had. (p. 68)

Jain (chapter 6) shared a similar experience of sexism in the academy. As a new faculty member, when she received her first student evaluations, they were laced with sexism, and Solórzano helped her process them, understand, and move forward. She wrote about discussing her teaching evaluations with Solórzano,

> Danny and I discussed how the impact of these evaluations was different for me than for him—regardless of rank and university, these evaluations carried a different weight because I am a woman. These students attacked me on my dress and appearance, something that male faculty often do not have to be conscious of. (p. 136)

The fourth theme, *dominant culture assimilation*, was present in three narratives: (a) González and Turner (chapter 2), (b) St. John et al. (chapter 4), and (c) Jain and Solórzano (chapter 6). St. John best recounted this, in explaining that there is a hierarchy of topics and methods, and critical issues are not at the top of that hierarchy. He wrote,

> If students seek to address critical social issues in their academic work, they will face greater scrutiny than their peers who stick to mainstream topics and methods, so they need highly rigorous standards, along with mentoring that supports them as they address these issues. (p. 78)

One reason St. John's students valued him is that he was the type of mentor who supported their work on critical social issues and allowed them the autonomy to develop into their own, with their own ideas and their own epistemologies.

Racism and institutional racism is the fifth theme. Wooden (chapter 4) shared an example from the University of Michigan, a predominantly White institution. At Michigan, his peers would question the legitimacy of his undergraduate degree from a historically Black college and university. He wrote,

> There were times I felt my sharing in class was devalued and that, because of not having attended a mainstream, predominantly White institution, I should remain silent. I remember being enrolled in a course, Diverse College Students, where it seemed my experiences were often discounted. Students openly questioned the value of my degree and my preparation for graduate school because I had attended a historically Black university; some of my classmates clearly did not think my degree was worth the paper on which it was printed. (p. 90)

Another experience of institutional racism is shared by Stanley and Louis (chapter 7). They wrote about being among the few Black people in their department:

> We were not the "typical" faculty member or student in our department, and our acknowledgment of that made us work harder to ensure the safety of one another. We had to look out for each other because there was no one else who understood us beyond the superficial level. We had to support each other in an environment that was not always supportive or welcoming to individuals of color. (p. 146)

Although Stanley and Louis shared a faculty–student mentorship, they nevertheless felt like family based on their cultural commonalities and on their similar experiences of institutional racism in academe.

Sixth, *external perceptions* were mentioned in two narratives. Wood and Turner talked about how some of Wood's peers perceived something other than work must be involved in their relationship because they spent so much time together. Regardless of the comments and rumors that Wood was subjected to, this did not stop Turner and Wood from building the strong working relationship that has continued as Wood has entered the academy as a faculty member. But in the case of Ramirez and Mirandé, comments and rumors did have a negative effect on their relationship. Ramirez (chapter 8) explained, "Alfredo and I did not forge a much closer relationship because of the greater public scrutiny that cross-gender mentoring relationships elicit." In the Ramirez–Mirandé mentorship, even Mirandé acknowledged that there were barriers in their cross-gender mentorship because of the potential rumors he may be subject to when mentorship begins developing into friendships. He explained,

> I have mentored a number of students over the years, but most of my mentees, particularly at the graduate level, have been men. I have often reflected on and pondered my tendency to work more closely with my male students. It is somehow always easier to develop close mentoring relationships that extend beyond the classroom with members of one's gender. For example, I would often invite students whom I worked closely with to go out for a drink at the Pub, which is the local watering hole on campus. . . . I have generally been more reserved in socializing with my female students, and I have worked hard to break down these barriers. (p. 172)

Mirandé's acknowledgment that it is easier to develop professional and social relationships with same-gender mentees demonstrates how it can be difficult for Latina mentees to find mentors when the majority of the professoriate is male.

The remaining six literature themes were each supported and reflected in one narrative. How *power dynamics affect relationships*, the seventh theme, was supported by the Wood and Turner narrative (chapter 3). Wood explained that although Turner would offer him suggestions and recommendations on choice related to his academic career, he felt he could not disagree with her because she was his mentor. However, as communication in the relationship evolved, Wood was to understand that these were indeed suggestions and recommendations. The eighth theme, *stigma with seeking help,* was explicated by González (chapter 2). González explained that prior to working with Turner he was always hesitant to seek mentoring and/or help, as he was taught that this was a sign of weakness or of lacking professional competence. It was Turner who helped him accept the idea of mentorship as being critical to academic and professional advancement, not a sign of weakness. Jain's narrative (chapter 6) is supportive of the ninth and tenth themes, *cross-cultural interactions* and *language, racial, and cultural barriers,* respectively. Jain, who identifies as a South Asian American woman, and Solórzano, a Chicano, experienced both cultural and gender differences. But Solórzano always made Jain realize the strength of their differences in mentoring relationships, something that Jain now uses as a faculty member mentoring diverse students. The eleventh theme, *mentees prefer same-race mentors*, is supported in chapter 4 by St. John's students. For some of St. John's students of color, he was their first White mentor, and this required building trust in and understanding of St. John and his commitment to students of color. The twelfth and final literature theme discussed here and described in the narratives is *lack of professional interactions.* This was explicated by Mirandé (chapter 8), stating that throughout his years of mentoring doctoral students, most had been males prior to Ramirez, in large part because it is easier to mentor males when the mentorship requires time outside the office and in the pub. Mirandé, however, also acknowledged that working with Ramirez has provided him with the opportunity to break down traditional mentoring barriers that exist in cross-gendered mentorships.

The seven mentor–protégé narratives presented in this book, taken as a whole, provide insights into the real-life development and growth of these mentoring relationships. The authors provided detailed descriptions of their own mentorship experiences, much of which is reflective of what scholars in the literature document as supports and challenges across race/ethnicity and gender. The mentor–protégé authors not only shared their unique stories with the reader but also further explicated the literature with their descriptions of the contemporary successes and challenges they faced. For example, the review of the literature resulted in the identification of a set of theoretical concepts or themes, detailed in Figures 1.1 and 1.2. When the themes from the literature were then compared with themes emerging from the personal narratives, themes reflective of the literature were noted in Table 9.1. The themes reflected in the literature are detailed in this chapter. Themes not found in the literature but revealed in the narratives will now be discussed in chapter 10, followed by an overview of the process used to develop the emerging unifying model, inclusive of all themes identified from the literature reviewed and from the mentor–protégé narratives. Following the presentation of the unifying model, a synthesis of results pointing to recommendations for mentors, protégés, and institutions is presented and discussed.

Reference

Casto, C., Caldwell, C., & Salazar, C. F. (2005). Creating mentoring relationships between female faculty and students in counselor education: Guidelines for potential mentees and mentors. *Journal of Counseling and Development, 83*(3), 331–336.

IO

ANALYSIS OF THE MENTOR–PROTÉGÉ NARRATIVES

Contributing to the Literature and Emerging Mentoring Model for Practice

Caroline Sotello Viernes Turner and Juan Carlos González

T his chapter provides an analysis of the coauthored mentor–protégé narratives, comparing the resulting themes to the themes emerging from the integrated literature review summarized in chapter 9. The previous chapter presented themes emerging from the narratives and also found in the literature, and this chapter presents new cross-race/ethnicity and cross-gender mentorship themes that were found in the narratives but not in the literature. It is these added themes that uniquely contribute to the current evidence presented in the literature on what works and what does not work with cross-race/ethnicity and cross-gender mentorships. The chapter will end with an overview of the entire process undertaken to derive a unifying thematic model from which recommendations for individual and institutional practices are presented.

Contributing Themes From Narratives

On the basis of the previous analysis of the literature, several themes overlap between the literature and the coauthored mentor–protégé chapters written for this book. This section discusses the themes that each mentor–protégé chapter adds to the literature presented previously. As we can see from Table 10.1, several successful pathways and challenges were described in the narratives but not found in the literature reviewed in this book.

TABLE 10.1

Successful Pathways and Challenges Across Race/Ethnicity and Gender, Contributing Themes and Narratives From Where They Originate

Successful pathways	Shared values and experiences	a, b, d, f
	Wholistic mentoring	b, c, d, g
	Intentional mentorship	c
	Existential component of mentoring	d
	Problem-posing mentoring	e
	Authority and rank as staple	f
	Observational mentorship	c, f
	Respecting mentees' career decisions	f
	Student-faculty ethnic-based writing groups	g
	Job-market support and knowledge	g
	Cross-disciplinary ethnic networking	g
Challenges	Different experiences	a
	Independent personalities	a
	Generational differences	a
	Race-based hostile work climate	g

Note. a: chapter 2 (González & Turner); b: chapter 3 (Wood & Turner); c: chapter 4 (St. John, Hill, Wooden, & Pasque); d: chapter 5 (Castellanos & Kamimura-Jiménez); e: chapter 6 (Jain & Solórzano); f: chapter 7 (Stanley & Louis); g: chapter 8 (Ramirez & Mirandé).

Successful Pathways

Although preference for mentors or protégés of similar backgrounds was noted in the literature, narratives from González and Turner, Wood and Turner, Castellanos and Kamimura-Jiménez, and Stanley and Louis provide the reader with a nuanced view of specific *shared values and experiences* that were critical to their successful relationships. Castellanos and Kamimura-Jiménez (chapter 5) reported sharing "similar struggles, a common language, histories, and similar oppressions" and stated that "eliminating the generational gap and our cultural familiarity [both Latino] facilitated a space to . . . [practice] our common values" (p. 116). They also indicated that they both share a multiracial, culturally mixed background and were interested in addressing "social justice for the greater whole" (p. 117).

Despite differences based on gender and age, González and Turner (chapter 2) have similarities such as they both come from large immigrant families. They noted that they "share a critical commonality in advancing a scholarly and personal commitment to access, equity, and social justice in higher education" (p. 45). Wood and Turner (chapter 3) stated the factors they had in common were being of mixed-race heritage, sharing similar research and advocacy interests, coming from small rural towns, and completing their doctoral education with family responsibilities. Stanley and Louis (chapter 7) also indicated that their commonalities resulted in a highly successful mentor–protégé relationship. Both entered an academic department in the same semester, both were highly driven individuals interested in diversity issues, both graduated from historically Black colleges and universities and both are of Caribbean background. For all of these mentor–protégé coauthors, these similarities greatly fostered communication, providing some fundamental ways in which they did not have to explain themselves to one another, as J. Luke Wood provides in this example:

> One other way in which we share similarities is that we are both from small rural towns. Dr. Turner grew up in farm labor camps in central California, and I grew up in a logging town in the far northern area of the state. There are certain experiences or lack thereof that we believe are part of growing up in "small town" America. Namely, these include relying on community for support during good and challenging times; knowing most people in our communities; standing out as a good student of color; and having a desire to prove oneself, a sense of trust in others, and an arduous work ethic. Not to say that these virtues are not held by individuals from other locales (e.g., urban, suburban), but the manner in which they occurred for us was similar and attributed to rural life. (p. 69)

Thus, although authors described differences causing tension in their relationships, these were mitigated, to a large degree, by the characteristics they had in common. Differences created conflict, whereas similarities created a level of comfort to overcome conflict and provided a foundation for the growth and development of successful mentorships.

Distinct mentoring relationships, touched on previously within the category of shared values and experiences, can be defined on a more profound level as the mentor and protégé enter each other's personal and family lives. This is referred to as *wholistic mentoring*. For example, several of the mentors got involved with their protégé's family, and protégés in turn were introduced to their mentor's family. St. John (chapter 4) stated,

> I frequently take graduate students to lunch. It was something Orville Thompson did frequently for me when I was a senior and graduate student. I view the lunches with my graduate students not only as payback to

Orville but also as a way to get to know them better. Often I have taken my wife on social lunches, more often with women graduate students than men. To be frank, I don't want any confusion about the nature of my relationships with students. (p. 102, note 4)

While addressing the challenge of potential external perceptions of sexual liaisons in cross-gender mentorship relationships, St. John shares lunches off campus with his students and introduces them to his wife. Furthermore, Pasque (chapter 4) provided an example of what can happen over time when such personal bonds deepen:

This is one example of how a mentor–mentee relationship can grow and change over time. As Ed has come to know Frank and me, as we have come to know Ed and Angie (his wife and life partner), and as we have read and reflected on each other's growing body of scholarship, there is a way in which we have come to "know" each other on a deeper level. As such, it takes less time to zero in on a problem, concern, dissonance, critical issue, or life challenge. (p. 99)

In an example of bonds that are as strong as those of family, Kamimura-Jiménez (chapter 5), with Castellanos as his mentor, saw himself as her younger brother who never had to worry about having to conform to non-Latino ways of being as an academic. Wood (chapter 3) also shared the following as he invited Turner to his wedding:

Viewing her simply as an advisor or colleague seemed insufficient, almost insulting. For example, Dr. Turner was included in many of my family celebrations. During the summer prior to entering the doctoral program, I married my wife, Idara. Even though I had known Dr. Turner for only a few months at that time, I invited her to the wedding to share this experience with my family and close friends. This speaks to how close Dr. Turner and I became in such a short period of time. Furthermore, the fact that Dr. Turner attended my wedding illustrates that the feeling of closeness was mutual. (p. 67)

For these mentors and protégés, having strong personal bonds, seeing each other as whole people rather than just as scholars, and knowing what's happening in their lives outside the walls of academia are vital parts of sustained lifelong mentoring relationships.

In addition to the factors of shared values, shared experiences, and wholistic mentoring, several authors provided conceptual descriptions of mentoring not found in the literature reviewed for this book but were supportive of their successful mentor–protégé relationships. Castellanos and Kamimura-Jiménez (chapter 5) identified the *existential component* in their mentoring relationship, by which life's purpose is examined by posing questions that they attempted to answer and discuss such as "why we are granted opportunities and what we must do with them" (p. 121). Jain and Solórzano (chapter 6) introduced the reader to the idea of Freirean *problem-posing mentoring*, supporting the creation of a two-way dialogue of cooperation as problems are defined and solved together. In this style of mentoring, issues are viewed

> as problems that can be resolved, not as a reality to be accepted. . . .
> Mentoring in this nonhierarchical, multidimensional, and problem-posing fashion creates a climate where students' ideas are important and central to their intellectual growth and in challenging dominant paradigms in their field. (p. 138)

On the other hand, Stanley and Louis (chapter 7) stated that their Caribbean cultures resulted in very similar modes of operating. In their relationship, hierarchical struggles were nonexistent, as "in our cultures, *authority and rank* are staples and are taken very seriously. Therefore, as a graduate student, Dr. Louis was 'subordinate,' and Dr. Stanley was the 'boss' in no uncertain terms" (p. 145, italics added). They also described their disagreement related to career choice. However, they were quick to caution the reader that "sharing a common culture does not mean that everyone from Jamaica or Trinidad or other Caribbean islands will have similar experiences. . . .We simply need more stories from other Caribbean scholars to either add to or counter our own experiences" (p. 158).

St. John et al., as well as Stanley and Louis, provided insights into how *observing a mentor* can transmit informative messages to the protégé. Louis stated that he learned "time management, research integrity, and professional posture," in large part, by observing his mentor (p. 149). St. John's protégés (chapter 4) described learning how to be a mentor by observation. In fact, Pasque contributed the idea of intentional mentoring to this discussion. She contended that although one is not required to take a course on mentoring, one learns from observing a thoughtful mentor. She named the idea of *mentoring with intentionality*, which is not leaving mentorship development to chance; it is only with intentionality that change takes place. Ramirez and Mirandé (chapter 8) introduced other specific, supportive factors. They described the establishment of *Onda Chicana*, an informal Chicano and Chicana *writing group* that provided a venue for faculty and graduate students from different disciplines to share critical feedback on each other's work. They underscored the importance of *cross-disciplinary ethnic networking* and described the *support received when negotiating the job market*.

A major lesson learned from these contributions to the literature on successful pathways in mentorship relationships is that practitioners must be cognizant of different cultures that serve as contexts for mentorship and understand that successful practices may be different for each mentor–protégé relationship and can even contradict the research in terms of "what works." Each of these mentor–protégé stories accounts for successful mentorships, but the elements for success are different, and implications for policy and practice may vary widely. Nonetheless, this book attempts to provide some recommendations for practice, which will be discussed later.

Challenges

The mentor–protégé narratives also allude to various challenges not found in the literature. For example, González and Turner (chapter 2) revealed that *varied life experiences*, including *generational differences*, shaped their *independent personalities*, leading to ways in which communication was, at times, a challenge. One example provided by Turner was her strong encouragement for González to complete his dissertation, not realizing that, in part, her own experience was laying a foundation as a guide. González had the flexibility to pursue more course work and to take advantage of opportunities to conduct research and teach abroad. Turner was a single parent while pursuing her degree, with a time limit of five years for her graduate assistantship. Her focus was completion as soon as possible to attain a full-time position to support herself and her family. Fortunately, González and Turner shared a relationship that not only allowed for such misunderstandings but also allowed for personal growth within such times. González and Turner now realize that their similarities and differences contributing to their times of conflict and misunderstandings emanated from the fact that they are also competitive and fiercely independent in their own ways. Otherwise, they would not have been where they were then and where they are now. Generational differences also influenced their perspectives of higher education. For example, González began college in the 1990s and Turner began in the 1960s (before broad financial aid programs were in place and during the farm labor movement and the struggle for civil rights). Partly because of generational differences, González and Turner have very different experiences and skills with technology. In addition, as González and Turner continued to work together, they came to realize that scholars who inspired González to pursue academia shared his ethnic background, and he eventually came to meet and to know them personally, whereas Turner's inspirational mentors were scholars who did not share her ethnic background and whom she would not come to meet and know personally. Such experiences can provide potential areas for misunderstanding, as documented in their chapter. One other critical challenge that Ramirez and Mirandé (chapter 8) brought forth in their narrative, not discussed in the literature, is the impact of a *race-based hostile work climate.* In this type of environment, in addition to research interests and perspectives of students of color being questioned, a mentor–protégé relationship may be compromised in that the mentor and/or protégé may not be able to easily access fellowships, internships, and other opportunities for professional growth.

These successful pathways and challenges emanating from the narratives add to the literature, illustrating detailed insights that provide deeper understandings of what facilitates and challenges cross-gender and cross-race/ethnicity mentoring relationships in academe. Through the analysis of the themes identified in the literature and the elaboration of these themes in the narratives, as well as the addition of new insight from the narratives, an emerging unifying model will now be presented, followed by implications for practice.

Model Encompassing and Comparing Literature Review and Narratives

After an extensive review of the literature and narratives, we found not only that the narratives support and extend the existing literature but that they also provide new themes that had not been explored in past literature. It was important then to create a model that could visually represent (a) the themes in the literature, (b) the themes from the narratives, and (c) how the narratives were similar to and different from the existing literature on cross-race/ethnicity and cross-gender mentorships. Table 10.2 shows the processes undertaken in the creation of this model, referred to as the *unifying model.*

Table 10.2 presents the data management and analytical processes undertaken that led to the creation of a model unifying all themes identified in the literature and narratives. The first column shows the steps taken to mine the cross-race/ethnicity and cross-gender literature for key themes, resulting in the development of visual representations of the themes identified (see chapter 1, Figures 1.1 and 1.2). Figures 1.1 and 1.2 display themes from the literature that specifically address cross-race/ethnicity and cross-gender mentorships (see Figure 1.1), as well as the literature that indirectly addressed these types of cross mentorships (see Figure 1.2). Once these themes were identified and discussed in chapter 1, the mentor–protégé narratives (chapters 2–8) were read and analyzed for thematic content.

The second column in Table 10.2 shows the process conducted to compare themes that were found in the narratives to the literature themes presented in chapter 1. To be able to conduct this comparison, we integrated Figures 1.1 and 1.2 into one visual representing all literature themes found (see Figure 9.1). Figure 9.1 was then used for comparison with the themes

TABLE 10.2
Process for the Creation of the Unifying Model

Extrapolate Themes From → the Mentoring Literature	*Create Model Derived From the Literature → Reviewed*	*Review Across Race/ Ethnicity and Gender Narratives*
• Across race/ethnicity • Across gender • With implications for across race/ethnicity • With implications for across gender • Model developed from the literature	• Review across race/ethnicity and gender narratives • Compare with themes identified in the mentoring literature • Identify themes that reflect the extant literature • Model from the literature expanded to include themes from the narratives that reflect those identified in the literature	• Compare with themes identified in the mentoring literature • Identify themes that add to the extant literature • Model from the literature and narratives reflecting the literature expanded to include themes from the narratives that add to those previously identified

emerging from the narratives. Only narrative themes that were reflected in the literature were presented in chapter 9, which focused on how the narratives were reflective of the literature, and we added the personal voices of the mentors and protégés that were largely missing in the existing literature on cross-race/ethnicity and cross-gender mentorships (see Table 9.1).

The last column in Table 10.2 shows the final process in the analysis of the literature and narratives. In this final stage, shown in Table 10.1, new themes that were not previously found in the literature were displayed. The analytic and comparative processes shown in Table 10.2 resulted in the creation of the unifying model, shown in Table 10.3.

Table 10.3 presents an overview of all the themes that emerged from an analysis of the literature and the narratives. Listed in the first two columns (successful pathways and challenges), are all the themes from the literature that pertained directly to cross-race/ethnicity and cross-gender mentorships. These are differentiated by race/ethnicity, gender, successful pathways, and challenges. The check marks represent the themes that were also present in the narratives (chapters 2–8).

TABLE 10.3

Unifying Model Encompassing Literature and Narrative Themes and Successful Pathways and Challenges, by Race/Ethnicity, Gender, and Both

| | Mentorship Literature | | | | New Themes From Narratives | |
| | On Cross-Race/Ethnicity and Cross-Gender | | With Implications for Cross-Race/Ethnicity and Cross-Gender | | | |
	Successful Pathways	Challenges	Successful Pathways	Challenges	Successful Pathways	Challenges
Race/Ethnicity	• Ally identification ✓ • Demystifying the academy ✓ • Diverse mentoring programs • Not academic cloning • Peer mentoring ✓ • Respect leads to openness ✓ • Mentoring as healing ✓ • Psychosocial support ✓ • Rich legacy of cross-race mentoring • E-mentoring • Cross-cultural support ✓	• Dominant culture assimilation ✓ • Isolation and marginalization • Racism and institutional racism ✓ • Stigma with seeking help ✓ • Power dynamics affect relationships ✓ • Cross-cultural interactions ✓ • Language, racial, cultural barriers ✓ • Mentees prefer same-race mentors ✓	• Cultural validation (diving for pearls) ✓ • Academic resiliency ✓ • Establishing caring communities ✓	• Lack of mentorship • Overwhelmed by student mentoring • Difficulty finding same-race mentors		
Gender	• Feminist mentoring • Politics of gender ✓ • Support of social needs ✓ • Respect leads to openness • Developing a culture supporting diverse mentoring and demystifying the academy ✓ • Characteristics that support relationships ✓ • E-mentoring	• Sexism ✓ • Tokenism and marginalization • External perceptions (sexual liaisons and favoritism) ✓ • Lack of professional interactions ✓ • Politics and power relations ✓ • Stereotypes • Gender differences (mentoring expectations and effects on careers) ✓	• Belay (peer support across institutions) • Musing (humanist/feminist community mentoring) • Same-gender mentors	• Same-gender mentors • Effects of science, technology, engineering, and mathematics fields	• Authority and rank as staple • Respecting mentees' career decisions • Student-faculty ethnic-based writing groups • Job-market support and knowledge • Cross-disciplinary ethnic networking • Existential component of mentoring	• Different experiences • Independent personalities • Generational differences • Race-based hostile work climate

(Continues)

TABLE 10.3 (Continued)

| | Mentorship Literature | | | | New Themes From Narratives | |
| | On Cross-Race/Ethnicity and Cross-Gender | | With Implications for Cross-Race/Ethnicity and Cross-Gender | | | |
	Successful Pathways	*Challenges*	*Successful Pathways*	*Challenges*	*Successful Pathways*	*Challenges*
Race/Ethnicity and Gender			• Shared power • Informal mentorships • Mosaic (group mentoring) • Formal mentoring programs	• Traditional (informal) mentoring • Formal mentoring • Peer mentoring	• Shared values and experiences • Wholistic mentoring • Intentional mentorship • Problem-posing mentoring • Observational mentorship	

Note. A check mark (✓) denotes a theme that is also found in the narratives.

The two columns that follow show the themes from the literature that talked about cross-race/ethnicity and cross-gender mentorships indirectly. These came from a rich literature base on cross mentorships. One critique of this literature base is that findings did not differentiate pathways of success or challenges specific to women faculty or faculty of color. Rather, many findings addressed implications for both women faculty and faculty of color. For example, the last row in these columns shows themes (e.g., shared power) where the authors did not differentiate implications for women faculty or faculty of color but addressed them collectively. Only three themes from this literature also appeared in the narratives (chapters 2–8), as shown by the check marks: (a) cultural validation, (b) academic resiliency, and (c) establishing caring communities.

The final two columns present new themes not found in the literature that emerged from the narratives. Although some of the narratives were written by cross-race/ethnicity mentors and mentees, there were no new race/ethnicity themes that had implications for cross-race/ethnicity mentorships. (For this reason, the last two columns in the first row were left blank.) All new themes from the narratives added to further understanding of cross-gender mentorship and mentorship across race/ethnicity and gender.

In reading the table from top to bottom, it is clear that the majority of the literature themes were in relation to cross-race/ethnicity mentorships, followed by cross-gender mentorships in the second row. When there were literature and narratives that did not distinguish struggles or successes for race/ethnicity or gender, we presented them in the last (bottom) row in the table, which encompasses both women faculty and faculty of color. Finally, the last column in the last row (challenges across both race/ethnicity and gender) shows no new findings from the narratives.

Mentoring for Organizational Change: Implications for Practice

Bozeman and Fenney (2007) concluded that, because of its multidisciplinary nature, "mentoring theory remains underdeveloped" (p. 735). They also concluded that mentoring relationships can be described as informal and voluntary, satisfying the needs of the participants rather than existing for the benefit of organizational goals and missions. In their view, this description differentiates itself from training and socialization, which has the benefit of the organization, not necessarily the individual, at its center. In a similar vein, Bernstein, Jacobson, and Russo (2010) concluded, "The goal of mentoring is not simply to teach the system, but also to change the system so that it becomes more flexible and responsive to the needs and pathways of its members—mentors and protégés" (p. 58). These statements place individual needs rather than existing organizational needs at the forefront. Implications for policy and practice, across gender and race/ethnicity, should focus on organizational change rather than on maintaining the status quo, which, over decades, has resulted in the continued underrepresentation of faculty of color and women faculty. The following overview of mentee and mentor experiences, recommendations for mentees and mentors, and implications for institutional practice emerged from the literature and narratives previously discussed.

On the basis of the literature and narratives presented, mentees of color and women have experienced the following:

1. Negative external perceptions from colleagues and peers (i.e., sexual liaisons, favoritism)
2. Isolation, tokenism, stereotyping, and marginalization
3. Negative cross-race/ethnicity and cross-gender mentorships that leave them with a desire for same-race/ethnicity and same-gender mentors
4. Negative cross-cultural interactions with mentors who do not understand their cultural backgrounds
5. Mentors who have tried to shape or transform their behaviors and beliefs
6. Language, racial, and cultural barriers
7. Use of power by mentors to exclude them from professional opportunities
8. Desire for their assimilation by mentors
9. Institutional racism and sexism

Again, on the basis of findings from the literature and narratives, mentees could do the following:

1. Rely on self-resiliency when mentoring falls short of expectations.
2. Establish mentorships in other disciplines, departments, colleges or schools, or universities to increase chances of positive mentoring outcomes.
3. Rely on mentors to explicate the politics of the academy.
4. Understand that cross- and same-race/ethnicity and gender mentors all can provide unique and valuable mentorship in various aspects related to demystifying the academy.

Mentors of color and women have experienced the following:

1. That some mentees of color and women may see mentoring as a sign that they are unable to succeed on their own and therefore associate mentoring negatively
2. That some mentees may be intimidated by power differentials in the relationship

3. That cross-cultural interactions require them to undertake learning about the backgrounds of their mentees
4. That if they are of a different race/ethnicity or gender, they may not be able to fully meet the mentoring needs of their mentees

The literature and narratives point to what mentors could do to support mentees:

1. Help them identify cross- and same-race/ethnicity and gender allies on campus.
2. Explain the politics of the academy.
3. Avoid attempts at cloning mentees.
4. Respect mentees' viewpoints and career and academic decisions.
5. Understand that mentoring includes academic and psychosocial support.
6. Share contacts, opportunities, and power with mentees.

Emerging from the analysis described previously, implications for institutional practices to support mentees of color and women include the following:

1. Build and/or expand mentoring programs that are robust and not one-size-fits-all.
2. Provide mentoring programs that include same- and different-race/ethnicity, gender, or academic discipline mentors; provide peer mentors, e-mentoring, (in)formal mentors, and group mentoring; and provide ways in which to enhance understanding of mentees' cultural backgrounds.
3. Understand that mentoring is fundamentally about relationships, and build programs that allow for a multitude of relationships to develop organically.
4. Develop institutional culture that supports mentoring faculty at all ranks and across ranks.
5. Provide support and opportunities for mentees beyond the institution.

Based on the varied experiences of mentees and mentors, a clear message is that one size does not fit all. At the institutional level, it is important that campus leaders understand their context and determine the ways in which it must change to meet specific mentorship needs of current and potential women faculty and faculty of color on their campuses.

With respect to organizational change, Bernstein et al. (2010) noted the importance of engaging the whole campus to effect successful change. All must take on the responsibility for change to take place. According to Verdugo (1995), organizational change, to be effective, must take place at the ideological and structural levels. In their interviews with senior scholars who are exemplar mentors, Espinoza-Herold and Gonzalez (2007) concluded that important solutions suggested are to develop "coping strategies [resiliency] among minority and all junior faculty and . . . networking . . . to form a collective force to infuse systemic change for sociohistorical factors (i.e., institutionalized racism and adverse cultural and ideological forces)" (p. 330).

Mentors and mentees presently in cross-race/ethnicity and cross-gender relationships, or those considering these types of relationships, can use these recommendations to begin a dialogue and to further understand the dynamics inherent in such relationships. The work of Davidson and Foster-Johnson (2001) focused on the improvement of relationships between White mentors and protégés of color. They underscored the need for training on cross-race mentoring and urged organizations to engage in "constructive dialogue about differences among individuals, whether they are due to race, culture, or other factors[, as such activities are] a hallmark of a mature organization" (p. 565).

Regarding the utility of e-mentoring, Bierema and Merriam (2002) stated, "E-mentoring could potentially make mentoring relationships more available to groups that have previously had limited access to mentoring" (p. 211). Bernstein et al. (2010) commented on the usefulness of e-mentoring, citing MentorNet and their *Career*WISE initiative as effective web-based interventions in the fields of science, technology, engineering, and mathematics.

Institutions may also use recommendations emerging from this book as a basis for the creation of an organizational climate supportive of faculty mentees and mentors involved in and/or interested in cross mentorships. Fostering caring campus climates (e.g., Chesler & Chesler, 2002) is critical not only for the persistence of women faculty and faculty of color but also for their ability to simply feel safe on campus. The literature and four of the seven narratives speak to the importance of safety as the authors described their experiences within hostile campus contexts. Furthermore, Bernstein et al. (2010) reported that women in science might leave their disciplines not because of low grades or low performance but because of a hostile working environment, an environment that largely ignores them, and/or an environment that does not encourage them.

Griffin and Reddick (2011) further urged departments and campuses to develop mentoring protocols and practices that "engage in frank conversations about historical and societal influences that affect Black men and women in academic settings and strategize about how these communities can challenge stereotypical perceptions" (p. 1053). Stein (1994) presented such concerns with regard to American Indian faculty. He painted a sobering picture of the challenges faced by American Indian faculty, concluding, "Higher education must continue . . . to encourage more American Indians and other minorities to become active and successful faculty. . . . The country is changing . . . at a rapid pace . . . none more rapidly than the numbers of its many minority citizens" (p. 113).

In addition to creating internal campus programs that serve on-campus faculty, campuses may support a broader academic community by creating programs that encourage mentorship relationships across the country and regionally. Regarding the provision of support for mentees outside the institution, Aryan and Guzman (2010) described a National Summer Institute as one model that brought together graduate students of color, aspiring to the professoriate and enrolled in various doctoral programs and disciplines, in order to provide opportunities for peer mentoring and mentoring from senior scholars. Belay is an example, described by Chesler, Single, and Mikic (2003), of peer mentoring for women engineering faculty from different academic institutions. These types of programs can work to combat isolation for women faculty and faculty of color by providing opportunities for them to interact closely with a broader academic community and to connect with others who may also be isolated on other campuses.

This discussion on implications for policy and practice is grounded in the literature and the narrative chapters presented in this book. These authors point to many ways in which an individual or an organization may pursue changes needed to promote effective mentoring across race/ethnicity and across gender. Questions remain as to whether higher education students, faculty, staff, administrators, and institutions can take the wisdom shared here and craft successful mentoring experiences for all in higher education. Given the current landscape of students and faculty in academe, effective mentorship across diverse backgrounds in order to achieve a representative professoriate is critical. Stanley and Lincoln (2005) elaborated on the importance of continuing this work, stating that cross mentorships are complex and, at times, present difficult challenges. However, the potential contribution to institutions and individuals that support and engage in these cross mentorships is invaluable. According to Pasque (chapter 4), the "seemingly little things, such as 'virtually introducing' you to a colleague with similar interests . . . are unquantifiable yet essential to mentorship and growth within academia" (p. 99). Cross mentorships can lead to new collaborative scholarship, increased engagement and retention for women faculty and faculty of color, and the breakdown of biases and stereotypes. For these and many other reasons, academe has much to gain if opportunities for cross mentorships are embraced, expanded, and supported.

Conclusion

Emerging from an analysis of the cross-race/ethnicity and cross-gender mentoring literature and of the cross-race/ethnicity and cross-gender experiences presented by the mentors and protégés in the narratives written for this book are successful pathways and challenges inherent in such mentoring relationships and implications for policy and practice. The analysis of the narratives revealed that cross-race/ethnicity and cross-gender mentorships can be very successful, resulting in productive academic careers and long-lasting connections. The contributors to this book provide exemplars of meaningful mentorship, in which people of different races/ethnicities and genders come together to grow and learn from each other, resulting in mutual understanding. This is a departure from the type of mentorship model in which a senior faculty member attempts to clone junior faculty who are their mentees. The narratives in this book describe relationships built on openness, trust, and mutual respect. Mentors and protégés reveal how their strong bonds held their relationships intact, even in times of struggle. The literature also reveals that some women faculty and faculty of color prefer mentorships with same-race/ethnicity or same-gender faculty, which they should continue to pursue. However, the literature also documents that in most predominantly White institutions, the availability of women faculty and faculty of color to fill the mentor role is almost nonexistent. For this reason, the contributors to this book undertook to share ways in which successful mentorships across race, ethnicity, and gender are created, maintained, and nurtured. As a collective, the mentor–protégé narratives not only add insight to the literature, providing examples of cross mentorships in action, but also point to ways in which successful practices can be implemented by higher education institutions that are working toward the retention and advancement of their women faculty and faculty of color.

In the foreword of this book, Christine Stanley asserted, "Two of the most fundamental questions about mentoring are as follows: (a) How do we know that mentoring makes a difference? and (b) What does effective mentoring look like or feel like" (p. x)? With the analysis of the literature relevant to mentoring across race/ethnicity and gender, combined with the narrative chapters written by those who have experienced the cross-race/ethnicity and cross-gender mentorship relationships presented in this book, we hope that the reader will come away with a deeper understanding of and insight into the complex constellation of individual and institutional factors inherent in programs, practices, and relationships that develop women faculty and faculty of color. Mentoring does make a difference, and what effective mentoring looks and feels like is voiced in these mentor–protégé narratives. It is time to remedy the challenges presented here and put in place practices that will make a difference in cultivating the next generation of diverse faculty.

References

Aryan, B., & Guzman, F. (2010). Women of color and the PhD: Experiences in formal graduate support programs. *Journal of Business, 1*(4), 69–77.

Bernstein, B. L., Jacobson, R., & Russo, N. F. (2010). Mentoring women in context: Focus on science, technology, engineering, and mathematics fields. In C. A. Rayburn, F. L. Denmark, M. E. Reuder, & A. M. Austria (Eds.), *The Praeger handbook for women mentors: Transcending barriers of stereotype, race, and ethnicity* (pp. 43–64). Westport, CT: Praeger.

Bierema, L. L., & Merriam, S. B. (2002). E-mentoring: Using computer mediated communication to enhance the mentoring process. *Innovative Higher Education, 26*(3), 211–227.

Bozeman, B., & Fenney, M. K. (2007). Toward a useful theory of mentoring: A conceptual analysis and critique. *Administration and Society, 39*(6), 719–739.

Chesler, N. C., & Chesler, M. A. (2002). Gender-informed mentoring strategies for women engineering scholars: On establishing a caring community. *Journal of Engineering Education, 91*(1), 49–55.

Chesler, N. C., Single, P. B., & Mikic, B. (2003). On belay: Peer-mentoring and adventure education for women faculty in engineering. *Journal of Engineering Education, 92*(3), 257–262.

Davidson, M. N., & Foster-Johnson, L. (2001). Mentoring in the preparation of graduate researchers of color. *Review of Educational Research, 71*(4), 549–574.

Espinoza-Herold, M., & Gonzalez, V. (2007). The voices of senior scholars on mentoring graduate students and junior scholars. *Hispanic Journal of Behavioral Sciences, 29*(3), 313–335.

Griffin, K. A., & Reddick, R. J. (2011). Surveillance and sacrifice: Gender differences in the mentoring patterns of Black professors at predominantly White research universities. *American Educational Research Journal, 48*(5), 1032–1057.

Stanley, C. A., & Lincoln, Y. S. (2005). Cross-race faculty mentoring. *Change: The Magazine of Higher Learning, 37*(2), 44–50.

Stein, W. J. (1994). The survival of American Indian faculty. *Thought and Action, 10*(1), 101–113.

Verdugo, R. R. (1995). Racial stratification and the use of Hispanic faculty as role models: Theory, policy, and practice. *The Journal of Higher Education, 66*(6), 669–685.

ABOUT THE EDITORS AND CONTRIBUTORS

Editors

Caroline Sotello Viernes Turner is a professor and graduate coordinator for the Doctorate in Educational Leadership program at California State University, Sacramento, and Arizona State University Lincoln Professor Emerita. She currently serves as president of the Association for the Study of Higher Education (ASHE). Turner's research interests focus on access, equity, and leadership in higher education. Her research has specifically advanced the dialogue on faculty gender and racial/ethnic diversity. Among her groundbreaking publications are *Faculty of Color in Academe: Bittersweet Success* (with Samuel L. Myers Jr.; Allyn and Bacon, 2000) and *Diversifying the Faculty: A Guidebook for Search Committees* (Association of American Colleges & Universities, 2002). Her research publications include contributions to *The Review of Higher Education*, *The Journal of Higher Education*, and *Harvard Educational Review*. She is also one of the founding editorial advisory board members and contributors to *Journal of Diversity in Higher Education*. Her current work addresses the preparation of the next generation of diverse higher education scholars and practitioners. Turner is the recipient of numerous awards, including the 2009 American Educational Research Association (AERA) Scholars of Color in Education Distinguished Career Contribution Award, the 2009 AERA Multicultural and Multiethnic Education (MME) Special Interest Group (SIG) Dr. Carlos J. Vallejo Memorial Award for Lifetime Scholarship, and the 2008 ASHE Council on Ethnic Participation Mildred Garcia Award for Exemplary Scholarship. Turner received her bachelor's and master's degrees from the University of California, Davis, and her PhD from Stanford University.

Juan Carlos González is an associate professor in the higher education master's program and doctoral program, at California State University, Fresno. He received dual bachelor's degrees from California State University, San Bernardino, in Spanish and philosophy, with a minor in history. His master's degree is from The Ohio State University in higher education, and his doctorate is from Arizona State University in educational leadership and policy studies. Presently he's an assistant professor at California State University,

Fresno, in the Department of Educational Research and Administration. His research interests include educational policy and history, multicultural and Latino educational issues, and ethics and diversity in higher education. His teaching interests include visual ethnography, the education of Chicanas and Chicanos, critical theory in education, and qualitative research methods. His recent publications include three coedited journal articles: "Teaching From a Critical Perspective/Enseñando de Una Perspectiva Crítica" (*The International Journal of Critical Pedagogy*, 2011, Vol. 4, No. 1), "Crime Control Strategies in School" (*The Urban Review*), and "Experiences of Central California Latino Male Youth" (*Diaspora, Indigenous, and Minority Education*).

Contributors

Jeanett Castellanos is a lecturer in the School of Social Sciences, teaching classes such as Ethnographic Research, Mixed Research Methods, Comparative Cultures, and Chicana/o Latina/o Families. Castellanos has coedited two books addressing Latinas and Latinos in higher education (*The Majority in the Minority: Expanding the Representation of Latina/o Faculty, Administrators, and Students in Higher Education* and *The Latina/os Pathway to the Ph.D.: Abriendo Caminos*) and has published in numerous national journals (including *Journal of College Counseling, Journal of Counseling and Development, Journal of Hispanic Higher Education, Psychological Reports*, and *Cultural Diversity and Ethnic Minority Psychology*). One of her most current research publications includes "Realidades Culturales y Identidades Dimensionadas [Cultural Realities and Dimensioned Identities]: The Complexities of Latinas' Diversities" in *The Oxford Handbook of Feminist Multicultural Counseling Psychology* (Oxford University Press, 2012). An upcoming publication is *SOMOS Latina/os—Ganas, Comunidad, y El Espíritu: La Fuerza Que Llevamos Por Dentro* [Latina/os—Drive, Community, and Spirituality: The Strength Within]. Castellanos is the recipient of the APA Division 12 (Clinical Psychology) Samuel M. Turner Mentorship Award, the 2012 NLPA Star Vega Community Service Award, and the 2012 AAHEE Outstanding Support of Hispanics in Higher Education. At the University of California, Irvine, she also received the Chancellor's Research Excellence Award, the Chancellor Teaching Excellence Award, the Lecturer of the Year, the Distinguished Women of UCI Award, and the 2014 Chancellor's Living Our Values Award.

O. Cleveland Hill is a retired dean of education and professor emeritus, Nicholls State University, and currently is an associate professor of educational leadership and coordinator of the Educational Leadership program at Our Lady of Holy Cross College in New Orleans, LA. His research interests focus on qualitative school action research, and his most current publication, with Gregg Stall, is in *Case Study Readings in Preparing for the School Leadership Licensure* (edited by Eugene Kennedy and Leslie Jones, 2011).

Dimpal Jain is an assistant professor in educational leadership and policy studies at California State University, Northridge. She received her PhD in higher education and organizational change from the University of California, Los Angeles, where she also worked with the Center for Community College Partnerships. She is a former community college practitioner and faculty member, and her research addresses women leaders of color, critical race theory, womanism, and the transfer function. She has coauthored several publications centered on community college transfer, most notably the necessary elements for a transfer receptive culture.

Mark A. Kamimura-Jiménez is the director of Graduate Student Success for the Rackham Graduate School at the University of Michigan. In this role, he is responsible for the development of programs to support academic and professional success and enhance the educational experiences for more than 8,200 highly diverse master's and doctoral students. He is currently the chair of the University Diversity Council, regional representative for the Hispanic Association of Colleges and Universities (HACU), and cochair of the Professional Latinos at the University of Michigan Alliance (PLUMA) and also serves on a number of university, state, and national committees. Kamimura-Jiménez previously served as the first director for Educational Partnerships at Cal State Fullerton, the first position of its kind developed in the California State University System. In this role, he garnered nearly $17 million in federal and private grants as a principal investigator to collaborate with school districts, community colleges, and four-year institutions to strengthen access in the P–20 educational pipeline. He received his BA from the University of California, Irvine; MA from Columbia University; and PhD in higher education and public policy from the University of Michigan.

Dave A. Louis is an assistant professor at Texas Tech University. His primary research strand is cross-cultural mentoring, specifically as it relates to faculty-student interactions via undergraduate research experiences. His research was spawned by his years as a university administrator and lecturer who noticed the many cultural factors that impacted the lives and learning of students and faculty. His most recent publication is titled "Frantz Fanon Ambivalence Revisited in America's Faculty: Narratives of Black and White Faculty Struggles With Cross Cultural Mentoring" in *National Journal of Urban Education and Practice* (2013, Vol. 4, No. 3), and he has an upcoming publication titled

"Cross-Cultural Peer Mentoring: Increasing White Faculty Adjustment at Black Colleges." Louis is a native of Trinidad and Tobago in the West Indies. He earned his bachelor of arts degree in psychology at Morehouse College, his master of education at Harvard University, and his PhD in educational administration at Texas A&M University.

Alfredo Mirandé is a professor of sociology and ethnic studies at the University of California, Riverside. His most recent publications include *Rascuache Lawyer* (University of Arizona Press, 2011) and *Jalos, USA: Transnational Community and Identity* (University of Notre Dame Press, 2014). His primary research areas are Chicano sociology; race, class, and gender; and Latinos and law. Mirandé is also a practicing attorney.

Penny A. Pasque is an associate professor of adult and higher education in the Department of Educational Leadership and Policy Studies, Women's and Gender Studies, and the Center for Social Justice at the University of Oklahoma. She is also a visiting scholar at the University of Michigan with the Center for the Study of Higher and Postsecondary Education and the Center for the Education of Women for the 2013–2014 academic year. Her research addresses in/equities in higher education, dis/connections between higher education and society, and complexities in critical qualitative inquiry. She has published articles in a number of journals and is author of *American Higher Education Leadership and Policy: Critical Issues and the Public Good* (Palgrave Macmillan), *Qualitative Inquiry for Equity in Higher Education: Methodological Implications, Negotiations and Responsibilities* (with Carducci, Kuntz, and Gildersleeve; Jossey-Bass), and *Empowering Women in Higher Education and Student Affairs* (edited with Errington Nicholson; Stylus).

Elvia Ramirez is an assistant professor of ethnic studies at California State University, Sacramento. She received her PhD in sociology from the University of California, Riverside. Her research interests include Chicanos/Latinos(as) in higher education; college choice; graduate education; race, class, and gender studies; and Mexican immigration. Some of her recent publications include "Examining Latinos/as' Graduate School Choice Process: An Intersectionality Perspective" (*Journal of Hispanic Higher Education*, 2013, Vol. 12, No. 1) and "The Politics of Welfare Inclusion: Explaining State Variation in Legal Immigrants' Welfare Rights" (coauthored with Ellen Reese and Vanesa Estrada, *Sociological Perspectives*, 2013, Vol. 56, No. 1).

Daniel Solórzano is a professor of social science and comparative education in the Graduate School of Education and Information Studies at the

University of California, Los Angeles. His teaching and research interests include critical race theory in education; critical race pedagogy; racial micro-aggressions in education; and the postsecondary access, persistence, and graduation of students of color in the United States. Solórzano has authored over 70 research articles and book chapters on issues related to educational access and equity for underrepresented student populations in the United States.

Christine A. Stanley is vice president and associate provost for diversity and professor of higher education at Texas A&M University. Her research interests are in faculty professional development, instructional development, multicultural organizational development, and college teaching. Stanley is a past president of the Professional and Organizational Development (POD) Network in Higher Education. Prior to joining the faculty at Texas A&M University, she was associate director of the Office of Faculty and TA Development at The Ohio State University, where she received the Distinguished Staff Award in 1999. Stanley has edited two books (*Faculty of Color: Teaching in Predominantly White Colleges and Universities* and *Engaging Large Classes*); has over 40 publications; has presented at 51 refereed national conference; and has consulted nationally and internationally with faculty and administrators on faculty development and diversity issues in the United States, Armenia, China, Mexico, and South Africa. Stanley is a native of Jamaica, the West Indies, and holds a BS in biology (cum laude) from Prairie View A&M University, an MS in zoology from Texas A&M University, and a PhD in curriculum and instruction from Texas A&M University.

Edward P. St. John, Algo D. Henderson collegiate professor of higher education at the University of Michigan's Center for the Study of Higher and Postsecondary Education, is concerned with education for a just society, an interest that stems from three decades of research on educational policy and practice. He is a fellow of the American Educational Research Association and has received awards for leadership and research from the Association for the Study of Higher Education. His most recent book, *Research, Actionable Knowledge, and Social Change*, launched the new book series Actionable Research for Social Justice in Education and Society with Stylus Publishing in 2013.

J. Luke Wood is associate professor of administration, rehabilitation, and postsecondary education at San Diego State University. Wood is codirector of the Minority Male Community College Collaborative (M2C3), chair of the Multicultural and Multiethnic Education (MME) Special Interest Group of the American Educational Research Association (AERA), and chair-elect for the Council on Ethnic Participation (CEP) for the Association for Study of Higher Education (ASHE). He is also the editor emeritus of *Journal of African American Males in Education* (JAAME). Wood's research focuses on factors impacting the success of Black (and other minority) male students in the community college. In particular, his research examines contributors (e.g., social, psychological, academic, environmental, institutional) to positive outcomes (e.g., persistence, achievement, attainment, transfer, labor market outcomes) for these men. He has authored nearly 70 publications, including 3 coauthored textbooks, 4 edited books, and more than 30 peer-reviewed journal articles.

Ontario S. Wooden is dean of the University College at North Carolina Central University. He has authored or coauthored more than a dozen publications and has presented at numerous conferences and symposia. He serves on the editorial board for *Journal for the Study of Sports and Athletes in Education* and the North Carolina Higher Education Research Council. His research interests include urban schooling, teacher preparation, college access and choice, higher education policy and finance, and multiculturalism and diversity in higher education. He holds a doctorate in higher education with a minor in African American and African diaspora studies from Indiana University Bloomington.

academic achievement gap, 85
academic capital, 96, 100
academic caretakers, women as, 15, 25
academic mentorship, 62, 66
academic resiliency, 28, 181, 187–88
Acosta, Oscar Zeta, 176
Action Science (Argyris), 85
ADVANCE program, 26
adventure education, 20
advisee-advisor relationship, 128–31
   boundaries defining roles as advisors
     and mentors, 78–79
   inappropriate, 128–29
   thought partners, 79
African Americans. *See also* Blacks
   Black Caribbean immigrants
     compared to, 145
   demographic distinction, 67
   doctoral students, 62
   experiences of, 84, 91–92
   studies of, 4, 7, 13–14
Albany State University, 90, 93
Alexander, M. L., 29
Allen, W. R., 162
Allen-Haynes, Leetta, 87, 88
alienation, 11
allies, 4–5, 185
ally identification, 4, 180, 184, 185, 205
American Indians, 30–31, 210–11
Anaya, G., 110
Angelique, H., 28, 33
apprenticeship, 62–63, 66, 126, 186.
   See also Research Apprenticeship
   Course (RAC)
Argyris, C., 82, 85
Arizona Education Policy Fellowship
   Program (Arizona EPFP), 66

Arizona State University (ASU), 47,
   59–60, 64
Aryan, B., 11, 15, 29, 34, 211
ASHE. *See* Association for the Study of
   Higher Education
Asian and Pacific Island Americans, 30
assimilation. *See* dominant culture
   assimilation
Association for Institutional
   Research, 89
Association for the Study of Higher
   Education (ASHE), 79, 98
Association for Women in Science
   (AWIS), 25
ASU. *See* Arizona State University
autobiographical sketch approach,
   43–45
autobiography, 44, 175
autoethnography, 164
AWIS. *See* Association for Women in
   Science

Balanced Access Model, 91
banking method, 137
barriers. *See* language, racial/ethnic, and
   cultural barriers
barrio, 50–51, 112, 164
Batiste, Donaldo, 87
belay, 28, 182, 211
belayer, 28
Bensimon, Estela, 78
Bernstein, B. L.
   on e-mentoring, 7, 10, 210
   on gender differences, 24, 25
   on gender stereotypes, 22
   on mentorship goal, 207
   on organizational change, 209

on politics and power relations, 22
on switch rates, 32
Beverly, C., 4
Bierema, L. L., 210
Blackburn, R. T., 3, 8
Black Greek letter organizations, 145
Blacks, 7
    Caribbean immigrants compared to
        African Americans, 145
    HBCUs, 145–46, 150
    hypersurveillance and, 11–12
    males in doctoral education, 60–61
    males' success, 69
    men as hypersexualized, 68
    narrative inquiry of women, 15
    professional and education
        attainment, 162
    on sexual relations and favoritism, 19
Blackwell, J. E., 2, 35
Blackwood, J., 5, 9, 24
Blake-Beard, S. D., 19, 20, 22,
    25, 114
Bogotch, Ira, 82
Boice, B., 33
Boyle, P., 33
Bozeman, B., 207
Bragg, A. K., 61–63, 70–71, 72–73
braids and disheveled hair
    (*Trenzas y Greñas*), 164
Bridges, Brian, 91
Brinson, J., 4, 11, 12
Brown, R., 7
Brown-Welty, S., 5, 9, 24
Buckner, J. P., 32
Bukoski, B. E., 12
Burkhardt, John, 94

Cafarella, R. S., 143
Caldwell, C., 189
Calhoun, J. A., 31
California Community College System,
    9–10, 24
California State University (CSU), 65
California State University, Sacramento,
    47, 64

Callahan Lijana, Kim, 94
Cameron, S. M., 3, 8
Campbell, D. E., 162
Campbell, T. A., 162
career development, 3
career/instrumental support, 162
*Career*WISE, 26, 210
Caribbean heritage and culture,
    143–48, 151–52, 155, 192, 201
caring communities, establishing, 28
Castellanos, Jeanett, 111–15, 185,
    187–88, 191, 198, 200
Castillo, L. G., 5, 17–18
Casto, C., 9, 15, 19, 20, 189
Caves, L., 61
Ceja, M., 28, 29, 33, 127
Cekic, Osman, 92
Center for Research on Learning and
    Teaching, 94
Center for the Study of Higher
    and Postsecondary Education
    (CSHPE), 95, 97
Cervero, R. M., 7, 21, 22
Chapman, D. W., 3, 8
checking in, 121
chemistry mentorship, 32
Chesler, M. A., 23, 32, 54–55, 155
Chesler, N. C., 20, 23, 32, 54–55,
    155, 211
Chicanas and Chicanos
    experiences of, 113, 125, 195
    research on, 29, 33, 50–52, 54,
        56, 108
    same-race, cross-gender mentorships,
        161, 164–75
class, 143–44
Clawson, J. G., 18
cloning, 5–6, 181
cohort mentorships, 86–88
Cole, D. G., 110
college access, 89, 90–91
*College Organization and Professional
    Development* (St. John), 78, 102n2
*College Prep: Transforming High Schools,
    Overcoming Failed Public Policy*,

and Preparing Students for Higher Education (St. John, Masse, Callahan Lijana, and Milazzo Bigelow), 94
Columbia University, 114, 156
Cominole, M., 61
Common Sense Racism, 176
community cultural wealth, 132
community service, 120
Community Service Internship Program (CSIP), 112
conformist resistance, 129–31
Confronting Educational Inequality: Reframing, Building Understanding, and Making Change (St. John), 96–97
conversations (*pláticas*), 112, 188
Cornell University, 95, 96
counterspaces, 126, 127
Cox, T., 11
Crawford, K., 35
Creswell, J. W., 44
critical race theory (CRT)
    analysis using, 78, 129, 132–33
    components of, 126, 140
    definition of, 125–26, 127–28
    leadership course evaluations and, 134–37
    research and, 139, 161
    testimonios, intersectionality and, 163–64, 175
Crosby, F., 21
cross-cultural interactions, 12–13, 110, 195
cross-cultural mentorships, 8
cross-disciplinary ethnic networking, 201
cross-gender mentorships. *See also specific individuals*
    autobiographical sketch approach, 43–45
    Caribbean heritage and culture and, 143–44, 151–52
    challenges in, 3–4, 14–26, 32, 110, 180–83
    characteristics supporting, 10, 186–87

demystifying the academy and, 9–10
diverse mentoring programs and, 9–10
diversity within, 45, 47, 54
e-mentoring and, 10, 181
gender differences and, 23–26
gender stereotypes and, 22–23
intimacy levels and, 18–19
lack of professional interactions and, 20
lack of understanding of, 68
marginalization in, 16–18
norms regarding, 17
power relations and, 8, 15, 20–22, 152–53, 162–63, 169
research on, 26–27
respect and openness with, 9
same-race, cross-gender mentorships, 161, 164–75
sexism and, 14–15
sexual relations and, 18–20, 163, 168, 175, 200
studies on, 3
successful pathways in, 3–4, 8–10, 28–29, 180–82
summarizing literature, 180–83
tokenism and, 16–18, 31
cross mentorships, 203, 207, 210, 211
cross-race/ethnicity mentorships
    academic resiliency and, 28, 181
    allies and, 4–5
    caring communities, establishing, 28
    challenges in, 3–4, 10–14, 29–31, 32, 180–82
    cloning and, 5–6, 181
    cross-cultural mentorships and, 8
    demystifying the academy and, 5, 181
    diverse mentoring programs and, 5
    dominant culture assimilation and, 11
    e-mentoring and, 7–8, 181
    healing power of, 6–7
    isolation and marginalization in, 11, 182
    language, racial/ethnic, and cultural barriers, 13, 182, 195

narratives on, 36
negative cross-cultural interactions
and, 12–13
peer mentorship and, 6
power relations and, 12
preference for same-race mentors,
13–14
psychosocial functions and, 7, 13
racism and, 11–12
research on, 26–27
respect and openness with, 6
rich legacy of, 7
same-race mentorships compared
to, 14
stigma with seeking help and, 12
studies on, 3
successful pathways in, 3–8, 27–29,
180–82
summarizing literature, 180–83
CRT. *See* critical race theory
Crutcher, B. N., 10, 13, 18–19, 22, 25
CSHPE. *See* Center for the Study
of Higher and Postsecondary
Education
CSIP. *See* Community Service
Internship Program
CSU. *See* California State University
Culp, J. M., 163
cultivation, 112
culture
Caribbean heritage and, 143–48,
151–52, 155, 192, 201
class, mentorships and, 143–44
community cultural wealth, 132
cross-cultural interactions, 12–13,
110, 195
cross-cultural mentorships, 8
cultural differences, 7, 11, 201
cultural validation, 27–28, 181, 185
dominant culture assimilation, 11,
182, 191, 193
language, racial/ethnic, and cultural
barriers, 13, 182, 195
supportive, 32, 189–90

Davidson, M. N., 13, 110, 210
Davies, A. B., 21
Davis, Leah, 91
DDP. *See* Disruptive Dialogue Project
Delgado Bernal, Delores, 129, 132
demographic distinction, points of,
67–68
demystifying the academy, 5, 9–10,
181, 185
Department of Education, U.S., 1
Department of Health and Human
Services, U.S., 20
desegregation, 82, 83
different experiences, 198, 205
Dirty 30, 136
dispositions, 71
Disruptive Dialogue Project (DDP),
97–98
dissertation
defense, 144, 156
finding one's voice, 145
process, 72, 131
research, 82, 84, 85
as student's work, 78
Diverse College Students course, 90
diverse mentoring programs, 5, 9–10
diving for pearls, 27–28, 181, 187
"Diving for Pearls: Mentoring as
Cultural and Activist Practice
Among Academics of Color"
(Okawa), 27–28
dominant culture assimilation, 11, 182,
191, 193
dropout prevention program, 85

East Carolina University School of
Medicine, 20
Eastern Michigan University, 96
Ebonics, 50
Ed Heads, 92
education
adventure education, 20
balancing family and doctoral
education, 69–70

Black males in doctoral education, 60–61
Blacks' professional and education attainment, 162
five educational pillars, 119
Latinas and Latinos educational pathways and degree attainment, 108–9
Latino men in education and mentorship, 109–11
prejudices in, 120
Ellis, E. M., 17
e-mentoring
    Bernstein on, 7, 10, 210
    cross-gender mentorships and, 10, 181
    cross-race/ethnicity mentorships and, 7–8, 181
    opportunities for, 25–26, 182, 210
engineering, women in, 20, 155, 211
epistemologies, 167, 169, 193
equal voice, giving, 101
Espinosa, L. L., 35
Espinoza-Herold, M., 6, 210
ethical issues, 162–63
ethic of care, 94, 100, 187
existential component of mentoring, 198, 200–201, 205
existentialism, 120–121
external perceptions, 18–19, 191, 194, 200
external resistance, 130–31

faculty
    diversity, 1, 3
    experience, 115–22
    nuances, expectations and stress of, 157
    by race/ethnicity, sex and academic rank, 1–2, 107–8
faculty-student mentoring relationships, 161
    taxonomy, 61–62, 72
failed mentorships, 173–75

familial capital, 132
family
    balancing family and doctoral education, 69–70
    balancing family and professional roles, 10, 181
    importance of, 119
Farm Labor Movement, 49
favoritism, 18–20
feedback, 62, 158
feminist mentorship, 8–9, 17, 168–69, 181
Fenney, M. K., 207
Ferreira, M. M., 23–24
first name, calling by, 155
Fisher, Hal, 83
Flowers, L. A., 60
Foley, P., 162
formal mentorships, 29, 34
Foster-Johnson, L., 13, 110, 210
Freire, Paulo, 129, 137
Freirean problem-posing mentoring, 137–40

gender. *See also* cross-gender mentorships; same-gender mentorships
    gender equity, 24, 152
    gender privilege, 68
    mixed-race and mixed-gender mentorship, 162
    opposite-sex mentors, 110
    politics of, 189
    stereotypes, 22–23
gender differences, 23–26, 54–55
    demographic distinction, 67–68
    impacts of, 73, 143, 183
    in narratives, 191
    roles and dynamics, 155
generational differences, 48–49, 183, 202
Gibson, S. K., 20, 25
glass ceiling, 31
The Global Gender Gap Report 2010 (World Economic Forum), 152

Goffman, Erving, 49
González, Antonio, 51
González, Joaquina, 50
González, Juan Carlos, 43, 50–56, 183, 186, 191–92, 202
Gonzalez, V., 6, 210
Gothard, K. A., 12
Gratz and *Grutter* decisions, 94
Griffin, K. A., 11, 15, 19, 25, 30, 210
Griffith, Alison, 82
group mentoring, 29. *See also* mosaic mentoring
Guggenbuhl-Craig, A., 79
Guzman, F., 11, 15, 29, 34, 211

habits of mind, 71
Hall, R. M., 12, 14, 16, 17, 18, 26
Harper, Shaun, 78, 91
Harris, A., 163
Harvard, 80
Harvard Educational Review, 80
Haskell Indian Nations University (HINU), 55–56
HBCUs. *See* historically Black colleges and universities
healing, 6–7, 189
help, stigma with seeking, 12, 34, 182
Herr, K. U., 33
Higher Education and Student Affairs (HESA), 90
Hill, O. Cleveland, 82
    reflections of, 83–88, 100–101, 185–86, 188
    work with, 77, 79
Hill, R. D., 5, 6, 10, 17–18, 21, 23
HINU. *See* Haskell Indian Nations University
historically Black colleges and universities (HBCUs), 145–46, 150
historical struggles (*La Lucha*), 117
Hoezee, Larry, 92
Holland, J. W., 61–62, 72
hostile campus climates, 52, 118, 127, 210

Howarth, W. H., 44
Hune, Shirley, 115
Hurtado, Sylvia, 115, 120
hypersexualized, Black men as, 68
hypersurveillance, 11–12

imitation, 62
imposter syndrome, 126
independent personalities, 198, 202, 205
Indiana Education Policy Center, 88, 89, 91, 92, 93
Indiana Project on Academic Success, 88, 93
Indiana University, 77, 88–93
informal mentorships, 29
initiation, 112
inspirational mentorship, 48–49, 64, 202
Institute for Higher Education Research, 65
institutional racism, 11, 182, 191, 193–94
Integrated Postsecondary Education Data System (IPEDS), 1
intellectual mentorship, 168
intentional mentorship, 101–2, 201
interdisciplinary approach, 126, 133, 139
internalization, 62–63, 71
internal resistance, 130–31
International Congress of Qualitative Inquiry, 98
intersectionality, 163–64, 175
intimacy levels, 18–19
IPEDS. *See* Integrated Postsecondary Education Data System
isolation, 11, 110, 182

Jacobson, R., 7, 207
Jain, Dimpal, 125–26, 187, 189, 193, 195, 201
Jamaica, 145, 147–49, 151–52, 155
Johnson, W. B., 110
Johnson-Bailey, J., 7, 21, 22
Johnsrud, L. K., 28, 29, 34

Kalbfleisch, P. J., 21
Kaltenbaugh, Louise, 87
Kamimura-Jiménez, Mark A., 185, 187–88, 198, 200
Kanter, R. M., 16
Kanter, Rosabeth Moss, 49
Kanuka, H., 10–11, 21, 29, 34
"Keeping Our Faculties of Color" symposium, 64–65
Kirkpatrick, L. A., 29
Kline, Kim, 92
Knefelkamp, L. Lee, 115
knowledge, 70, 137
Kottler, J., 4, 11, 12
Kram, K. E., 9, 14, 18, 31, 112
Kuck, V. J., 32
Kuykendall, John, 91

language, racial/ethnic, and cultural barriers, 13, 182, 195
Latina Filipina, 45, 49, 59
Latinas and Latinos
    educational pathways and degree attainment, 108–9
    faculty experience, 115–22
    Latino men in education and mentorship, 109–11
    mentee perceptions of Latina mentor, 113–15
    representation, 107–8
    research on, 54, 69
    theoretical framework, 109
leadership course evaluations, 134–37
Lechuga, V. M., 5
Lick, D. W., 33
Lincoln, Y. S., 5, 6, 11, 211
López, Haney, 176
Louis, Dave A.
    on lessons learned, 156–57
    reflections of, 153–54, 192, 194
    Stanley and, 144–58, 199, 201
Lovell, N. B., 29
Lu, C., 12
La Lucha (historical struggles), 117

lunch with graduate students, 94, 102n4, 167, 199–200
Lynch, R. V., 7

macroaggressions, 151
male-dominated society, 24, 68
Mansson, D. H., 10
marginalization
    in cross-gender mentorships, 16–18
    in cross-race/ethnicity mentorships, 11, 182
    isolation and, 11, 110, 182
    tokenism and, 16–18, 182
Marini, A., 10–11, 21, 29, 34
Mark, S., 20, 23
Marzabadi, C. H., 32
Masse, J. C., 94
McClure, Michelle, 91
MCP Hahnemann School of Medicine, 20
MCSP. See Michigan Community Scholars Program
MEChA (Movimiento Estudiantil Chicana/o de Aztlan), 131
medicine, 20, 23
Meharry Medical College School of Medicine, 20
men. See also gender
    Black males in doctoral education, 60–61
    Black males' success, 69
    Latinos, 107–8, 109–11
    male-dominated society, 24, 68
Mendez, Jesse, 92
mentee
    experiences, 111–13
    perceptions of Latina mentors, 113–15
    as term, 2
mentoring dynamics, 64–72
MentorNet, 26, 210
mentor–protégé relationship, 62–66. See also specific individuals
    commonalities, 69–70, 73, 144–51, 181

demographic distinction, points of, 67–68
differences, 151–53
initial experience, 65–66
lessons learned regarding, 156–58
origins of, 64–65
mentors
benefits of, 70–71
boundaries defining roles as advisors and, 78–79
mentee perceptions of Latina, 113–15
multiple, 9, 118
opposite-sex, 110
preference for same-race, 13–14, 182, 195
role of, 7, 158
St. John as, 96–98
student-centered, 61
mentorship narratives, 3, 164. *See also testimonios; specific individuals*
analysis of, 179, 197, 212
of Black women, 15
challenges and, 190–96, 202–3
contributing themes from, 197–203
cross-race/ethnicity mentorships, 36
function of, 36
successful pathways and, 183–90, 198–202
mentorships. *See also specific individuals; specific types*
academic, 62, 66
benefits of, 72, 125
career development and, 3
challenges of, 118–22
chemistry, 32
class, culture and, 143–44
cohort, 86–88
components of, 62–63, 110, 120
definition of, 1–2, 25, 35, 85, 110, 162
through example, 102
failed, 173–75
feminist, 8–9, 17, 168–69, 181
formal, 29, 34

four ideals influencing, 81
four phases of, 112
functions, 162
goal, 207
informal, 29
inspirational, 48–49, 64, 202
intellectual, 168
intentional, 101–2, 201
Latino men in education and, 109–11
lessons learned regarding, 169, 173–75
as lifelong process, 99
multigenerational, 118
networks compared to, 100
peer groups and, 79–81
peer mentorships, 6, 35, 98, 187
psychology graduate students' perceptions of, 152
questions about, 212
reciprocal component of, 33, 48, 174
Reddick on, 3, 210
research on, 162–63
socialization and, 61–63, 70–71
successful, 16–17
systematic mentoring, 33
theoretical underpinnings of, 61–64
types of, 62–63, 140
methodology, 133
Meyer, James H., 80, 81
Michigan Community Scholars Program (MCSP), 95
microaggressions, 118, 127, 151
Mikic, B., 20, 211
Milazzo Bigelow, V., 94
Miller, Jacob, 115
Mills, Billy, 56
minorities
academic achievement gap and, 85
low expectations and sympathy for, 86
model, 30
Mirandé, Alfredo, 164–75, 189–90, 194, 195, 201, 202
Mirón, Louis, 82

mixed-race and mixed-gender
    mentorship, 162
mixed-race heritage, 69, 73, 113,
    114, 199
model minorities, 30
modification, 62
Montoya, M. E., 164
Morales, E. E., 110
Morehouse College, Georgia,
    145, 151
Morelon, Carla, 91
mosaic mentoring, 22, 29
Movimiento Estudiantil Chicana/o de
    Aztlan. *See* MEChA
Mullen, C. A., 29, 33
multigenerational mentorship, 118
multiple mentors, 9, 118
musing, 28, 33
Musoba, Glenda, 92
Myers, S. A., 10

narratives. *See* mentorship narratives
National Center for Education
    Statistics, 1, 89, 91
National Center for Institutional
    Diversity, 94
National Centers of Leadership in
    Academic Medicine, 20
National Forum on Higher Education
    for the Public Good, 94, 95
National Science Foundation, 26
National Summer Institute, 34, 211
networks, 17
    cross-disciplinary ethnic
        networking, 201
    developing, 71
    mentorships compared to, 100
    'old boys,' 14, 97, 99
Ngu, L. Q., 5
Nicholls State University (NSU), 77,
    82, 83, 88
Noe, R. A., 17
Nolan, S. A., 32
nonverbal behavior, 152
NSU. *See* Nicholls State University

observation, 62, 201
Office on Women's Health (OWH), 20
Ohio State University, 47
Okawa, G. Y., 27–28
'old boys' networks, 14, 97, 99
Olsen, Louise, 87
Onda Chicana writing group, 166,
    172, 201
O'Neill, R. M., 19, 20, 22, 25, 114
Ong, M., 35
openness, respect and, 6, 9, 181, 183
opposite-sex mentors, 110
Orfield, G., 35
organizational change, 207–11
Orozco, V., 110
otherness, 156
OWH. *See* Office on Women's Health

Paredes, A., 175
Parker, V. A., 9, 14, 31
Pasque, Penny A.
    on cross mentorships, 211
    reflections of, 95–99, 101–2,
        187–89, 201
    work with, 77, 79, 94
Patton, Lori, 78, 91
pedagogies of the home, 132
Pedagogy of the Oppressed (Freire), 137
peer groups
    formation of, 168
    mentorships and, 79–81
    as vital to academic success, 79
peer mentorship, 6, 35, 98, 187
Pepion, K., 5
personal growth, opportunities for, 66,
    107, 202
Peterson-Hickey, M. M., 29, 30
pláticas (conversations), 112, 188
politics
    of gender, 189
    power relations and, 20–22, 191–92
Ponjuan, L., 54
power, shared, 28–29
Power in the Helping Professions
    (Guggenbuhl-Craig), 79

power relations
  conflict in balance, 67–68
  cross-gender mentorships and, 8, 15,
    20–22, 152–53, 162–63, 169
  cross-race/ethnicity mentorships
    and, 12
  ineffective, 17
  politics and, 20–22, 191–92
  power dynamics, 12, 15, 114, 195
Prairie View A&M University, Texas,
  145, 147, 149
prejudices
  in education system, 120
  racial, 88
  reinforced, 18
professional development, 8, 81
professional effectiveness, 82
professional interactions, lack of,
  20, 195
Promotion and Tenure (Tierney and
  Bensimon), 78
proportional representation ratios
  (PRRs), 60–61
protégé, 2. *See also* mentor–protégé
  relationship
PRRs. *See* proportional representation
  ratios
psychosocial support, 7, 13, 162, 186
psychosociocultural (PSC) framework,
  109, 112
Puerto Ricans, 108

Quijada, D. A., 111

RAC. *See* Research Apprenticeship
  Course
race/ethnicity. *See also* critical race
  theory; cross-race/ethnicity
  mentorships; same-race
  mentorships; *specific race/ethnicity*
  demographic distinction, 67–68
  language, racial/ethnic, and cultural
    barriers, 13, 182, 195
  mixed-race and mixed-gender
    mentorship, 162

mixed-race heritage, 69, 73, 113,
  114, 199
race-based hostile work environment,
  202–3
race blindness, 163, 164
racial prejudices, 88
racial justice, 88, 163
racism, 11–12, 113. *See also* prejudices
  Common Sense Racism, 176
  elimination of, 163, 164
  institutional, 11, 182, 191, 193–94
  sexism and, 15–16, 36, 78
Ragins, B. R., 162
Ramirez, Elvia, 164–75, 187, 189–91,
  194, 201, 202
reactionary resistance, 129–30
recommendations and implications for
  practice, 207–11
Reddick, R. J.
  on cultural validation, 27
  on demystifying the academy, 5
  on gender differences, 25
  on mentorships, 3, 210
  on peer mentorship, 6
  on racism, 11
  on rich legacy of cross-race/ethnicity
    mentorships, 7
  on same-gender mentorships, 28
  on sexual relations and
    favoritism, 19
  on women as academic caretakers,
    15, 25
redefinition, 112
reflexivity, 95
Regan, Mary, 80, 81
Research Apprenticeship Course
  (RAC), 126–28, 136, 139,
  140, 186
resistance, 126, 129–31
respect and openness, 6, 9, 181, 183
Rex, Lesley, 94, 96
Riccobono, J., 61
Rivas, M., 28, 29, 33
Rodriguez, S., 12
Rosaldo, R., 163

Rosen, J., 61
rural settings, 69, 86–87
Russo, N. F., 7, 32, 207

Sáenz, V. B.
  on cultural validation, 27
  on demystifying the academy, 5
  on Latinas and Latinos research, 54
  on mentorship narratives, 3
  on peer mentorship, 6
  on same-gender mentorships, 28
  on stigma with seeking help, 12
Salazar, C. F., 189
Sally Casanova Predoctoral
    Fellowship, 65
same-gender mentorships
  challenges for, 31
  findings regarding, 33
  same-race, same-gender mentorships,
    28, 29, 33, 162
same-race mentors, 13–14, 182, 195
same-race mentorships
  benefits of, 13, 29–30
  cross-race mentorships compared
    to, 14
  cultural validation within, 27–28
  findings regarding, 33
  same-race, cross-gender mentorships,
    161, 164–75
  same-race, same-gender mentorships,
    28, 29, 33, 162
Sanchez, Vera, 111
Sandler, B. R., 12, 14, 16, 17, 18,
    26, 33
Sands, R. G., 30
Schlosser, L. Z., 162
Schön, D. A., 82
Schramm, S., 8–9, 15, 17
science, technology, engineering, and
    mathematics (STEM), 10, 23–24,
    26, 32, 35, 183
sciences, women in, 8, 22–23, 25–26,
    32, 210
scientism, 163
segregation, 88

selection bias, 79
self-defeating resistance, 129–30
self-portrait, 44
separation, 112
sexism
  cross-gender mentorships and, 14–15
  definition of, 14
  experience of, 182, 191, 192–93
  racism and, 15–16, 36, 78
sexual relations, 18–20, 163, 168,
    175, 200
shared power, 28–29
Siegel, P., 61
Singh, D. K., 7
Single, P. B., 20, 211
skills, 70
Smith, D., 35
social capital, 96
socialization, 17
  five stages of, 62–63
  mentorships and, 61–63, 70–71,
    72–73
  proficiencies of, 70–71
social justice
  advocate for, 87, 101
  commitment to, 77, 81, 82, 88
  equity and, 43, 45, 47, 52–53, 64
  issues, 84–87, 95
  work toward, 129–30
social needs, support, 9, 189–90
social oppression, 129–30
Society of Women Engineers, 25–26
Solórzano, Daniel, 125–27, 129, 189,
    193, 201
South Asian American, 125, 195
Southern University at New Orleans
    (SUNO), 88
Stanley, Christine A.
  on allies, 5
  on cloning, 6
  on cross mentorships, 211
  on demystifying the academy, 5
  on isolation and marginalization, 11
  on lessons learned, 157–58
  Louis and, 144–58, 199, 201

on questions about mentorships, 212
reflections of, 154–56, 192, 194
on respect and openness, 6, 9
Stein, W. J., 30, 210
STEM. *See* science, technology, engineering, and mathematics
stereotypes
    debunking, 118, 119
    gender, 22–23
    about women, 17, 163, 183
St. John, Edward P., 77
    College Organization and Professional Development, 78, 102n2
    College Prep, 94
    Confronting Educational Inequality, 96–97
    as mentor, 96–98
    reflections of, 78–83, 88–89, 93–94, 100, 185, 186–87, 193, 199–200
Stoloff, D. L., 7
student-centered mentors, 61
SUNO. *See* Southern University at New Orleans
Swisher, Karen, 55
switch rates, 32
Syracuse University, 96
systematic mentoring, 33

Taylor, Gloria, 115
testimonios, 161, 176
    CRT, intersectionality and, 163–64, 175
    of Mirandé, 170–73
theory
    as term, 133
    theories in use, 84, 85
Thomas, D. A., 6, 12, 14
Thompson, Orville, 80, 81, 102n4
thought partners
    advisee-advisor relationship, 79
    definition of, 80
    inner images of, 100
    work with, 81, 82, 91, 94
Tierney, W. G., 44, 78
Tillman, L. C., 7, 13, 15, 16–17

Title III of Higher Education Act, 80
Title IV federal financial aid programs, 1
tokenism
    cross-gender mentorships and, 16–18, 31
    marginalization and, 16–18, 182
traditional mentoring
    drawbacks of, 33, 122
    expansion of, 13
transformational resistance, 126, 129–31
Trenzas y Greñas (braids and disheveled hair), 164
Trinidad, 145, 147–48, 151–52
Turner, Caroline S. V.
    awards, 72, 73n3
    background of, 43, 45–50, 59, 67
    González, Juan Carlos, and, 43, 50–56, 183, 186, 198, 202
    mentoring dynamics, 64–72
    Wood, J. Luke, and, 59–60, 192, 194, 195, 199–200

UCD. *See* University of California, Davis
UCI. *See* University of California, Irvine
UCLA
    Dirty 30 at, 136
    experiences at, 138
    RAC at, 126–28, 136, 139, 140, 186
UCR. *See* University of California, Riverside
UM. *See* University of Michigan
underrepresented students, 54, 60–61, 117, 169–70
unifying model, 203–7
University of California, Davis (UCD), 45, 80, 81, 100
University of California, Irvine (UCI), 112–13, 116
University of California, Riverside (UCR), 165–66, 168, 170, 173
University of California, San Diego, School of Medicine, 20

University of Hawaii, 34
University of Michigan (UM), 77,
    93–99, 193
University of Minnesota, 47, 65
University of Missouri, Kansas City, 53
University of New Orleans (UNO), 77,
    81–88, 102nn2–3
University of Oklahoma, 77, 102
UNO. *See* University of New Orleans
urban settings, 86–87

Váldes, F., 163
values, 70–71, 87, 100–101, 116
Verdugo, R. R., 209
voice
    equal voice, giving, 101
    finding one's voice, 145

Weathersby, George, 80
Western Interstate Commission of
    Higher Education's (WICHE)
    Doctoral Scholars Program, 10,
    17–18
West Indies, 148, 152
White, Joseph L., 116
White privilege, 5
wholistic mentoring, 199–200
WICHE. *See* Western Interstate
    Commission of Higher
    Education's (WICHE) Doctoral
    Scholars Program
Willie, C. V., 7

womanist theory, 128
women. *See also* gender
    as academic caretakers, 15, 25
    balancing family and professional
        roles, 10, 181
    Black, narrative inquiry of, 15
    in engineering, 20, 155, 211
    in sciences, 8, 22–23, 25–26,
        32, 210
    stereotypes about, 17, 163, 183
    strong female influences, 114–15
    successful pathways for, 181–82
Wood, Idara, 66, 67
Wood, J. Luke
    background of, 59, 67, 73n2
    experiences of, 186, 193
    mentoring dynamics, 64–72
    Turner and, 59–60, 192, 194, 195,
        198, 199–200
Wooden, Ontario S.
    reflections of, 89–93, 101, 183
    work of, 78
    work with, 77, 79, 89
World Economic Forum, 152
Wright, C., 35
write and revise process, 97
writing groups, 34, 166, 187, 190, 198,
    201, 204. *See also* Onda Chicana
    writing group
Wunsch, M. A., 15, 21

Yosso, Tara, 127, 132

Also available from Stylus

Faculty Mentoring
A Practical Manual for Mentors, Mentees, Administrators, and Faculty Developers
Susan L. Phillips and Susan T. Dennison
Foreword by Milton D. Cox

The book provides step-by-step guidelines for setting up, planning, and facilitating mentoring programs for new faculty members, whether one-on-one, or using a successful group model developed and refined over 25 years by the authors. While it offers detailed guidance on instituting such programs at the departmental level, it also makes the case for establishing school or institutional level programs and delineates the considerable benefits and economies of scale these can achieve.

The authors provide guidance for mentors and mentees on developing group mentoring and individual mentor–protégé relationships, the corresponding chapters being available online for separate purchase. Also available online are detailed outlines and advice to department chairs, administrators, and facilitators on how to establish and conduct institution-wide group mentoring programs and how to apply or modify the material to meet their specific needs.

Sty/us

22883 Quicksilver Drive
Sterling, VA 20166-2102   Subscribe to our e-mail alerts: www.Styluspub.com